PATRICK DiDOMENICO

KNOWLEDGE MANAGEMENT FOR LAWYERS

AMERICAN BAR ASSOCIATION
Defending Liberty
Pursuing Justice

ABA LAW PRACTICE DIVISION
The Business of Practicing Law

Cover design by Andrew Alcala/ABA Publishing.

Printed in the United States of America

19 18 17 16 15 5 4 3 2 1

Library of Congress Cataloging-in-Publication Data

DiDomenico, Patrick V., author.
Knowledge management for lawyers / by Patrick V. DiDomenico. — First Edition.
pages cm
Includes index.
ISBN 978-1-62722-271-6 (print : alk. paper)
1. Knowledge management—United States. 2. Law firms—United States—Management. 3. Practice of law—United States—Management. 4. Law offices—United States. 5. Project management—United States. I. Title.
KF318.D53 2015
340.068'4—dc23

2015015351

Contents

About the Author

Recipient of the 2013 International Legal Technology Association (ILTA) Knowledge Management Professional of the Year Award, Patrick DiDomenico has been in the legal knowledge management industry since 2005. He is the Director of Knowledge Management for Ogletree, Deakins, Nash, Smoak & Stewart, P.C., an international labor and employment law firm with more than 750 attorneys in more than 40 offices. He has also held knowledge management positions at Gibbons, P.C. (Chief Knowledge Officer) and Debevoise & Plimpton, LLP (KM Manager). Before his knowledge management career, Patrick was a practicing litigation attorney for more than eight years.

Patrick volunteers as a member of the ILTA Knowledge Management Peer Group Steering Committee and has served on the ILTA Conference Committee and the ILTA SharePoint Symposium Committee. In his spare time, Patrick publishes the LawyerKM blog (www.LawyerKM.com), tweets as @LawyerKM, and manages the 7,000-plus-member Knowledge Management for Legal Professionals LinkedIn group and the 4,000-plus-member Legal Project Management LinkedIn group, both of which he founded. He is a frequent speaker on KM and legal technology topics. He is also an aspiring minimalist.

About This Book

This book is about how knowledge management can benefit lawyers in law firms and corporate law departments. It addresses what knowledge management is about, why law firms and law departments should consider investing their time and resources in knowledge management efforts, and how to take action toward those efforts. Throughout the book, I sometimes refer only to law firms, but readers should note that my comments typically apply to law departments, as well, and I only omit law departments for the sake of brevity.

Because legal knowledge management, at its core, is about improving the practice and business of law, the topic should be interesting to almost anyone in the legal services industry. However, not every part of the book will be of interest to all readers. There are two main target audiences for this book, which I call Lawyer Leaders and Administrative Leaders.

Lawyer Leaders are those lawyers (usually partner-level) who have some leadership role in their organizations and who want to improve their businesses and find ways for their fellow lawyers to improve how they practice law. Lawyer Leaders would include managing partners, chief legal officers, general counsel, practice group leaders, and lawyers who are members of executive or management committees, technology committees, practice committees, and the like. Also included in the Lawyer Leader category (even if they are not lawyers) would be high-level executives, such as law firm chief operating or chief executive officers.

Administrative Leaders are those mid- to high-level administrators who are charged with operating the business of the law firm or legal department. This group would include members of knowledge management departments but also legal administrators in other departments who wish to learn about the benefits of knowledge management. Senior management staff and those who aspire to become part of the senior management would fall into this category, as well.

Because my intention is for this book to be a practical guide to implementing knowledge management, some of the content may be too detailed for certain readers. I suspect that just about all of the content will be of interest to Administrative Leaders, whereas some of the more detailed content will be of less interest to some Lawyer Leaders. Because there is a diversity of content that is more appropriate for some readers than others, the target audience(s) that will likely find the content of particular value is stated at the beginning of each chapter. I encourage all readers to read the entire book, but these indicators will help busy readers focus on the parts that will be most relevant to them.

Finally, as a bonus, Appendix B includes the stories of how several knowledge management professionals got started in their careers. I included this information to inspire people who have decided that knowledge management might be the right career path for them.

Introduction

The Diamond Appraiser: A True KM Story

A diamond appraiser almost derailed my knowledge management career before it started.

In 2005, after recently leaving the practice of law to take on a new career in knowledge management, I traveled to Chicago to attend a KM seminar. I was excited, as I had hoped to learn all there was to know about my new field. The seminar was fantastic, and although I hadn't learned everything there was to know about KM, I left the Windy City enthusiastic about returning to New York with some new knowledge about knowledge management.

I boarded the plane and sat next to a middle-aged man; he kept to himself, but he seemed a little nervous. We exchanged the sort of nod-of-the-head "hello" that really tells a fellow passenger that we'll agree not to talk for the next few hours. Well, that tacit agreement was broken about 30 minutes into the flight, after my fellow passenger had finished off his first mini bottle of whiskey, mixed with diet cola. Apparently feeling that he needed to justify his beverage, my seatmate told me that he was a nervous flyer. He didn't like to travel, and when he did, he preferred to drive. Joe introduced himself as a diamond appraiser and asked me what I did for a living. I told Joe about my new career and how it was about helping lawyers work more efficiently by sharing their knowledge among their colleagues (at this point in my KM career I hadn't formulated my elevator pitch). I didn't get into details, and he didn't seem that interested. But I'm always interested in hearing about what people do, and I thought it was the least I could do to try to make him feel less nervous about the flight, so I asked him about his business.

Joe may have been nervous, but he was not modest. Not only was he a diamond appraiser, but he was the best in the business. He worked for himself, in New York's Diamond District, and his services were sought all over the country. Joe ordered another whiskey and diet cola. He described to me the basics of how to identify a good diamond—the four Cs that just about everyone has heard of: carat (weight), cut, color, and clarity. Clarity was the most important, he said. "I don't know why I'm telling you this." But I was interested and happy that he continued. Joe recounted his lengthy career in the diamond business. He learned the trade from his late mentor, who at the time was the best in the business. The diamond community was small, one where everyone knew everyone else, and your reputation was crucial. It reminded me of the way my father had spoken about the way the legal community used to be decades ago.

We were well into the flight, and now that Joe's second drink had begun to take effect, he really started to open up. "I don't know why I'm telling you this," he repeated, "but do you want to know the key to diamond appraisal—the *one* technique that makes me the best?" This got my attention. I straightened up in my seat and refocused my attention, which had drifted a little from Joe's story, probably after he had repeated some less-fascinating part of his trade. Yes, I did want to know. Very much. For a moment, thoughts of a quick career shift raced through my head. This (self-proclaimed) diamond guru was about to tell me the One Thing that makes him the Michael Jordan of diamond appraisal. Armed with this one piece of information, I too could set up shop on 47th Street in Midtown Manhattan and get to work and make a fortune. Joe had my full attention.

"A diamond's clarity is the key," Joe repeated. "Everyone uses expensive instruments to look for inclusions, but there is a simpler way. I can tell you about the clarity of a diamond like that," he said, snapping his fingers. Joe explained that an inclusion was a flaw in a diamond—something inside the stone that shouldn't be there, like a fleck of carbon. The fewer inclusions, the better the clarity, and the higher the value of the diamond. "The best way to judge clarity—better than any microscope—is tissue paper," he said. Come again?

Joe went on to tell me how when you wet a piece of tissue paper and hold it over the stone, the inclusions appear right through the tissue paper, as plain as day. “Nobody knows about this trick, and why I’m telling you, I don’t know,” he said, as he poured the rest of his third airline-sized bottle of whiskey into what was left of his cola. “Tissue paper,” I thought to myself, “In vino veritas.”

“The problem with what you do for a living,” he said, “is that all that ‘knowledge sharing’ creates competition. When I tell someone my techniques, I no longer have the edge. People don’t need me. They can go to the next guy.” At first, I was surprised that Joe had even listened to what I told him about knowledge management. But I was instantly deflated when I realized that competitive lawyers might be resistant to the idea of sharing their knowledge because, just like Joe, they could lose their edge. Could this competitive nature be the undoing of KM? Are lawyers genetically predisposed to competition and averse to sharing? I was reminded of my law school days, when students would use razor blades to cut pages out of court reporters and treatises so that their classmates would be unable to find the right research to prepare for class. Backstabbing among lawyers, even in law firms, is the stuff of legend. I needn’t cite examples, I’m sure.

Joe’s statement made me question the very foundations of KM. It also made me wonder how to defend KM from those naturally competitive lawyers who would argue that sharing their knowledge would put them at a competitive disadvantage, even among their partners and colleagues. I had heard the arguments before. “If I give everyone my work product, they will no longer come to me when they need my help. They’ll just copy my work and pass it off as their own.”

I thought long and hard about this. At the time, I didn’t have all the answers (and unfortunately, I still don’t), but I believed that most people, lawyers included, want to succeed and want their colleagues to succeed, as well. I knew that there would always be those lawyers who are hypercompetitive and think of lawyering as a zero-sum game, even among their teammates. However, I had worked as an associate in law firms long enough to know that the most truly successful lawyers are generous, collaborative, and team players. Backstabbing, sabotage, and infighting may be effective tactics for short-term gain, but those gains are not sustainable in the long term. The organizations that tolerate such bad behaviors are usually undesirable places to work, have high turnover, or both. Those that embrace the idea that "a rising tide lifts all ships," on the other hand, are more enjoyable, positive places that foster loyalty, long-term growth, and prosperity.

I also realized that there is a fundamental difference between the technique that purportedly made Joe the best diamond appraiser and what makes an outstanding lawyer or law firm. Joe's single technique is akin to a trade secret, such as the secret formula for Coca-Cola. Unlike Joe after a few drinks, The Coca-Cola Company fiercely guards its secret formula, because it knows that if it were to fall into the wrong hands, their flagship product could theoretically be produced by anyone, potentially ruining the entire company.[1] Lawyers' skills, abilities, and work product are different. Just having a copy of a lawyer's Supreme Court brief will not make another lawyer proficient in writing a similar brief or arguing a case before the Court. But embracing knowledge management principles and enabling lawyers to locate work product and other attorneys with specific experience or skill sets can help the firm as a whole better represent clients, develop business, and be more successful.

My short time with Joe made me think more deeply about the knowledge management journey on which I was about to embark and the challenges I would face in trying to convince lawyers of the way of KM. Since that flight, I have run into some lawyers who shared Joe's competitive attitude and reluctance to share. I'll never forget the partner at one firm who refused to save his documents to the firm's document management system or add his contacts to the firm's contact relationship management system for fear that his colleagues would steal his work product and his clients. He didn't stay at the firm very long. For the most part, however, I've had the good fortune to work for law firms where the majority of the lawyers valued teamwork and collaboration. That's not to say there haven't been challenges. And in this book I hope to share with you some ways to overcome your KM challenges. But I am getting ahead of myself. We'll get into all of that shortly. First, let me tell you one more story, from before I met Joe, about how this all started for me.

1. Jamal Booker, "The Secret Formula Is Still Safe!", April 13, 2011, http://www.coca-colacompany.com/stories/2011/04/the-secret-formula-is-still-safe.html.

How I Got Started in Knowledge Management

In Appendix B of this book, I have recorded the stories of how several knowledge management professionals got started in their current roles. I have also interspersed parts of those stories throughout. I encourage you to read their stories, as they are not just chronologies of how they got where they are, but they contain pearls of wisdom that will give you greater insight into the fascinating world of knowledge management. When I thought about my own story, I had planned to include it in the appendix, as well, but I was encouraged to put it here, up front, to help readers understand my perspective—where I'm coming from.

What put me on that plane, where I met the diamond appraiser, was a feeling that I didn't want to be a lawyer forever. I had been practicing law as a general commercial litigator in the New York City office of Gibbons P.C. (then called Gibbons, Del Deo, Dolan, Griffinger & Vecchione). I didn't hate it, the way some practicing lawyers unfortunately do, but I knew that I needed to find something else to do with the rest of my working life. This was not an overnight decision; the feeling had been brewing for a couple of years. I mulled job options, not knowing where to go from here. I didn't want to continue practicing, but I also didn't want to discard my experience as a lawyer and all those years of education that got me there. And I had even less interest in taking a huge pay cut to start over in some foreign industry. That's probably why it took me so long to make my move. I had student loans to repay, after all.

Slowly but surely, things came together in my mind. I was still working the sort of full-time hours that are typical of a litigation associate in New York City, so I had little time to think deeply about my move. I found myself increasingly busy and frustrated, working weekends when there were no pressing deadlines. I realized that I spent a lot of my spare time—to the extent that any time was spare—trying to figure out how to make my work life easier. With relatively few good technology tools to help me manage my work and my cases (this was the early- to mid-2000s), I found myself using basic Microsoft Office applications, Excel and Word, to organize my matters. My firm had not adopted a digital case file approach, so I took it upon myself to make my own. I scanned all of the key documents in all of my cases, saved them as PDF files, and organized them in folders and subfolders on my PC hard drive so that I would have instant access to all of my files right from my desktop. I created matter indexes of all of my cases, with key facts, key players, and issues outlined in Excel spreadsheets. I started to amass my own personal collection of sample and template motion papers, briefs, legal memos, etc., so that I could reuse them and cut my document drafting time down significantly. At this point, I had never even heard of the term "knowledge management."

While all of these techniques helped me cope with the busy, inefficient, and sometimes tedious practice of law that I had come to know, I started to think that I could not be the only one feeling frustrated, spinning my wheels, putting in lots of time and energy, but not getting the expected results. Others must feel the same. If only there was a way to make what I was doing in my spare time into a career helping other lawyers be more efficient. By the middle of 2005, I had had enough. I was mentally and emotionally done as a practicing lawyer. I needed a change. That thought, "if only there was a way . . . ," kept returning, and I found myself writing up a job description for a job that didn't exist.

I scheduled a meeting with the firm's managing partner, marched into his office, and with crossed fingers and a racing heart, explained that I had come up with a proposal for me to stay with the firm but discontinue my role as a practicing attorney. "I want to help improve the way our lawyers practice law," I said, "to help make us more efficient and effective, and to help improve the way we approach the business of law, as well." I told the managing partner about the way I had managed my cases, collected samples and templates, and generally made my work more efficient. I went on and on, explaining my ideas, while he sat there silently. I couldn't read his poker face, and as I ran out of things to say, he paused for a moment, picked up a sheet of paper from his desk, and handed it to me. "It just so happens that we are looking to create a new role at the firm," he said. "What do you know about knowledge management?"

Scanning the page, and realizing that it contained the essential description of what I wanted to do for the firm (only far better articulated), I resisted the urge to say, "What's knowledge management?" I had no idea that the things I had been working on, the things that comprised my proposed made-up job, were elements of an actual, established discipline. I withheld my proposed job description and told the managing partner, "Wow. This is exactly what I had in mind."

This serendipitous series of events led to me consuming all I could find about this exciting new thing called knowledge management and starting my new job as the firm's first Chief Knowledge Officer. It also led to my lesson in diamond appraisal, and everything else you're about to read. I hope it helps you on your knowledge management journey.

Chapter 1

The Fundamentals of Knowledge Management

> Taoists declared there is a knowledge not accessible by language. As the *Tao Te Ching* announces in its opening line, "The Tao that can be put into words is not the real Tao."
>
> —Thomas Hoover, *The Zen Experience*

1.1 Chapter Preview and Target Audience

Chapter preview:

1. There are many different definitions of knowledge management, but there is no universal definition.
2. You'll gain an understanding of how KM has been defined and what it is about.
3. You'll learn some ways to communicate KM to busy lawyers that will pique interest rather than create confusion.

Target audience:
Chapter 1 will be of interest to Lawyer Leaders, Administrative Leaders, and even casual readers. It contains information that will form the foundation of your understanding of knowledge management and will prepare you for your knowledge management journey.

This book is not a deep dive into the theoretical and scholarly depths of knowledge management (KM). I will not dwell on the details and try to come up with the ultimate or universal definition of KM. Those in KM circles know, all too well, that there is no universally accepted definition of knowledge management. Oh, how we would love to just open a dictionary and point when someone asks, "What is knowledge management?"

That said, it is important that we have a common understanding about what we mean when we talk about knowledge management. Therefore, we will spend some time on the fundamentals to make sure that we are all on the same page.

When I discuss KM, I tend to be a bit of a chameleon. My description of it, and the way I talk about it, changes based on my surroundings. Like lawyers, we KM folks have our own jargon. Those of us who are KM folks *and* lawyers, like me, are at even greater risk of the jargon trap. If you were a fly on the wall at some of my industry gatherings, you would hear terms like "tacit knowledge," "communities of practice," "enterprise search," and "taxonomy." But if you were to catch me evangelizing KM to one of the lawyers in my firm, you would hear plain language, terms that lawyers (and just about anyone else) can understand. As lawyers know, after having been criticized about the use of legalese for decades, people want plain language.

I despise jargon. I praise simplicity, clarity, and plain language. I shall strive for all three throughout this book.

1.2 A Brief History of Knowledge Management

As the well-known author and professor of management Peter Drucker noted, the "knowledge society" is upon us.[1] We are no longer a community made up of a majority of farmers, manual laborers, craftspeople, or the like. However, this condition is relatively recent. At the start of the 20th century, the majority of workers in the world were farmers, but by the mid-

1. Peter Drucker, *The Essential Drucker* (New York: HarperCollins, 2001).

1990s, they made up only 5 percent of workers in the United States and other developed countries. This agrarian society of the early 20th century yielded to blue-collar workers, and by the mid-1900s, "industrial blue-collar workers had become the largest single group in every developed country." By the 1990s, however, the blue-collar worker was "in total and irreversible retreat" and "had become marginal in numbers," accounting for less than one-fifth of the workforce.[2]

One can see that with the rise of the knowledge society, as Drucker calls it, how to manage knowledge workers and their work has become increasingly important. The knowledge worker does not earn her living by "making or moving things," as her blue-collar predecessor did. Knowledge workers are not making, and their employers are not selling, widgets. Their value is not derived from their ability to push a button or pull a lever. Their value is based on their ability to "apply theoretical and analytical knowledge."[3]

I provide this truncated, and selective, history of the American workforce not to educate the reader (many authors can do that far better and much more thoroughly than I have), but rather merely to provide some context and to point out what is likely a nagging thought for almost everyone reading this: Legal professionals have been knowledge workers all along! We have never sold widgets, and the only buttons we've ever pressed were on typewriter or computer keyboards (and that development is relatively recent). What's more is that we have always understood the value of our intellectual capital. We, in the legal profession, have *always* been knowledge workers.

It's not the knowledge that's the problem, it's the management of the knowledge that leaves a little to be desired. Some readers (KM practitioners and academics, for sure) will recoil at this pronouncement, possibly for various reasons, but I can practically hear some saying all the way from here: "But you cannot manage knowledge! Knowledge is personal!" Drucker himself once said at a conference: "You can't manage knowledge. Knowledge is between two ears and only between two ears."

2. Ibid., 301.
3. Ibid., 305.

1.3 What Is Knowledge Management (And Why It Doesn't Really Matter)?

Please don't misunderstand me. Knowledge management matters. If it didn't, then I wouldn't have written this book. What doesn't really matter is whether we can agree on a universal definition of KM that is acceptable to everyone across all industries and fields. It is more important that we understand what knowledge management is *about.*

Even more important, as members of the legal services industry, is that we understand what knowledge management is about *in our field.* And for each of us individually, it is important to have a solid understanding of what KM is about *in our particular organizations.*

This is not a cop-out. It's not a way to avoid answering the question "What is knowledge management?" (although many KM professionals would rather do just that). Rather, it is a call to action for you to understand what is important for your law firm, law department, or company. Only by understanding what is important *to your organization* can you employ the appropriate KM efforts and initiatives that will really make a difference.

That last point is important. Don't overlook it. You'll be tempted to do just that. You'll be tempted to skip ahead and look for some quotes that tell you exactly what knowledge management is. Although you won't find exactly what you think you want, I won't leave you hanging. I'll tell you what others think KM is, and I'll tell you what KM is (and has been) about for me and the organizations I've been associated with at various times.

1.4 What Is Knowledge Management (According to Others)?

Many people will tell you their definition of KM. Many of these definitions are good. They help us understand the nature of knowledge management. They help us grasp the concepts. But they are slow, contemplative, and often laden with jargon. There is nothing wrong with slow, contemplative thinking. I highly encourage it. But these days, law firms are fast-paced, high-pressure environments where you need to make your point, make it quickly, and make it count. If you can't communicate your point simply, quickly, and meaningfully to a busy lawyer, then you've missed an opportunity that you may never have again. What's more, as a wise man once said, "If you can't explain it simply, you don't understand it well enough."[4]

We are all competing for attention. Think of all the things going on in your law firm or company. Communicating KM is only one of dozens of things that compete for lawyers' attention. As Steve Jobs told his employees at Apple about marketing in 1997, "This is a very complicated world, it's a very noisy world. And we're not going to get the chance to get people to remember much about us. No company is. So we have to be really clear on what we want them to know about us."[5] The same is true of communicating about KM.

As mentioned, there is no agreement about the definition of knowledge management. David Gurteen, a well-known KM consultant and speaker, has compiled a group of video clips in which he asks several people the simple question: "What is knowledge management?"[6] The more than 20 answers (some verbose, some concise) are interesting and diverse, and they underscore the point that there are common themes, but there is still disagreement about the definition of KM. Following are some published definitions of KM:

- In his seminal work, *The End of Lawyers? Rethinking the Nature of Legal Services*, Richard Susskind describes the essence of knowledge management as characterized by "formal organization of procedures, knowledge, and expertise . . . gathered on a collective basis from across a firm." He notes that these characteristics "should bring greater quality, consistency, and speed of turn-around [of work product to clients]."[7] The idea of KM, he says, is "straightforward enough—it is about systematically organizing and exploiting the collective knowledge of a business."[8]

4. Albert Einstein, http://www.brainyquote.com/quotes/quotes/a/alberteins383803.html.
5. http://www.forbes.com/sites/carminegallo/2011/01/17/steve-jobs-people-with-passion-can-change-the-world/.
6. http://www.gurteen.com/gurteen/gurteen.nsf/id/wiskm.
7. Richard Susskind, *The End of Lawyers? Rethinking the Nature of Legal Services*, revised edition (New York: Oxford University Press, 2010), 35.
8. Ibid., 41.

Although this is true, in part, KM is so much more than that, and we shall explore the farther-reaching aspects of KM later. Susskind also points out that, in many firms, there has been disappointment in the field of knowledge management. He discusses this letdown in a section about "apparent failures." It is important to note that many of these failures are actual, but some are merely, as he puts it, "apparent"—they only seem to be failures. Later, we will explore the reasons for some such failures, but we will spend more time focusing on how to avoid them and on implementing successful KM programs and initiatives.

- In his book, *Knowledge Management*, Carl Frappaolo succinctly defines knowledge management as "the leveraging of collective wisdom to increase responsiveness and innovation."[9]
- Despite its self-denigrating title, *The Complete Idiot's Guide to Knowledge Management*, by Melissie Clemmons Rumizen, also sets out a good, concise definition of KM. She defines it as "the systematic processes by which knowledge needed for an organization to succeed is created, captured, shared and leveraged."[10]
- In her book about knowledge management for lawyers, Gretta Rusanow defines KM as "the leveraging of your firm's collective wisdom by creating systems and processes to support and facilitate the identification, capture, dissemination and use of your firm's knowledge to meet your business objectives."[11]
- More recently, although not in the context of the legal profession, Carla O'Dell and Cindy Hubert of the American Productivity and Quality Center (APQC) defined knowledge management as "a systematic effort to enable information and knowledge to grow, flow and create value."[12]

9. Carl Frappaolo, *Knowledge Management* (West Sussex, UK: Capstone Publishing, 2006), 8.
10. Melissie Clemmons Rumizen, *The Complete Idiot's Guide to Knowledge Management* (New York: Alpha Books/Penguin, 2002), 9.
11. Gretta Rusanow, *Knowledge Management and the Smarter Lawyer* (New York: ALM Properties, 2003), 7.
12. Carla O'Dell and Cindy Hubert, *The New Edge in Knowledge: How Knowledge Management Is Changing the Way We Do Business* (Hoboken, NJ: John Wiley & Sons, 2011).

- There are other definitions of KM—many, many others. Matthew Parsons lists several in his 2003 book, *Effective Knowledge Management for Law Firms*. And Ray Sims once posted in his blog[13] a list of "43 knowledge management definitions—and counting." That list of 43 definitions grew to more than 60 before the blog went offline.

These definitions, although diverse and somewhat incongruent, include several common concepts, most of which revolve around what we call "explicit knowledge" (a term we will explore later). The common concepts included in these definitions—creation, capture, organization, accessibility, sharing/transfer, and reuse/application—are depicted in Figure 1.1.

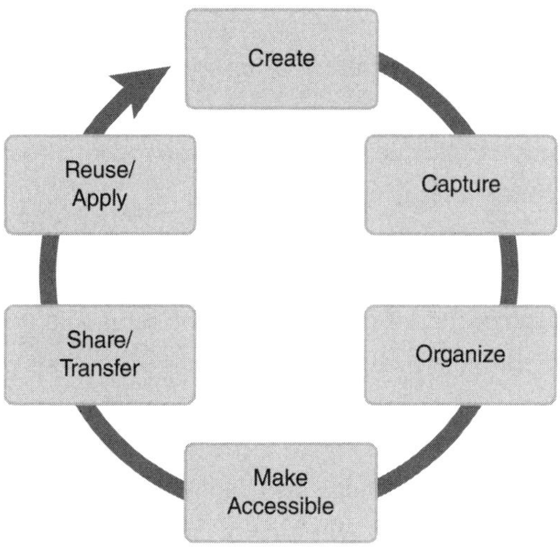

Figure 1.1
A typical representation of the scope of knowledge management. However, this is a limited view of KM, and I believe KM to be much broader and farther reaching.

13. The blog appears to be currently offline, but an archived copy is available via the Internet Archive Wayback Machine: http://web.archive.org/web/20081219112728/http://blog.simslearningconnections.com/?p=279.

Let's briefly address these concepts in the context of some of these definitions:

Create. The concept of creating knowledge is a bit of a misnomer. Most would agree that knowledge is not really created, but rather it is acquired through experience or education. We know things because we have learned about them, either through training or doing. So, when we talk about creating knowledge, we are really talking about creating environments in which people can obtain knowledge through learning or experiencing. In a law firm environment, that may consist of lawyers performing research or taking part in various activities, such as negotiating contracts, arguing motions, or trying cases, just to name a few. Creating these opportunities for knowledge acquisition can be intentional (e.g., through training and mentorship) or simply a byproduct of doing the work of a lawyer (or, as some may call it, on-the-job training). Creating knowledge in a legal industry context is often thought of as creating legal work product (e.g., some form of document). Work product is not knowledge, but it is widely considered to be the manifestation of one's knowledge.

Capture. The concept of capturing knowledge is also technically a misnomer. In reality, knowledge is tacit—a personal possession that, some may argue, cannot be captured, except in one's own mind. So, what most KM professionals mean by capturing knowledge is turning one's tacit knowledge into explicit knowledge by recording or codifying it (or a representation of it) in some medium.[14] Practically speaking, capturing knowledge in this way is easy. We do it every day when we write notes, briefs, memos, contracts, e-mail messages, letters, and books. Whether we scribble thoughts or ideas on a piece of scrap paper or save them digitally in a word processing application, we are constantly capturing our knowledge, in a sense.

Organize. Compared to capturing our knowledge, which is relatively easy, organizing our knowledge (or at least the representation of our knowledge) as it is captured is more difficult and requires more

14. The concepts of tacit and explicit knowledge are addressed more fully in Chapter 3.

deliberate effort. This can be done in a low-tech way: for example, think of a classic filing cabinet full of paper records arranged or sorted logically. Or it can be done with the assistance of higher-tech tools, such as digital storage media (like networked computer hard drives) or more complex document or content management systems. Although these technologies are often simultaneously used to capture our knowledge, they also help us organize it. There are also more advanced technologies, such as automatic classification systems, tagging, labeling, etc., and approaches, such as employing taxonomies or classification techniques, that enable better or more detailed organization of our captured knowledge.

Make Accessible. For knowledge management efforts to be successful, it is not enough to create, capture, and organize our collective knowledge. A crucial step is to make that knowledge accessible to others. Knowledge management is a communal endeavor. The purpose is to share (see the next step) our knowledge to the benefit of others in our community. If we don't make our collective knowledge (on which we spent so much time creating, capturing, and organizing) accessible, then it is *almost* worthless. Knowledge that is trapped in someone's mind (tacit knowledge) is valuable but only to the single person who possesses it. Likewise, even explicit knowledge that is trapped in a locked file cabinet or on an inaccessible computer server is similarly of limited value.

Share/Transfer. The easiest way to share knowledge is for one person to communicate it directly to another; nothing complicated here. The ability to share or transfer knowledge on a larger, enterprise scale, however, is related to the level of accessibility of that knowledge. Arguably, if knowledge is appropriately accessible, then it is being shared (or at least it is able to be shared or transferred). Thus, in one respect, sharing or transferring knowledge is simply a matter of setting up systems or processes to enable it to happen. But on another—more fundamental—level, sharing and transferring knowledge is a cultural challenge. As the attitude of the diamond appraiser in the Introduction section of this book demonstrated, and as we will explore further, developing and encouraging a knowledge-sharing culture is sometimes the greatest challenge that KM professionals will face. Technology is relatively easy, but people can be difficult.

Reuse/Apply. Once an organization's collective knowledge is captured, organized, made accessible, and shared, the final step is to reuse that knowledge. This is the most visible step in the process—the tip of the proverbial iceberg. It is what lawyers and other legal professionals do on a daily basis. Whether they are using checklists, template documents, or precedent documents to eliminate the need to reinvent the wheel on a current matter, or applying an argument articulated in one matter to the facts of a new matter, reusing existing collective knowledge is where the rubber hits the road for your lawyers. It is important to realize, however, that this is not the end of the road for this KM model. Notice that the diagram does not stop at reuse/apply. It circles back to creation and continues its flow, because knowledge that is reused (and inevitably altered when that happens) becomes newly developed knowledge that can be reused repeatedly.

The elements of the aforementioned scope of knowledge management are a good start in understanding the basics of KM. Although many KM concepts and activities fall under one or more of these elements, I believe that the scope of KM is broader than what is depicted and described here. As you will see, I am not alone in this opinion. Several law firm KM efforts, although diverse in their scopes, go beyond this more traditional model. Even the way I communicate knowledge management to lawyers hints at the broadening scope of knowledge management.

1.5 Communicating Knowledge Management to Busy Lawyers

If you are going to undertake knowledge management efforts or initiatives in a law firm or legal department setting, you will need to be able to communicate KM simply and effectively. Communicating what KM is *about* is different than what KM *is*. Defining a concept (what something *is*) can be abstract and lead to a shallow understanding. Expressing what something is *about* adds relevance, context, and applicability, ultimately leading to greater understanding.

I always address what KM is *about* before I address what KM *is*, because I want to ensure that my audience understands what's in it for them in the context of what they do. I want them to care about KM, because I know how much KM can help lawyers improve their practice and business. Answering the question "What's in it for me?" is fundamental to acceptance of anything new. "Why would I do that?" and "Why should I care?" are valid questions. Addressing what something is *about* is really addressing these questions of why. Answer the why question first and then address the what and how questions.

1.5.1 What Is Knowledge Management *About*?

Over the years, I have attempted to communicate KM to lawyers in various ways. Along the way, I've seen some glazed-over eyes, some semiconfident nods of understanding, and some aha! moments when light bulbs have suddenly appeared over people's heads. I prefer to see light bulbs. And to achieve light bulbs, it's important to know your audience. Craft your message so that it is meaningful to the person you're talking to.

Although the KM definitions noted previously are good and valid, in my view, they are geared toward KM practitioners, not lawyers. If you are among the growing number of KM practitioners in law firms and law departments today, then you will likely appreciate and can digest, comprehend, and use these definitions to help further your understanding of the field and discipline of KM. But these definitions don't do much to promote a true understanding of KM among those who are not in the KM business. They don't answer the "What's in it for me?" question for busy lawyers.

But there are a few ways to quickly and effectively answer the question, "What is knowledge management about?" To answer this question—to really get the point across—and capture the essence of what knowledge management is about *for your audience*, I recommend using some catchy mantras that I've adopted over the years. They are "The Right Stuff," "Who, What, How," and "Connections."

1.5.2 The Right Stuff

The first catchy mantra used in KM circles is "Knowledge management is about getting the *right* information to the *right* people at the *right* time." KM professionals will recognize this immediately. Some will dismiss this catchphrase as trite, meaningless, and simplistic. Others will claim it as their own. Librarians, information management professionals, big data pundits, and even news media professionals have used this slogan—or a variation of it—for years to describe what they do. It's the catch-all way to describe a whole host of activities and efforts that are employed to deliver information. But in the right context, this phrase can be an effective way to describe *at least part* of what KM is about. Thus, I typically use this refrain in conjunction with the others described as follows to set the stage for a more meaningful discussion about connections. We'll discuss more on connections in a moment.

I have found that communicating KM to busy lawyers is easier with visual aids. Some of the graphics that I often use during presentations are included in Figure 1.2.

Figure 1.2
In part, KM is about "getting the right information to the right people at the right time." I use this image in presentations about knowledge management.

As mentioned, this theme is common, and it has been used by several KM professionals, including O'Dell and Hubert, who wrote that KM "is about creating and managing the processes to get the right knowledge to the right people at the right time and help people share and act on information in order to improve organizational performance."[15]

Picture the scenario in which a frazzled lawyer comes to you for help. He is inundated with a daily flood of e-mail messages, news alerts, and other media, and he just can't keep up. Worse yet, this flood is washing away the important stuff, so he's missing things that he really should be seeing. In simple terms, he suffers from the effects of what is commonly referred to as "information overload." He has lost his focus and his *ability* to focus. The clutter of so much stuff is obscuring what is truly important—the actionable information that he can use to develop business, learn or expand his understanding of an important topic, or make some decision that has an immediate impact on a current matter. Sound familiar? You don't need to be a lawyer to know how that feels. We all feel the effects of information overload.

Some people, such as author and New York University professor Clay Shirky, argue that the problem is not information overload, but "filter failure." In his fascinating September 2008 presentation at the Web 2.0 Expo in New York,[16] Shirky posited that what many call information overload is not the real problem. Rather, the ever-increasing torrent of information that comes at you every day is simply a fact of life in the Information Age. Simply put, Shirky claims that it is a fact, it is not likely to let up anytime soon, and we must deal with it.

The cause of this torrent—and its derided effects—is accessibility. With the advent of the Internet, and affordable access to it, the once seemingly insurmountable barriers to producing content for all to see have been eliminated. Anyone with Internet access can create a blog, social network post, or website that will be indexed by web search engines like Google. Once indexed, this content is accessible by anyone else with Internet access. Add to this the continued abuse of today's most popular communication medium: e-mail. The ever-increasing number of e-mail messages is oft-cited as one of

15. O'Dell and Hubert, *The New Edge in Knowledge.*
16. "It's Not Information Overload, It's Filter Failure," http://www.youtube.com/watch?v=LabqeJEOQyI.

the biggest complaints about work life, and there is no shortage of authors willing to prescribe methods and systems to deal with it.[17]

There is no way to stop the ever-increasing amount of information that the world produces, argues Shirky, so we should not try. In addition, we should not use that volume of information as an excuse for our inability to get things done. Instead, we need to improve the filters we use to control what information reaches us and what does not. This is sort of an Information Age variant of the old adage that we cannot control other people's behaviors, but we can control how those behaviors affect us.

As KM professionals, it is our responsibility to help members of our organizations control how the information-blasting behaviors of others affect them. We must provide our lawyers with tools, techniques, tactics, and methods for dealing with the inundation of information. In Shirky's terms, we must help with the filtering. Ultimately, we need to help get the right information (the relevant, actionable information) to the right people (our lawyers and other legal professionals) at the right time (when they need it, not when others feel like sending it).

There are many ways that KM professionals can help address this problem. For example:

- Encouraging the use of traditional communication methods, such as face-to-face discussion
- Developing intranets with news and announcements that can be used in place of sending firm-wide e-mails
- Enabling discussion forums, wikis, or blogs
- Enabling enterprise social networking features, like micro blogging, sharing, and promotion applications
- Using shared task lists
- Using shared note-taking applications

1.5.3 Who, What, and How

The second mantra I use to communicate knowledge management is simply to say that "KM is about who we know, what we know, and how we do

17. Amy Gallo, "Stop Email Overload," http://blogs.hbr.org/hmu/2012/02/stop-email-overload-1.html.

things." (See Figure 1.3.) This phrase will also be immediately recognized by legal KM professionals.[18] Again, it is important to notice the word "about." I don't claim that this is a *definition* of KM. This who-what-how mantra is one of the many things that KM is *about*, and it is an effective way to help busy lawyers understand how KM can help them in a meaningful, practical, and jargon-free way.

Figure 1.3
"Who we know, what we know, and how we do it" is a popular way to describe part of what knowledge management is about. I use this image in presentations about knowledge management.

Who we know refers primarily to your colleagues and coworkers. Who are the other lawyers in your firm or law department? What are their specialties? Who do they know? How can their experiences help you—and therefore help the firm as a whole—succeed? Answering the "who we know" question was easier in the past, when law firms weren't the massive international entities that many are today. For most law firms, gone are the days when everyone knew everyone else. Today, lawyers at law firms come and go. Not too long ago, law firms were places of great loyalty, and

18. I first heard this concept articulated by Tom Baldwin, who has served as chief knowledge officer to law firms such as Sheppard Mullin Richter & Hampton LLP and Reed Smith LLP and is currently chief information officer at Cadwalader, Wickersham & Taft LLP. www.linkedin.com/in/tombaldwin.

the typical career path for a lawyer was a relatively straight line. It went something like this:

1. Secure a summer associate position in a law firm while in law school
2. Work hard and get an offer to join the firm as an associate upon graduation
3. Work hard for several years as an associate
4. Make partner (and make good money)
5. Retire

But in the past 20 to 30 years, that model has slowly changed. The straight-line career path of the traditional lawyer has been forever altered. These days, you would be hard pressed to find a lawyer who graduated law school after 1990 who had not made a lateral move from one law firm to another or to an in-house law department. This is not a commentary on the state of law firms today but rather a realization that lawyers are much more mobile than they were in the past. This means that you are likely to be working in a law firm where most of the lawyers did not "grow up" working together. They don't know each other as well as they did in the old days when lawyers picked a firm and stuck with it. For any lawyer in a law firm today, knowing who your colleagues are, what experiences they have had, and what they have to offer to the firm as a whole can be a challenge.

Add to this the challenge of numbers. Although this is not a particular issue for smaller firms, large law firms today are larger than ever before. At some point, as a law firm grows, it is simply impossible to know all of the attorneys. According to the 2014 NLJ 350, the *National Law Journal*'s survey of the largest law firms in the United States by number of lawyers, the largest law firm in the United States, Baker & McKenzie, has more than 4,000 attorneys, while the smallest firm on the list, Farella Braun + Martel, has only 115. The average number of attorneys in the largest 350 law firms in the country is 419. That's far too many to know everyone personally. In fact, if we accept the idea of Dunbar's Number,[19] people can only maintain stable social relationships with between 100 and 250 others. Knowledge

19. British anthropologist Robin Dunbar suggests that people can have a maximum of about 150 stable social relationships; beyond that number, the relationships start breaking down.

management, in part, addresses how we can better know our colleagues when, increasingly, law firms are too big to know.

This is not to imply that knowledge management is only for large law firms and legal departments. As we will see, knowledge management principles, concepts, and tools can help lawyers at law firms and law departments of all sizes.

"Who we know" is also not limited to the people inside a law firm. Knowledge management also addresses the people outside the walls of our own organizations. Familiarity with our colleagues and coworkers is essential, but knowledge about people outside of our organizations is also critical to law firm success. Knowledge about our clients, business partners, vendors, co-counsel, adversaries, and others can often be equally important to the business and practice of law.

Although some KM purists might argue that KM professionals have no business focusing outside the walls of an organization, modern KM professionals are seldom bound by such theoretical restraints. They focus on the business of knowledge management and don't dwell on whether they are overstepping the traditional bounds of KM that might otherwise restrict those in academic KM circles. They see the application of KM principles as a means to an end and not an end in itself. They ask: "How can we use the powerful concepts and approaches of knowledge management to help our law firms succeed as businesses?" We will explore more about the who we know aspect of KM in later chapters.

What we know, the second part of the who-what-how mantra, is closely related to who we know, because people possess knowledge (i.e., the "what"). But when we talk about what we know, we primarily mean the firm's collective knowledge, which is usually captured in documents and, increasingly, in digital repositories such as databases, document management systems (DMSs), e-mail, and other content-driven applications.

Many law firms have DMSs or some other document repositories (e.g., shared network storage, or even cloud-based storage) in which they collect the firm's work product. The bulk of this work product is contained in documents such as letters, briefs, memoranda, agreements, and other legal documents.

Many lawyers would like to think that their work product or area of law is truly unique and that they cannot possibly use previous work product to help them create new work product, but this is rarely the case. In truth, many legal documents are, for the most part, boilerplate. If lawyers can find a document that is similar to the type of document that they need to create for new matter, then they can use that preexisting document to shorten the time it takes for them to draft the new document. This approach not only makes document drafting more efficient, but it also helps ensure document drafting quality and consistency. Most lawyers will recognize the practice of using prior documents as the basis of future documents. In fact, most lawyers probably use *their own* prior work product as the basis for new documents on which they are working. Extending this idea to a firm-wide practice can further enhance the ability of lawyers to be more efficient and consistent with their work product, because they are able to leverage their colleagues' work as well as their own.

Legal work product is not restricted to official legal documents that were created for matters. Legal professionals can seek to leverage other work product beyond matter documents captured in their DMSs or other document repositories. For example, a law firm's collective knowledge is also captured in places like databases, time entry narratives, note-taking software, biographical marketing documents, and especially e-mail conversations. Today, almost all work product is digital and therefore easily captured in some system, software, or repository. If this information is captured, then it is subject to being accessed by others. This ease of capture creates a great opportunity for knowledge sharing throughout a law firm.

However, certain practices can make meaningfully capturing work product more difficult, even in this digital age. When I was a practicing litigation attorney, I was often asked to research and write briefs about various legal issues. These memoranda were typically drafted in the formal internal memo style in Microsoft Word and saved to my firm's DMS, captured for future generations of lawyers to access as needed. At the tail end of my days as an attorney (in 2005), however, I was typically asked to forego the formal memo format and simply send the memo as an e-mail. This made it easier for the partner to access and read the memo, but the e-mail memo was only captured in two e-mail boxes (my sent items and the partner's inbox). It was not captured in a firm-wide DMS for all attorneys to access. Some firms now capture e-mail in their DMSs or have other integrations with dedicated e-mail repositories to make e-mail more widely accessible, but it is not all that common, and thus it can be a challenge for some firms.

In addition to legal work product, another aspect of what we know is information about clients. This information can be direct knowledge about clients contributed by lawyers at the firm or it can be information gathered from various sources outside of the firm. Gathering and capturing such information, which is often done with customer relationship management (CRM) tools, can be useful not only to enhance the practice of law for lawyers, but also to assist lawyers with business development. Thus, contrary to what some people think, the what we know aspect of knowledge management is not just about traditional legal work product. It can also help lawyers with the business of law. We'll discuss more on this topic later.

How we do things, the third part of the who-what-how mantra, is about how we implement practices, procedures, and technologies to support maximizing the use of who we know and what we know. When most people hear this, they think about the technology part and ignore the practices and procedures part. After all, it's fun—especially for technologists—to address challenges with technology tools. DMSs, enterprise search systems, intranets, databases, etc., are grand endeavors that, when done well, can have a profound impact on the way lawyers and staff members get their work done more efficiently and effectively. However, addressing KM challenges with a sole focus on technology—without considering people and processes—is almost guaranteed to fail miserably.

We will talk more about technology in later chapters, but it's worth noting early and often that KM is not about technology. Using technology is only part of how we do things in KM. Failing to consider how you will address your KM challenges from a holistic perspective (where technology is merely one of the factors) is a recipe for disaster. Ignore this advice at your own peril. The mantra is not "who we know, what we know, and how we do *technology*."

1.5.4 Connections Are the Key

My favorite (and primary) way to communicate KM to lawyers—and the representation in the KM card in Figure 1.4—is to speak in terms of connections:

> Knowledge management is about connecting people with people, connecting people with knowledge and information, and the processes, procedures, and technologies required to make those connections.

I like this approach because it is broad yet meaningful. It allows me to talk about various aspects of KM from culture to behavior to technology, without eyes glazing over.

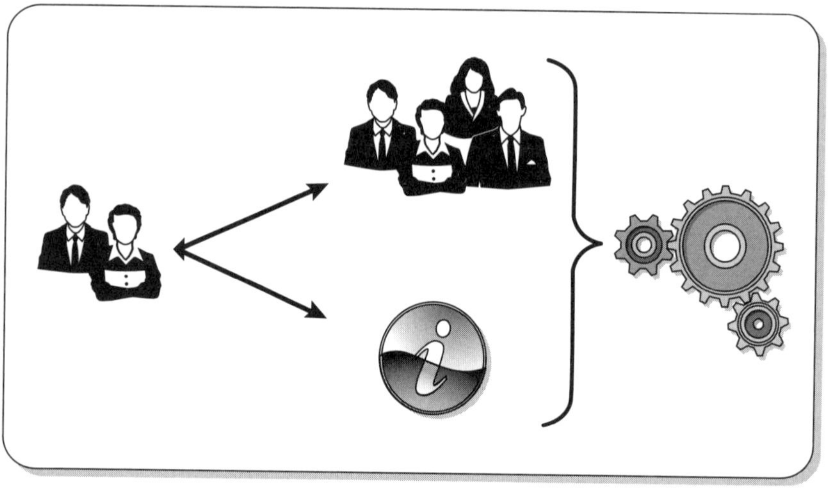

Figure 1.4
This is my KM Connections business card that I carry around and give to people when I describe what knowledge management is about. The KM department's e-mail address is printed on the back of the cards. I also use this image in presentations about knowledge management.

I carry the KM Connections cards with me at work (and elsewhere). When I need to explain KM to someone, I talk about connections. After my elevator speech, I hand them a card as a takeaway mnemonic. "Here's an easy way to remember what we do," I say. "The KM department's e-mail address is on the back."

The more complex definitions of KM, noted earlier, are fine when talking to people in KM circles and getting into the depths of KM, but when talking to busy lawyers, spouting some convoluted, jargon-bloated nonsense is the surest way to lose their attention. Lawyers are no strangers to jargon. They know it—and will reject it (and you)—the second they hear it.

This card has been highly effective in helping me to communicate what KM is all about. It has also become a part of our KM brand and the KM experience that I seek to create for my audiences. I include it in presentations, and I ask my KM department members to have the cards handy when they promote the department and our mission.

Connections are a common theme among KM professionals when describing what KM is all about. Well-known KM consultants Clara O'Dell and Cindy Hubert, of APQC, discuss the importance of connections in their book, *The New Edge in Knowledge*: "KM programs should: Connect employees to one another to help them excel at their jobs; connect employees to knowledge assets (just enough, just in time, and just for them); [and] connect those with experience or know-how with those who need it."[20]

Many law firm KM professionals also rely on the connections theme to describe what they do. Chris Boyd, Senior Director of Professional Services at Wilson Sonsini Goodrich & Rosati, who is head of knowledge management efforts there, agrees: "With KM specifically, we focus on connecting attorneys and legal support staff with the firm's three Ps: work product (model forms and sample documents), projects (matter profiles and documents), and people (internal and external experts)." Chris also focuses on the process improvement aspect, which has been a driving force behind his KM career choice. As he puts it, "I really like making things work better, and leading KM enables me to do just that for the legal profession."[21]

You can see how the theme of connections incorporates the two previous mantras. Connecting people with people is akin to the "who we know" and the "right people" concepts. Because people—not documents or databases—are the real knowledge possessors, connecting lawyers to each other within a firm or law department is often the most important first step in knowledge transfer. Very often, lawyers are not necessarily seeking model or sample documents. Rather, they want to pick each other's brains about various experiences they've had. One example you may have seen in your

20. O'Dell & Hubert, *The New Edge in Knowledge*.
21. Read about Chris's KM story in Appendix B.

own organization is when an attorney sends a firm-wide e-mail asking if anyone knows a particular adversary or has argued a motion before a particular judge.

Connecting people with knowledge and information is akin to the "what we know" and the "right information" concepts. The ability to make "knowledge assets," as O'Dell and Hubert call them, searchable and available to the people in your organization is a crucial part of knowledge management. There are many ways to do this, and although most of them do incorporate the use of some technology, it is not the technology that's important. More important is the culture of the organization—one that understands the value of making this codified knowledge widely accessible. Also important is the willingness of the workforce to make knowledge sharing a priority and to take personal responsibility to make it happen—to act on it by following the practices and procedures that ensure that the knowledge assets are properly stored and organized.

The processes, procedures, and technologies part of the mantra is akin to the "how we do it" and the "right time" concepts. As noted, and as we will explore more later, there are many ways to manifest your knowledge management efforts. They will be communicated to your organization through processes and procedures, and people will interact with, and benefit from, your efforts through various tools and technologies that you will create and maintain.

All three aspects of the connections model of knowledge management (or the other two models described) are necessary for a holistic, effective knowledge management program. Being able to communicate your efforts clearly, concisely, and meaningfully will be important. In the end, however, it's not about definitions. Once you've started your KM initiatives, you won't often find yourself *defining* KM. After all, do we ever define human resources or information technology or marketing or any other function of our law firms or legal departments? We usually just describe what people with those functions do or can offer. So, you will be spreading the word about what you are *doing*. The mantras described previously can help you communicate the value that KM can bring to your legal professionals and your firm or company.

1.6 Key Points

- There are many different definitions of knowledge management, but there is no universally accepted definition.
- Traditional views of knowledge management focus on creating, capturing, organizing, making accessible, sharing, and reusing institutional knowledge assets, but modern views are much broader.
- Defining KM can be useful to some people (primarily other KM professionals), in some circumstances, but communicating to lawyers what KM is *about* is more important.
- Communicating what KM is about to busy lawyers can be done with three mantras:
  a. Getting the right information to the right people at the right time
  b. Who we know, what we know, and how we do things
  c. Connecting people with people, connecting people with knowledge and information, and the processes, procedures, and technologies required to make those connections

Chapter 2

Why Knowledge Management, Why Now?

> Knowledge has become the key economic resource and the dominant—and perhaps even the only—source of competitive advantage.
>
> —Peter Drucker

2.1 Chapter Preview and Target Audience

Chapter preview:

1. You'll learn how, at its core, the goal of knowledge management is to help build better businesses.
2. You'll learn how knowledge management initiatives and techniques can deliver a mutual benefit to clients and law firms.
3. You'll learn how to overcome the challenges of skeptical lawyers who might, at first, be resistant to the idea of pursuing knowledge management.

Target audience:
Chapter 2 will be of interest to Lawyer Leaders, Administrative Leaders, and even casual readers. It addresses the all-important question "Why should we consider investing in knowledge management?" and gives tangible reasons to support the decision to pursue it.

2.2 How Knowledge Management Benefits Clients and Law Firms

Despite struggles and pronouncements of death (see Section 2.6), knowledge management has survived and thrived because KM initiatives, when executed well, benefit both law firms and clients. This happens in many ways, some of which we have discussed and others that will be addressed later, but fundamentally, KM is about *creating value* for clients in a way that is also beneficial for law firms. By definition, value is "a fair return or equivalent in goods, services, or money for something exchanged."[1] Thus, providing value in the legal services industry is not about charging the cheapest price (nobody wants to win a race to the bottom). Rather, it is about delivering appropriate, high-quality legal services as efficiently and cost effectively as possible, in a manner that clients find valuable.

At the very core, the main reason that any organization should pursue knowledge management is to help build a better, more sustainable, and more profitable business. Law firms are businesses. Corporate law departments are parts of businesses. Although businesses may exist for many laudable reasons, such as providing quality legal services to clients, in the long run, a for-profit business (such as a law firm) will cease to exist if it is not profitable. It just so happens that knowledge management focuses on efficiency, effectiveness, increasing quality, and promoting innovation to help businesses succeed. Knowledge management can help law firms and law departments provide quality legal services at good and reasonable costs to clients (whether those clients are external or internal). When clients receive high-quality legal services for a fair cost, they find that valuable. When clients, like any consumers, find value in what they receive for what they pay, they are happy. Happy clients provide the revenues that allow law firms to be successful businesses. Unhappy clients—those who don't find value in the legal services they receive—fire their law firms (or don't hire them in the future) and don't recommend their services to others. Unhappy clients lead to decreased revenues, which contribute to failing law firms. Thus, knowledge management benefits law firms by benefiting clients.

1. Merriam-Webster, http://www.merriam-webster.com/dictionary/value.

As many lawyers (both those in law firms and in law departments) know, however, happiness is a moving target. For decades, many clients were happy to hire the best law firms without much consideration of cost. Those clients paid their bills, perhaps not happily but without much challenge or pushback. Then things changed with the global financial crisis of 2007–2008, which has had a lasting, and some believe permanent, effect on many businesses. These changing and challenging economic and market conditions have a great impact on a business's ability to succeed. General counsel and other law department leaders are feeling unprecedented pressure from their clients (the companies and business units they serve) to reduce legal spending. "We need you to do more with less" is a common message that just about every law department leader has been hearing for several years now. That message is passed along to outside counsel. Happiness is now measured by how much more law firms can do with less. By establishing efficient processes and procedures, and enabling them with the tools to help lawyers work more efficiently, knowledge management can help both parties do more with less.

Reducing the impact of employee turnover is another important reason to pursue knowledge management. The ability of a law firm or law department to operate efficiently and effectively depends heavily on the expertise of individual lawyers. Because individuals have varied knowledge and experience, and turnover (in one way or another) is inevitable, knowledge sharing and transfer is important to prevent loss of knowledge from the organization when a lawyer departs. Later in this book, we will discuss several examples of how to share and transfer knowledge so that the knowledge of individual lawyers becomes institutional knowledge.

For a simple example of how knowledge management benefits clients and law firms, consider the following case study about document automation at my law firm.

2.3 Case Study: Document Automation at Ogletree Deakins

James Pennington is a labor and employment lawyer in the Birmingham, Alabama office of Ogletree, Deakins, Nash, Smoak & Stewart, P.C., where

I serve as Director of Knowledge Management. Several years ago, a large client with operations in several states asked James to help with a series of layoffs across its many locations. The assignment required knowledge of the employment laws in several jurisdictions and the delivery of severance agreements for the more than 1,500 employees who would be affected. James knew that this work was important to the client, but he also knew that the client was looking for efficiency in the delivery of the legal services.

Because there were employees in various jurisdictions, all with different laws and regulations, the severance agreements for each jurisdiction would be unique. Complicating the situation was that various categories of employees were being laid off, and each category of employee was entitled to different benefits. Even though there were multiple employees in each jurisdiction—and some at the same level who would have relatively similar severance agreements—these variables created slight differences in the documents that made this a difficult logistical task to accomplish efficiently yet accurately.

James and his team initially sought to make the process of developing the agreements more efficient by using word processing templates. Although this approach was somewhat effective, it was still relatively cumbersome and too time consuming; even with this approach, each agreement still took about an hour to complete. The client needed a more efficient solution. So, James and his team, which included Chris Mixon, who later became the firm's General Counsel, investigated a document assembly approach, using software called HotDocs.

The document assembly software allowed James and Chris to set up a template for the standard parts of the severance agreements and leave the variable parts to be filled in when the data became available. Once the template was created, a paralegal entered the data for each affected employee. The data entry was done via a questionnaire-based interface, so the paralegal did not have to be concerned with the structure and format of the end product. This variable data included the employee's name, title, position, location, benefits, etc. Factors such as position and location would trigger the inclusion or exclusion in the agreement of certain provisions and references to various state and local laws, regulations, or notices that were required. For example, the template presented the data entry user with the question, "Is this employee over 40 years of age?" If the user selected "yes," then the system inserted language into the agreement that advised the employee, among other things, of his or her statutory right to a certain number of days to review the document in accordance with the Older Workers Benefit Protection Act.

When all data for a particular affected employee was entered, the severance agreement was generated in either Microsoft Word or as a PDF with the appropriate variables, including statutes, contact information, rate of severance pay, etc. Workflow settings routed the draft document to James or Chris for review and any required revisions.

The document assembly approach not only made the process far more efficient by reducing the amount of time to prepare and review each agreement, but it also ensured the quality and consistency of each document, because it eliminated the potential mistakes that are possible when someone is editing an actual document or template. A task that originally took about one hour per agreement was cut down to a little over 12 minutes (or 0.2 billable hours); that's a huge savings considering the scale of the project. The client was extremely pleased with the cost savings and quality—so much so that they proposed that the firm handle each of the agreements for a fixed fee of 0.3 billable hours. The result was a true win-win solution for the client and the firm. The client received the high-quality work product they expected at a significantly reduced cost (saving 0.7 billable hours per agreement). The firm also benefited because it was paid for the time it took to prepare the document (0.2 hours) plus the extra 0.1 hour premium, which amounted to a built-in profit on the work.

To make the efforts even more efficient and cost-effective for the client, James worked with the firm's practice support group to make the document assembly questionnaire available to the client's regional human resources managers on the firm's extranet. This allowed the client's managers to directly input the various data about affected employees. After the HR managers input the data, workflow settings routed the assembled document directly to James or Chris for review and finalization. This revision in the procedure streamlined the process even more and allowed the attorney to return the completed work product even faster and with the same high quality—a further benefit to the client. The initiative worked so well that the client asked the firm to prepare additional severance agreements. So instead of the initial 1,500 agreements, the firm ended up delivering almost 6,000 agreements over a four-year period.

2.4 Communicating the Why: Challenges When Developing Knowledge Management Programs

Some of the greatest challenges when developing a KM program will come from the very people you are trying to help: lawyers. Let's face it, lawyers can sometimes be (ahem) difficult and resistant to change. However beneficial your KM efforts may be, they still constitute a change with which the lawyers, and others at your firm, must deal. Most people don't like change. Lawyers like it even less. These are not simply stereotypes or generalizations about lawyers. There is some hard science behind these assertions. Specifically, the lawyer personality contributes to the difficulty of successfully implementing a KM program.

Dr. Larry Richard, JD, PhD, has studied the personality traits of lawyers for more than 20 years and has measured multiple traits among thousands of lawyers. His research has revealed certain personality traits among lawyers that offer insight into why it can be difficult to convince some lawyers to adopt some management decisions. The six traits, in particular, that may have an impact are skepticism, autonomy, urgency, abstract reasoning, sociability, and resilience. Dr. Richard's research reveals that lawyers score above average in skepticism, autonomy, urgency, and abstract reasoning, and below average in sociability and resilience. As my colleague, Jennifer Mendez, Ogletree Deakins' KM Firm Solutions Manager, noted, "while these may be the traits of a successful lawyer, these tendencies pose a serious problem for KM initiatives in law firms."[2]

The first trait is skepticism, for which lawyers score in the 90th percentile, while the general public scores in the 50th percentile. "People who score high on this trait tend to be skeptical, even cynical, judgmental, questioning,

2. "Psychology of Lawyers and Knowledge Management: Encouraging Collaboration," http://blog.ogletreedeakins.com/psychology-of-lawyers-and-knowledge-management-encouraging-collaboration/.

argumentative and somewhat self-protective," Dr. Richard claims. "People who score low tend to be accepting of others, trusting, and give others the benefit of the doubt."[3] Skepticism, while a good trait when it comes to lawyering, is not necessarily beneficial when trying to make changes that come along with implementing a knowledge management program or initiative.

In addition to the basic difference between the general public and lawyers, it is interesting to note that Dr. Richard found that rainmakers—those lawyers who are particularly good at bringing in business to the law firm—are an even rarer breed, whose characteristics are even more exaggerated than non-rainmaker lawyers. Beyond interesting, it is important to understand these rainmakers because, in most law firms, they are the ones who rise to power and often take on leadership and management roles at firms.[4] That means they are the decision makers, the ones whom you will need to convince of the importance of knowledge management.

So, how do you convince skeptical lawyers (and hyperskeptical rainmaking lawyer leaders) of the importance of knowledge management? The short answer is that you must communicate the why of knowledge management.

2.5 Who Else Is Doing This?

A common refrain from lawyer leaders who are asked to opine about KM initiatives is "How many other firms are doing this?" This could be good or bad, depending on the reason for the question. If the lawyer's inquiry is to assess the possibility of an opportunity for a marketing position that truly differentiates the firm from its competition, then the question may be welcome. Perhaps implementing the program or initiative can serve as a way to market to clients and the public that the firm is forward-thinking and innovative.

3. Larry Richard, "Herding Cats: The Lawyer Personality Revealed," Hildebrant International, http://www.managingpartnerforum.org/tasks/sites/mpf/assets/image/MPF%20-%20Herding%20Cats%20-%20Richard%20-%203-5-121.pdf.
4. Some, including Bruce MacEwen, publisher of the popular Adam Smith, Esq. blog and the excellent book *Growth Is Dead, Now What?*, might argue that rainmakers are not particularly suited to take on such management roles. See also "Is Your Managing Partner Still Making Jet Engines?," http://www.adamsmithesq.com/2008/01/is_your_managing_partner/.

If, however, the question is based on the more common reason that lawyers are skeptical and reluctant to try something that has not been adopted by their peers, then this position can be very limiting. After all, if a law firm is only ever doing things that its competitors are already doing, then true market differentiation is impossible. Unfortunately, expressing this truism can be a hard sell, but there is hope in the pages ahead, which include stories and examples of how and why knowledge management can help law firms truly differentiate themselves from the competition.

At the other end of the skeptic spectrum, far from those who are wondering who else is doing it (and therefore at least leaving the door open to being convinced), are the naysayers. Some of these naysaying lawyers will claim—based on a blog headline they read or cocktail party conversation they had—that knowledge management is dead and that KM efforts will only lead to failure.

2.6 KM Is Dead, Long Live KM

For many years, people have declared, for one reason or another, that KM is dead. It's a popular statement among everyone from technologists and software developers to so-called social media experts and consultants. But just as Mark Twain declared about his own purported demise in 1897, reports of KM's death are an exaggeration.[5] Many have made the bold declaration simply to sensationalize the issue and drive web traffic to their blogs; controversial blog titles tend to have that effect. A Google search for the phrase "KM is dead" returns about 60,000 hits, and the variant "knowledge management is dead" returns about 10,000 more. I didn't have time to read them all, because I had a book to write.

In fact, there is much evidence of the contrary. In January 2014, Ron Friedmann, a notable law firm KM consultant, published the results of a private KM survey of large law firms. The survey found that "KM professionals continue to focus on 'new' (relative to a decade ago) priorities: alternative fees, budgeting, legal project management, and process management."

5. http://en.wikiquote.org/wiki/Mark_Twain.

But he also found that other, more traditional KM activities were still on the minds of KM leaders in large law firms. "Traditional KM, however, is not dead: search, matter management, forms and precedents, and portals continue to be important," said Friedmann.[6] There are also many examples of firms that have recently started, expanded, or rebranded their KM programs. In fact, while writing this chapter, I happened on a posting on my LinkedIn Group, Knowledge Management for Legal Professionals[7] (which currently has more than 7,000 members), indicating that a large Canadian law firm is looking for a Chief Knowledge Officer. The post reads, in part:

> Reporting to the Executive Committee, the CKO will articulate a vision for KM that is consistent with and builds on the Firm's strong tradition of excellence in client service, research, professional development, and knowledge sharing. The CKO will lead the Firm's KM team in implementing this vision, working with the Firm's practice groups and its leading edge information technology and marketing professionals.

Here in the United States, I learned of another large firm (more than 600 lawyers in 20 offices) looking for a CKO who

> will serve as the senior executive leader for the firm's overall knowledge management function . . . work closely with the Practice Group Chairs and Chairman & CEO to develop strategies, drive initiatives, and promote and monitor the use and effectiveness of the firm's knowledge management systems and services.

(See more about the various roles of CKOs and other KM team members in Chapter 7.)

Also while writing this book, I was contacted by a partner at a large U.S. law firm (with more than 700 lawyers in more than 15 offices), who was looking for resources to help guide the firm in the development of a knowledge management program. Additionally, in recent years, many firms,

6. http://prismlegal.com/knowledge-management-priorities-large-law-firms-2014-survey/.
7. http://j.mp/LinkedIn-KMLP.

my own included, have officially established KM programs where previously none existed or where the firms were merely conducting unofficial or unstructured KM activities. Finally, if the incidence of cold calls from professional recruiters is any indication, there are plenty of opportunities, as I was contacted by several headhunters seeking to fill director of KM positions at two large U.S.-based international law firms, one in New York City and the other in San Francisco, just in the past several weeks.

Why is the death of KM such a popular pronouncement? Why do so many people want to declare the end of KM as we know it? One reason for the death knell is the "as we know it" part. As I noted earlier, there is a misunderstanding of what knowledge management is all about. Many who have declared it dead have done so to promote their own technologies, including search engines, databases, social networking applications, or enterprise collaboration platforms. As we will see in Chapter 9 and elsewhere, KM is not about technology, software, or the next fancy app.

A different kind of misunderstanding is the basis of some death pronouncements. This misunderstanding arises from the fact that KM is an amorphous field. Its borders are not bright lines; they are blurred and they ooze into and blend together with the territory of other fields, such as technology, training, business development, application development, professional development, research, library services, legal project management, and others. For those of us with a broad vision of knowledge management, we see far beyond brief banks and best practices documents. However, when we talk about how KM can help connect lawyers with their clients, the marketing or business development folks may say, "Hey, we do that!" And when we explain how KM helps our lawyers practice more efficiently, the IT department may say, "Hey, we do that!" And when we say that our practice support lawyers can expedite your research by helping you find resources more quickly and easily, the reference librarians may say, "Hey, we do that!" And when we emphasize the importance of continuous learning and development among lawyers and other legal professionals, the trainers and professional development department members say, "Hey, we do that!"

This is the blessing and the curse of knowledge management. In the right environment—a collaborative one—it can foster cooperation among various administrative functions in an organization. In the wrong environment, it can be the start of turf wars—administrators of various groups feeling that KM is trying to edge in on their territory. Smart KM professionals will nip this competition in the bud at the first sign of tension and reassure their colleagues that they are not trying to swoop in and take away jobs or responsibilities, but rather, that they are simply seeking to collaborate.

A related reason for premature reports of KM's demise is that some confuse death with an identity change or makeover. "Practice Support," "Client Support," and "Professional Services" are some popular alternatives to labeling a firm's knowledge management department, initiatives, or efforts with the K Word. To the extent that a KM leader is responsible for other fields and is also responsible for the activities that typically fall under knowledge management, that leader may choose to abandon the term KM in favor of terminology that might be more palatable—or at least familiar—to lawyers. I am not opposed to alternative names, because a rose by any other name smells just as sweet (and in this case, offers just as much value to lawyers and clients). The importance is not the name knowledge management, but rather the value that the efforts can bring. If a name change will resonate better with your lawyers, then by all means, call it whatever works. However, my hope is that this book provides you with some ways to communicate the nature and value of knowledge management in a way that will be a positive experience for your lawyers and other legal professionals.

If KM has, in fact, died, then it has surely been reborn and is stronger than ever. To the extent that KM was ever in peril of an early demise, I would argue that KM's rebirth, or rejuvenation, in the legal industry (and perhaps in others) is a result of the global financial crisis of 2007–2008. It has also spawned increased interest in a previously little-known field called legal project management (addressed in Chapter 10). One law firm KM colleague declared at an industry gathering that this economic downturn was the best thing that ever happened for knowledge management. His point wasn't to gloat or delight in the misery of most of the developed world, but rather to point out an opportunity for improvement in the way that lawyers deliver legal services. Previously, some lawyers saw KM efforts as an option that was nice to have or something that could be undertaken in an attempt to merely appear to be concerned about delivering greater value to their clients. But today, in this post–global financial crisis world in which we live, known to many as the new normal, value is king. Clients who truly suffered, and continue to suffer, from the effects of the global financial crisis are exerting unprecedented pricing pressure on law firms. Those same clients are demanding that their lawyers worship at the altar of efficiency and deliver greater value.

Please don't take my hyperbole as alarmism. Rather, it is a call to action. My purpose is to help you understand that law firms need to be more efficient to survive in the long term and that KM can help. These client demands are real, and they show no sign of going away anytime soon. As any rain-making lawyer or law firm marketing/business development professional who has completed a request for proposal (RFP) in the past few years can tell you, clients want to know, specifically, how you will handle their matters in an efficient and cost-effective manner. The queries in RFPs are no longer the softball questions like, "What are your technological resources?" or "How will you handle our legal work efficiently?" Those are the sorts of questions that just about any law firm can fake their way through and answer adequately enough to pass muster. Today's RFP questions, such as the following, are much more detailed and specific and zero in on knowledge management initiatives:

- "Describe your knowledge management staff, roles, and functions."
- "What software applications will you use to ensure you handle our matters efficiently?"
- "Describe how your firm uses efficient search technology to enable your lawyers to locate and reuse work product to help reduce the time it takes to prepare legal documents."
- "What legal project management resources does your firm provide to ensure quality and efficiency in handling our matters?"

Having an established knowledge management program in place can not only help you answer these questions and client demands, but it can also help your organization and lawyers operate more efficiently and effectively and become better and more profitable.

If KM is dead, then the afterlife may not be as much like retirement as I thought it might be.

2.7 Knowledge Management's Health by the Numbers

Although client demand, as discussed in the last section, is one indicator of the continued need and viability of knowledge management in the legal profession, law firm efforts (many in response to those client demands) are another. The 2008 International Legal Technology Association (ILTA) KM Survey, conducted by ILTA's Knowledge Management Peer Group, reported on data about various aspects of knowledge management efforts at law firms.[8] One clear theme arising out of that survey is that KM—at the time, and still today—is a young, but maturing, discipline at law firms. The 2008 data showed that only 9 percent of respondent firms/law departments started their KM groups by designating a full-time KM role 10 or more years ago. The vast majority of respondents (49 percent) had only designated a full-time KM role within the prior three years (2005–2008). (See Figure 2.1.)

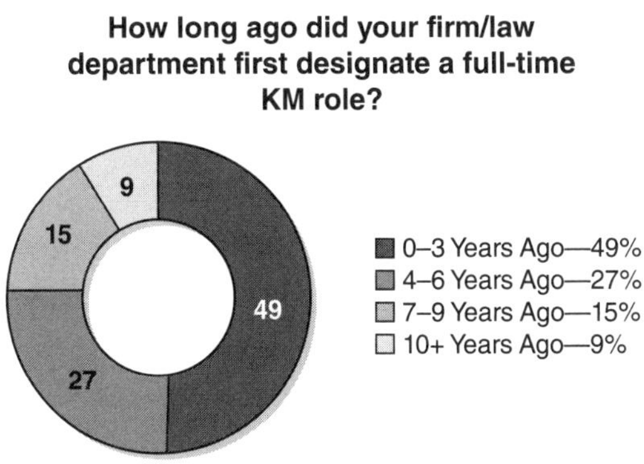

Figure 2.1
ILTA KM survey results measuring the age of KM departments at law firms.

Mixed indications of the strength of KM in the legal profession also come from the ILTA KM surveys. The number of survey respondents is one measure of KM's proliferation. In the latest survey (2014), a record 147 organizations responded, which is in line with expectations. The single

8. The biennial ILTA KM surveys were published from 2008 to 2014.

anomaly since the inaugural 2008 survey was in 2012, when only 74 organizations took part. This was an unexpected drop from previous years (141 respondents in 2010 and 131 respondents in 2008). The cause of the 2012 drop is unclear, but ILTA reports that the greatest decline in respondents "was from organizations with fewer than 50 attorneys." This makes sense, as the prevalence of formal KM departments or programs at smaller firms and law departments is less than in larger ones.

If we were to look solely at the number of ILTA KM survey respondents (especially 2012) as the indication of the strength of KM in the legal industry, then we might join the vocal few in the KM is dead refrain. However, I would argue that this single number is not a significant factor. In fact, as a part of my own research into the prevalence of KM in law firms, I have found that among the 100 largest law firms based in the United States, no less than 57 percent have formal KM programs or at least one employee with a KM title. This is in addition to the hundreds of smaller firms that have knowledge management programs. This is an important point, because the 100 largest law firms in the United States, according to the *National Law Journal* 350, have an average of 892 attorneys and range from the smallest of 433 to the largest, with 4,036 attorneys. These are very large law firms, and while the larger the firm, often the greater the need for KM, firms of all sizes can benefit greatly from KM programs, activities, and initiatives.

Focusing on the 50 largest U.S.-based law firms measured in the NLJ 350, my research revealed that 36 (72 percent) have formal KM programs or at least one employee with a KM title. The remaining 14 (28 percent) either did not have KM programs or I could not confirm that they did. Among the second 50 largest law firms, the numbers are different, with the majority (29 firms, or 58 percent) lacking KM programs and 21 firms (42 percent) having formal KM programs. Measuring KM at smaller firms is difficult. Anecdotally, we can be relatively sure that smaller firms are less likely to have formal KM departments or KM programs, as we will explore later.

How do the numbers of U.S.-based law firms with KM programs stack up against another major legal market, namely the United Kingdom? A recent study by the Legal Support Network (LSN)[9] reveals some interesting

9. http://www.legalsupportnetwork.co.uk/knowledge-management/news/top-100-directors-research-knowledge-management-report-2013-released.

findings. The study, conducted in early 2013, revealed that 53 of the United Kingdom's top 100 law firms have an employee in charge of KM efforts. Two more of the top 100 have open positions. That's a full 55 percent of the top 100 U.K. firms that have formal KM functions.[10] Looking more closely at these numbers, we find that, like U.S.-based firms, the larger U.K. firms are more likely to have formal KM programs. As reported by LSN, 88 percent of the top 25 law firms and 76 percent of the top 50 firms have formal KM programs. However, among the bottom 50 of the largest law firms, only 36 percent have formal KM programs.[11]

You can see from this data that knowledge management efforts are more prevalent at larger firms. This makes sense, for many reasons, as we will explore more fully later. However, lawyer leaders and administrative leaders at smaller firms—even substantially smaller firms—should not take this as a message that KM is just for large firms. Many smaller firms are applying knowledge management principles and practices with great results (see Chapter 4 for examples). In addition, the KM approaches, strategies, and tactics discussed throughout this book can be applied to law firms and law departments of just about any size.

2.8 Start KM Initiatives Now to Prepare for the Future

Throughout this chapter, I have tried to convince you why *now* is the right time to start your KM program or initiatives, but that's not entirely accurate. Yesterday was actually the right time. Fortunately, you haven't missed the boat. You've taken a step in the right direction (by reading this book), but don't get lazy. These ideas won't implement themselves. Envision what your firm will look like after you start down the path of knowledge management. Chapter 4 will help by showing you what knowledge management organizations look like. But first, Chapter 3 will describe, in a little more detail, some of the concepts and ideas behind knowledge management.

10. LSN keeps the list of the Top 100 KM leaders at U.K. law firms updated: http://www.legalsupportnetwork.co.uk/knowledge-management/top-100.
11. LSN's research measures whether firms have at least one person in charge of knowledge management, which I have translated as having a formal KM program.

2.9 Key Points

- Knowledge management has always been able to help businesses grow and prosper, but ever since the global financial crisis of 2007–2008, KM has become something that every law firm and law department should seriously consider.
- Corporate law department leaders (who often hire law firms) recognize the value of knowledge management, and they want their law firms to adopt KM to help ensure that they are delivering the highest-quality legal services at a reasonable cost.
- A misunderstanding of the nature of knowledge management leads some people to believe that KM has failed or that it is losing popularity, but the contrary is true.
- Having an established knowledge management program enables law firms to answer specific questions from prospective clients about the law firms' KM capabilities.
- Although legal knowledge management is still a relatively new field, it is becoming more prevalent in both large and small law firms and legal departments.

Chapter 3

A Deeper Dive into Knowledge Management

Information is not knowledge. The only source of knowledge is experience.

—Albert Einstein

3.1 Chapter Preview and Target Audience

Chapter preview:

1. You'll learn the differences and distinctions among data, information, experience, and knowledge.
2. You'll learn about the two different types of knowledge—tacit and explicit—and how they impact our knowledge management efforts.
3. You'll learn why it is important to share tacit knowledge or convert it to explicit knowledge so that it is accessible and can be shared more easily in your organization.

Target audience:
Chapter 3 will mainly be of interest to Administrative Leaders who lead or plan to lead knowledge management efforts in a law firm or law department. The content will enhance every reader's understanding of knowledge management, but it may be slightly too detailed for busy Lawyer Leaders, who may wish to only skim this chapter.

3.2 Data, Information, Experience, and Knowledge

Now that we know what knowledge management is about and why law firms and law departments should pursue it, let's spend a little time exploring some terms and concepts to help frame the context of what we will discuss throughout this book. I will not dwell on these definitions, because the *practical application* of these concepts is what really matters, rather than a philosophical or theoretical understanding of them. In a business context (remember: law firms are businesses), more attention should be focused on knowledge management activities and initiatives than on the hair-splitting, navel-gazing, pedantic traps that can suck some KM practitioners into infinite loops of inaction. That said, a fundamental understanding of some key concepts may be helpful.

Data, information, experience, and knowledge are interrelated concepts that are often confused and misused. Most people have a general understanding of these terms, but they are often used loosely and interchangeably in everyday discussions. Much like the definition of knowledge management that we explored in the last chapter, I am not sure that having a lexicographer's grasp on the precise definitions of the words "data," "information," "experience," and "knowledge" is all that important. Perhaps it is enough to "know it when I see it," as Justice Potter Stewart described of his understanding of pornography in his concurring opinion in *Jacobellis v. Ohio*, 378 U.S. 184 (1964).

An extensive examination of the differences between and among the terms is a discussion for a different day and a different book. Search "differences among data information knowledge and experience" in your favorite web browser for some interesting discussions on the topic. That said, unlike knowledge management, there are established definitions of these terms. So, we will briefly review them and try to understand enough about them to extract their value and apply them practically to our understanding of knowledge management, with the goal of getting closer to practical application. According to relevant excerpts from *Merriam-Webster*, the terms in question are defined as follows:

- **Data**[1]: "factual information (as measurements or statistics) used as a basis for reasoning, discussion, or calculation"
- **Information**[2]: "the communication or reception of knowledge or intelligence"; "knowledge obtained from investigation, study, or instruction"
- **Experience**[3]: "*a*: direct observation of or participation in events as a basis of knowledge; *b*: the fact or state of having been affected by or gained knowledge through direct observation or participation"
- **Knowledge**[4]: "(1) the fact or condition of knowing something with familiarity gained through experience or association; (2) acquaintance with or understanding of a science, art, or technique"

You can see the interrelation I mentioned. (See Figure 3.1.) Data is factual information; information is the communication of knowledge; knowledge is gained through experience; and experience is having gained knowledge through observation. Dictionary definitions are great, and we could dissect and probe them for hours, but good examples help with true understanding.

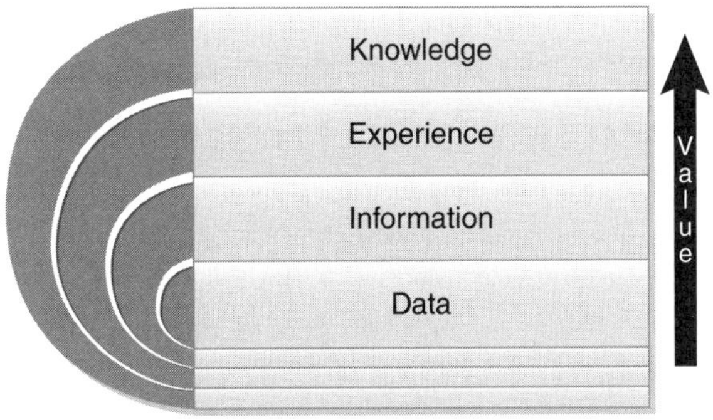

Figure 3.1

The value of data, information, experience, and knowledge. The real value, however, is the ability to act that is generated.

1. "Data" defined, http://www.merriam-webster.com/dictionary/data.
2. "Information" defined, http://www.merriam-webster.com/dictionary/information.
3. "Experience" defined, http://www.merriam-webster.com/dictionary/experience.
4. "Knowledge" defined, http://www.merriam-webster.com/dictionary/knowledge.

Nick Milton, a well-known knowledge management consultant from the United Kingdom, has an interesting and effective way to communicate the differences among data, information, knowledge, and experience, using the metaphor of a mineral map used to mine for gold:

> Each point on the map is a datum—a mineral sample point, with a location in space. The map itself is information; built up from the data points in such a way that it shows patterns which can be interpreted by a trained geologist. However, to interpret that map needs knowledge. I could not interpret it—I am not a mining geologist—and unless you are a mining geologist, you could not interpret it either. The knowledge—the know-how, acquired through training and through experience—allows a mining geologist to interpret the map and come to a decision—to site a gold-mine, to take more samples, or to declare the area worthless.[5]

Another well-known knowledge management consultant, David Gurteen, uses the metaphor of a cake to distinguish data, information, knowledge, and experience.

> An analysis of [a cake's] molecular constituents is data—for most purposes not very useful—you may not even be able to tell it were a cake. A list of ingredients is information—more useful—an experienced cook could probably make the cake—the data has been given context. The recipe though would be knowledge—written knowledge—explicit knowledge—it tells you how to make the cake. An inexperienced cook however, even with the recipe might not make a good cake. A person, though, with relevant knowledge, experience, and skill—knowledge in their heads—not easily written down—tacit knowledge—would almost certainly make an excellent cake from the recipe.[6]

5. http://www.nickmilton.com/2013/03/how-to-explain-difference-between.html.
6. http://www.gurteen.com/gurteen/gurteen.nsf/id/ksculture.

These examples are particularly helpful because you can see from them one concept that is missing from the dictionary definitions: action. Action is the key. The actions of deciding where to dig (or not) in Milton's example and baking a cake in Gurteen's example point to the most important aspect of using the data, information, knowledge, and experience. Taking action is the purpose—the reason—for addressing these concepts and for focusing our efforts on knowledge management initiatives.

A legal example of the distinctions among data, information, knowledge, and experience may revolve around a litigation matter. You could consider laws or statutes as data; they are individual pieces that often don't amount to much without context. When a law or statute is challenged in court, the data points are argued by adversaries, and a judge issues a ruling or opinion about the legal issue at hand, which could be considered information. But interpreting the ruling or opinion requires knowledge gained through training in or practicing law. Only the experienced attorney, one who has the knowledge and has handled similar matters, will make the right decision—take the right action—that is best for the client, based on all of the factors. Again, irrespective of all the details, the action is what's most important.

We could come up with other examples from the legal profession that help us grasp the concepts, but this academic depth of understanding and ability to analogize is not what's important. Some KM scholars and theorists spend ample time on the distinctions and differences among data, information, knowledge, and experience. However, practitioners who see KM as a means to an end, rather than an end in and of itself, are satisfied with a working knowledge of these terms. Although it may be interesting to explore the semantics of these concepts, in practice, some of the details are practically irrelevant, because life in a law firm or law department requires that we are interested in, and take advantage of, all of it: data, information, experience, and knowledge.

3.3 Types of Knowledge—Tacit and Explicit

Let's explore just a little bit more of the details of knowledge management (and then we'll move on, I promise). It will be quick and worth the time.

At the core of knowledge management are a pair of concepts that address the availability and accessibility of knowledge: tacit knowledge and explicit knowledge. We won't go too deep, as many other books have done this well. In fact, some authors spend considerable time on this topic, and there is great value in it for those who desire a more academic approach. For a good list of some of these works, visit my blog, www.lawyerkm.com, and check out the KM resources tab. My intention here is to give you a basic working understanding of these concepts.

The common word in the terms tacit knowledge and explicit knowledge, of course, is "knowledge," so let's start there. We saw earlier a definition of "knowledge" from *Merriam-Webster*: "(1) the fact or condition of knowing something with familiarity gained through experience or association; (2) acquaintance with or understanding of a science, art, or technique." A variation of that definition, also from *Merriam-Webster*, is "information, understanding, or skill that you get from experience or education."[7] Those are the dictionary definitions of the term, but when most people use the word "knowledge" in simple terms, they are talking about know-how or what they know.

What I know seems personal, almost private in some ways. It seems to be in my mind, locked away there, unless and until I am ready to share it. These two aspects of knowledge or know-how—that it is *personal* and *sharable*—are the essentials of tacit and explicit knowledge.

Tacit knowledge is fundamentally personal. It is the knowledge that resides in an individual's mind. Authors Thomas Koulopoulos and Carl Frappaolo define tacit knowledge as "personal knowledge embedded in individual experience and involving such intangible factors as personal belief, perspective, instinct and values."[8] Tacit knowledge has also been defined as the intuitive, difficult-to-define knowledge that is based in experience. Examples of tacit knowledge include one's knowledge about how to take a deposition, try a case, structure a merger, plan an estate, argue a motion, get along with a particular judge, or even find the courthouse.

---

7. http://www.merriam-webster.com/dictionary/knowledge.
8. Thomas Koulopoulos and Carl Frappaolo, *Smart Things to Know about Knowledge Management* (West Sussex, UK: Capstone Publishing, 1999), 42.

Unlike tacit knowledge, explicit knowledge has been codified or captured in some medium. In other words, explicit knowledge has been written down or recorded somewhere. Because it has been recorded, it tends to be easily transferred or shared with others. It is also easier to organize, make accessible, and reuse. Explicit knowledge is found in documents, memoranda, legal briefs, databases, spreadsheets, presentations, e-mail messages, practice guides, and other documented or recorded media.

Contrast this with tacit knowledge. Because it is in one's mind, tacit knowledge has not been codified, recorded, or captured in any way. It is also not easily shared, except through direct, synchronous communication. For example, one person verbally telling another about something is a direct transfer of knowledge from one person to another. But some tacit knowledge—even when shared through direct, synchronous communication—is not easily shared or understood. Take the example of explaining to a boy how to ride a bicycle. You could go into minute detail about the handlebars, pedals, seat, etc., and explain how forward momentum helps keep the rider balanced and prevents him from falling over. But a boy who has learned all there is to know about riding a bicycle does not *know* how to ride a bicycle. It is only when he has gotten on a bicycle and applied the theory (and perhaps fallen once or twice) that we would consider him to know how to ride a bicycle.

When thinking about tacit versus explicit knowledge, I am always reminded of the 1988 film *Twins*, starring Danny DeVito and Arnold Schwarzenegger, in which the two main characters are twins who were separated at birth. Julius, played by Schwarzenegger, was raised on a remote island by a professor and is extremely intelligent (book smart), but he is naive when it comes to things in the modern world. Vincent, played by DeVito, although not formally educated, is more street smart. In a classic scene, Vincent asks Julius to drive a car, which he is really stealing, unbeknownst to Julius. Julius, having never driven a car because there were no cars on the remote island, reaches in the glove box, opens the owner's manual, and starts speed reading it. Vincent asks Julius what he's doing, and he responds, "learning to drive." The following scene shows Julius driving horribly with jerky motions, stopping and starting, swerving all over, and at one point striking a curb, which sends the car on two wheels, almost crashing into pedestrians. Julius may have learned—but he didn't know—how to drive.

In the legal context, even well-educated, book-smart lawyers could have difficulty with some legal tasks. If an experienced attorney were to tell a junior attorney how to try a case or to structure a deal, the junior attorney would not necessarily be able to do these things effectively. It takes more than simple instruction. Perhaps assisting with trial preparation, "carrying the trial bag," and taking on the role of second chair can help the junior lawyer develop his or her own knowledge about how to effectively try cases. Of course, being thrown into the deep end can help someone gain experience pretty quickly, too.

Remember that knowledge management is an institutional endeavor. It is concerned with the *collective knowledge* of a group of people. Thus, a core goal and challenge of KM is sharing tacit knowledge or converting it to explicit knowledge so that it is more accessible and can be shared more easily. Some would say that this is an oversimplification, arguing that knowledge is not either tacit or explicit, but rather exists on a spectrum, or a continuum between tacit and explicit. For practical purposes, however, we don't need to delve into the theoretical weeds. Suffice it to say that when it comes to knowledge sharing and knowledge transfer within an organization, explicit knowledge, by its nature, is easier to share more widely.

Ultimately, we are concerned with sharing knowledge and ensuring that it is accessible to others within our organizations. We may have to take different approaches to sharing different types of knowledge, but the overall goal remains the same. The following chapters will provide guidance on how to better share collective knowledge and make it more accessible throughout your organization.

3.4 Key Points

- Data, information, experience, and knowledge are interrelated concepts that are often confused, but knowing their differences will help you better understand the practical application of knowledge management.

- Knowledge management professionals don't need to get hung up on the differences among these concepts, because in practice, you will use data, information, experience, and knowledge to accomplish your knowledge management initiatives and goals.
- Tacit knowledge is personal knowledge that resides in an individual's mind. It is intuitive, difficult to define, and based on individual experience, such as knowing how to ride a bicycle or try a case. It is therefore not easily shared, made accessible, and reused by others.
- Explicit knowledge, which is typically found in documents and digital media, has been codified, recorded, or otherwise captured in some form. It is therefore more easily shared, organized, made accessible, and reused by others.
- Sharing tacit knowledge or converting it to explicit knowledge so that it is accessible and easily shared is a core goal and challenge of knowledge management.

Chapter 4

The End Game: What Does a Knowledge Management Organization Look Like?

He who receives ideas from me, receives instruction himself without lessening mine; as he who lights his taper at mine receives light without darkening me.

—Thomas Jefferson

4.1 Chapter Preview and Target Audience

Chapter preview:

1. You'll learn many of the ways that knowledge management efforts originate in law firms and law departments.
2. You'll see that considerable variation exists in the structure of knowledge management departments, even in law firms that appear to be quite similar.
3. You'll learn how smaller law firms approach knowledge management differently from some of their larger firm counterparts.
4. You'll see several examples of the organizational structure of knowledge management departments at law firms of various sizes.
5. We'll explore the roles libraries and librarians can play in knowledge management departments.

Target audience:
Chapter 4 will be of great interest to Lawyer Leaders, Administrative Leaders, and even casual readers. It contains several descriptions of law firm knowledge management departments, as well as tips and ideas about how they are managed and operated. Some descriptions also contain guiding principles that create the foundations of the KM departments. The KM leaders I interviewed for this chapter shared some valuable information that you will find helpful when you create or refresh your KM program.

Let's imagine that you could fast-forward to a day when your law firm or law department has fully adopted knowledge management. What are the characteristics of this knowledge management organization? What does your firm do differently today—as a KM organization—than it did before you started your KM endeavors? This chapter contains descriptions of several law firm KM departments and includes their organizational structures and other features. These examples demonstrate that there is some variation in how firms have decided to approach knowledge management. So, while you will notice differences, you will also notice similarities and themes that recur. No matter how similar law firms or law departments may be, there will always be some differences in the ways they are organized, who is involved in the administrative operations, and KM maturity levels.

In some ways, asking what KM looks like in organizations is an unfair question. It's like asking someone to describe a landscape. Some people may describe an arid, flat desert with sparse vegetation and red rocks in the distance. Others may describe an ice-capped mountain surrounded by snow. Still others may describe a green forest bordered by a stream with rolling hills and expansive fields. Describing landscapes is in some ways similar to describing KM in law firms: What you see not only depends on the unique characteristics of the environment (your law firm or law department and your organization's strategy), but it also depends on the vantage point of those who champion KM (including senior lawyers and senior KM administrators). Each organization will have a different approach, and people with different backgrounds will have different ideas about what is important for a KM program. There is no standard for what constitutes the right organizational structure for knowledge management in the legal services industry.

I have interviewed dozens of legal industry KM practitioners, and there are some similarities and trends among them, but no two stories are the same. The diversity in KM is not limited to what KM organizations do, but also who is involved and how they are governed.

On the other hand, describing natural landscapes may not be the best metaphor for KM. Other than the fact they are varied and unique, natural landscapes develop . . . naturally, without the influence—or interference—of people. That's not so with knowledge management efforts. KM requires deliberate action. A more accurate metaphor may be a *man-made landscape*, like your backyard. Perhaps it's of your own design, or perhaps you hired a professional landscape architect to help you design it. Either way, your landscape might be similar to your neighbor's, but they are not identical. They may have common features, like shrubbery, a lawn, and a vegetable garden, but they can never be exactly the same. They were designed (or influenced) by different people in different environments at different times. Even if they are right next door to each other, they are not identical. As with KM programs, the grass is not necessarily greener on the other side of the fence. Just about every homeowner has challenges with landscapes, and just about every law firm has challenges developing a KM environment.

4.2 How Knowledge Management Efforts Originate in Law Firms

There are many ways that KM efforts can originate in law firms. Some are grass-roots campaigns that spring up from far corners of the firm, whereas others are top-down initiatives born out of competition with other firms that are "doing KM." Others are generated from the frustration of inefficient processes and procedures, which causes an interest in improving the way the firm gets work done. Still others are direct responses to client demands for a firm to possess tools and demonstrate practices to promote efficiency, often in connection with request for proposal (RFP) requirements. More often than not, law firms are already doing some KM—that is, they are performing some KM activities—and they may not even know it. Some of the most fundamental KM activities, such as identifying and reusing exemplar or model documents, have been common for as long as lawyers have been practicing.

Just as law firms have been doing what could be considered KM activities for several decades, the origins of KM in general are loosely based on activities that were not labeled as knowledge management at the time. Authors Michael Koenig and Kenneth Neveroski claim that KM, "as we now know it, evolved as a concept in the late 1980s,"[1] while Ron Friedmann has written that some law firms began assembling brief banks in the 1970s.[2]

Take, for example, my own story about how KM originated at my first firm, which was a combination of planning and serendipity (see Introduction). Contrast this with the story of Rick Kryzminski, who spearheaded KM at Mayer Brown several years ago, when his interest in a firm intranet platform sparked a KM program (see Appendix B). However KM initiatives start, they will be unique to the particular organizations. The following sections describe the various ways that several law firm KM departments are structured and came to be. My hope is that this will give you ideas and inspiration about how to begin a KM program in your organization.

4.3 Variations in Knowledge Management Approaches at Different Law Firms

For many readers, this section will be the most valuable part of the book. I have profiled several different law firms and will discuss their demographics, KM organizational structure, and in some cases, their approach to knowledge management. It is useful to learn about the KM environments at various law firms, because the attributes of law firms have an impact on how KM can and should be approached, just as a physical environment influences how a landscape architect may plan a design. Some factors that come into play when developing a KM program include firm size (number of attorneys), practice areas, number of offices, the geographic footprint

1. Michael Koenig and Kenneth Neveroski, "The Origins and Development of Knowledge Management," *Journal of Information and Knowledge Management* 7 (2008): 243–254, http://j.mp/OriginsofKM.
2. Ron Friedmann, "A Brief History of Legal KM," Prism Legal, September 4, 2014, http://prismlegal.com/a-brief-history-of-legal-km/.

of those offices, and perhaps most important—and most challenging—the culture of the firm itself.

Although knowledge management can benefit firms and law departments of all sizes, the size of an organization is a factor, because it will affect how you approach KM. Furthermore, size may even dictate whether a firm is ready to take on the effort and expense required to implement formal KM initiatives in the first place. Take, for example, a very small firm (two to ten attorneys) in a single office location. Such a small law firm will not likely invest the time and money in a KM program that would be appropriate for a very large firm of several hundred or several thousand lawyers. Scale is obviously a factor. But I believe there is a sweet spot in terms of attorney headcount when it comes to the need to initiate a formal KM program, with at least one employee who is 100 percent dedicated to KM efforts.

Firms may be able to manage with part-time KM efforts for a while, but at around 150 attorneys, more formal KM initiatives are really needed. As noted, other factors come into play, but attorney headcount is an important factor. That number, 150 attorneys, is not random. Anecdotally, it seems that many peers in the KM field have started their more formal KM efforts when their firms have reached that critical mass number, but there is also some science behind it. A theory called Dunbar's Number, proposed by British anthropologist Robin Dunbar, suggests that there is a limit to the number of stable social relationships—150—that people can have before those relationships start to break down. Knowledge management efforts can help maintain and improve connections (both people-to-people and people-to-content connections) when the sheer size of an organization makes it difficult to do so. Again, other factors contribute, and your experience may vary, but as a general rule, when your firm approaches this size, more structured and formal KM approaches are warranted. That said, even some smaller firms, as you will see, have formalized their KM efforts before growing this large. This is wise, as it's never too early to consider KM initiatives.

The number of offices a firm has, or how geographically dispersed an organization is, may be another factor in how to approach knowledge management. A firm with many offices—even if it does not have that many attorneys—may require different KM initiatives and technologies to connect their attorneys with their fellow attorneys, which is a key part of any KM effort. Although it is relatively easy to know a great number of coworkers when they are all in the same physical office, this becomes a challenge when they are spread across the country or the world. Overcoming the challenges of physical separation of colleagues is usually addressed with technology tools, such as video conferencing, expertise location systems, online collaboration applications, and increasingly, enterprise social networking applications. Single-office or regional firms often do not see as much value in such technologies, because they have more frequent face-to-face contact with their colleagues and coworkers. Technology is not the only way to connect widespread colleagues. Many firms with geographically dispersed attorneys find great value in periodic attorney retreats or all-attorney meetings when lawyers can connect in the old-fashioned way. Such get-togethers remain popular, even in these challenging economic times, despite the great cost of travel and the associated lost opportunity cost when participating lawyers are connecting rather than billing hours to their clients.

Firm or organizational culture is probably the most significant factor at play when deciding how to approach knowledge management. Company culture is about values. What does your firm stand for? What does it value? Is your firm collaborative or cutthroat? Is it an eat-what-you-kill, blood-and-sand battleground where knowledge sharing is mocked and a sign of weakness? Or do your lawyers see the opportunities that come when knowledge sharing causes a rising tide that lifts all ships? This company cultural spectrum is wide and diverse. Your firm or organization probably falls somewhere quite distant from the extremes.

Sometimes company culture is not about the organization itself, but rather it develops from a combination of the individuals that constitute the organization. This is often, but not always, a sign of a lack of foundational vision and leadership. Other times, company culture is woven into the fabric of an organization from the start and is fiercely guarded and nurtured. In these instances, new members of the organization are often selected based, in part, on their willingness to uphold and promote the culture. Either way, company culture is something with which knowledge management professionals will need to deal. Understanding the culture will help you make decisions about how to communicate about, promote, and initiate your knowledge management efforts.

4.4 Smaller Law Firm Knowledge Management Efforts

In the next section (and in Appendix A), we examine several examples of law firms that have implemented formal knowledge management programs. Many of these are what most people would consider large law firms, as they have several hundred attorneys and multiple office locations. As noted previously, this size makes sense, because most organizations reach a critical mass before they decide to invest the time and money into formal KM efforts. But three of these firms are smaller (fewer than 120 attorneys), and they show that law firms need not be massive to enjoy the benefits of knowledge management.

For the most part, however, smaller firms tend not to have formalized KM programs or departments. The data from the biennial knowledge management surveys conducted by the International Legal Technology Association (ILTA) show this to be the case. The 2010 survey results are especially revealing, because they reported results based on firm size. For example, for small firms (those with fewer than 50 attorneys), only about 10 percent had separate KM departments. Contrast this with larger firms (those with 500 or more attorneys), where approximately 60 percent had separate KM departments. Another survey metric—the existence of a KM budget—also supports this finding. Fewer than 10 percent of small firms had separate KM budgets, whereas larger firms had separate KM budgets about 55 percent of the time. The type of KM leadership at small firms versus larger firms is also indicative of the lack of KM formalization. At smaller firms, the head of knowledge management tends to be a practicing lawyer (about 43 percent of the time), which indicates that his or her time is split among KM, practicing law, and everything else that comes with it. At larger firms, nonpracticing lawyers tend to lead KM efforts approximately 40 percent of the time, and it is rare to have practicing lawyers at the helm.

However, this is not to say that smaller law firms cannot and should not engage in knowledge management efforts. To the contrary, organizations of all sizes can benefit from KM initiatives. The main difference between KM efforts at small firms and larger firms is the number of people who are dedicated to full-time KM efforts. This should come as no surprise. In smaller organizations of all types, administrative professionals tend to take on a jack-of-all-trades role. At very small firms, say with one to five attorneys, it is not uncommon to see a single administrator taking on all office operations from office manager to secretary to paralegal and beyond. At such firms, it is not uncommon for this person to add certain KM efforts to his or her list of responsibilities. This is not to say that KM efforts are the exclusive responsibility of some administrative employee. As we will see, in the most mature KM organizations, all employees embrace and take part in KM activities and initiatives.

4.5 Examples of Law Firm KM Organizational Structures

The next section outlines the profiles of KM departments in seven law firms. However, this chapter contains fewer than half of the firms that I profiled for this book. The remaining ten profiles are in Appendix A. I selected the following seven firms to highlight in the chapter not because their KM departments are somehow superior to those in Appendix A, but rather because of the diversity among the firms. Here, there is a mix of larger and smaller firms, whereas in Appendix A, the firms are all larger. I excluded those ten additional large firm profiles from this chapter simply to make it a quicker read. I encourage you to read the profiles in Appendix A, as each firm approaches knowledge management differently, and you are likely to gain valuable insights from them. The firms profiled in Appendix A include the following:

- Addleshaw Goddard, LLP
- Faegre Baker Daniels, LLP
- Foley & Lardner, LLP
- Fox Rothschild, LLP
- Goodwin Procter, LLP
- King & Wood Mallesons (Australian Partnership)
- Littler Mendelson, P.C.
- Pillsbury Winthrop Shaw Pittman, LLP
- Two anonymous firms

The firms profiled in the following pages are a healthy mix of large and small, and their KM departments are diverse in terms of number of members, background of KM leaders and staff, and KM program maturity level. They include the following:

- Ogletree, Deakins, Nash, Smoak & Stewart, P.C.
- Levenfeld Pearlstein, LLC
- O'Melveny & Myers, LLP
- Lawson Lundell, LLP
- Debevoise & Plimpton, LLP
- Bradford & Barthel, LLP
- Bracewell & Giuliani, LLP

4.5.1 Ogletree, Deakins, Nash, Smoak & Stewart, P.C.

My current law firm, where I serve as Director of Knowledge Management, is Ogletree, Deakins, Nash, Smoak & Stewart, P.C.[3] It is an international labor and employment law firm that has grown rapidly since its founding with 16 lawyers 38 years ago. In the three years since I joined the firm, at the end of 2011, it has grown from approximately 600 lawyers to more than 750 lawyers practicing in 47 offices.

I joined the firm to formalize the various KM efforts that were in place and to create the firm's first official knowledge management department. The KM department's current structure includes five groups, which are distinct but work together to serve the firm and our clients.

The KM Firm Solutions group focuses on developing and maintaining internal, or firm-facing, applications, databases, and content, most of which are based on our award-winning[4] SharePoint-based intranet platform, ODConnect. The group also creates and/or maintains other internal systems, such as our enterprise search tool, ODSearch. On a day-to-day basis, the Firm Solutions team helps practice groups manage their practice-specific content on ODConnect, helps client teams collaborate by creating and

3. http://www.ogletreedeakins.com/.
4. 2014 Intranet Innovation Gold Award winner for intranet redesign, http://www.steptwo.com.au/iia.

maintaining client-specific intranet pages, helps administrative departments manage their ODConnect content and make it accessible to others throughout the firm, maintains the firm's current-awareness and alert systems, provides end-user training for ODConnect content owners on SharePoint tools and resources, works with developers to create solutions for intranet sites, and provides just-in-time assistance to lawyers and administrative staff in locating and managing the firm's vital content. The group has three members: a manager, an analyst, and a coordinator.

The KM Client Solutions group focuses on developing and maintaining client-facing applications, creating custom reports for clients, and helping to manage large client engagements. This group is responsible for creating and developing the firm's client extranet/collaboration platform and various other client-facing tools and web-based products. These products are specialized applications that clients can use to help manage their matter information and/or obtain particular information on such things as labor and employment compliance and regulation issues. This group works closely with lawyers and clients to ensure that the firm is providing clients with the information, tools, and support they need to ensure they receive the highest value service. This team consists of a manager, an analyst, and two coordinators.

As you can see from the organizational diagram (Figure 4.1), there is a dotted line connecting the KM & SharePoint Development Team to the KM department. This team reports into the firm's technology department but focuses its work specifically on knowledge management department projects. Because of this focus, there is a tight bond between and among these developers and the members of the KM Firm Solutions and KM Client Solutions groups, and they work closely together every day. The cooperation and collaboration among these teams help them operate very efficiently and effectively. The KM & SharePoint Development Team has a manager and three developers.

The KM Counsel group at Ogletree Deakins is made up of two experienced labor and employment attorneys who formerly practiced with the firm. One was a senior associate, and the other, Evan Shenkman, who is profiled in Appendix B, was a shareholder with the firm. KM Counsel, otherwise known as practice support lawyers or professional support lawyers (PSLs), at Ogletree play a more expansive role than at some other law firms.

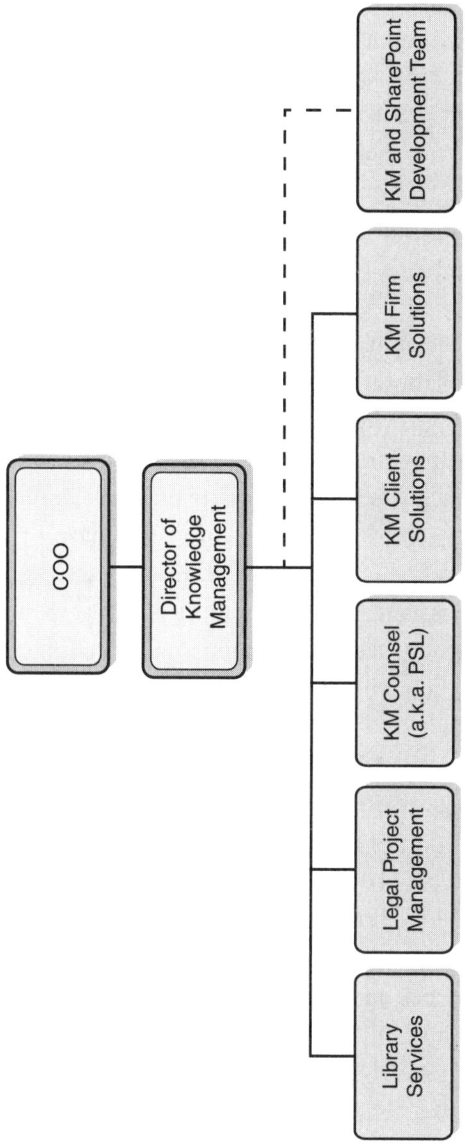

Figure 4.1
Ogletree Deakins' knowledge management department organization chart.

They do perform the more traditional work of PSLs, such as creating and maintaining model, sample, and form documents and assisting practicing attorneys with finding substantive, internally created legal work product, but they also work closely with the other KM department groups. For example, KM Counsel use their practical knowledge of labor and employment law, and their perspective as former practicing attorneys at the firm, to help the KM Client Solutions and KM Firm Solutions groups create software applications, databases, client collaboration sites, etc. They even use their unique perspective to consult on technical aspects of certain projects, such as the development of our enterprise search engine.

This sort of collaboration helps ensure that the views of practicing lawyers are represented when the KM department is developing tools and applications to help attorneys work more efficiently and effectively. Having lawyers (especially lawyers who formerly practiced at the firm) on the KM team is a great benefit. It opens lines of communication with the current practicing lawyers and creates instant credibility for the whole KM team. KM Counsel are assigned to every practice group at the firm and routinely attend practice group meetings to maintain connections, make suggestions for practice-specific KM initiatives, and generally make themselves available for assistance.

Ogletree Deakins has implemented project management principles into its practice and has created a dedicated Legal Project Management (LPM) group, which is a part of the KM department. This group, which currently consists of two legal project managers who are former practicing attorneys, is responsible for creating, implementing, and promoting our LPM program. The legal project managers help attorneys develop budgets and project plans for their matters and assist with creating reports that track matter progress and budget-to-actual spend analyses. In addition, they work closely with members of the business development team to conduct pricing analysis to assist in pricing alternative fee-arrangement proposals and create budget templates. As part of their efforts to find better ways to deliver the firm's legal services that are more valuable to clients, they create workflow diagrams and process maps to analyze current approaches to handling matters and create models designed to improve the processes and thereby improve efficiency.

The Library Services group is also a part of our KM department. Although they are not the same as knowledge management, library services (especially research) are often very closely related to knowledge management services. At many firms, including Ogletree, the library function reports into KM.[5] Library research services and KM research services (frequently provided by KM Counsel) are often considered to be opposite sides of the same coin. While library researchers typically focus on third-party resources, KM Counsel typically focus on firm-generated resources. The Library Services group performs all of the traditional library functions, such as collecting and cataloging the firm's print materials, but it also performs specialized research, including competitive intelligence. From an administrative perspective, the group handles all aspects of the firm's relationships with providers of computer-assisted legal research tools and platforms, from contract negotiations to providing our users with training.

One of the more interesting and unique aspects of the KM department as a whole is that we get to collaborate with just about everyone in the firm—both on the administrative side and the practicing lawyer side. For example, the KM Firm Solutions group role of managing and maintaining our intranet requires that we stay in continuous contact with every administrative group and practice group at the firm, because they all have sites on the intranet. Keeping all of that information current requires collaboration and interaction. KM Client Solutions, KM Counsel, Library Services, and LPM also have extensive interaction with attorneys and often clients.

This extensive collaboration makes sense considering our broad view of what KM is all about, what the department's subgroups do, our innovative and entrepreneurial spirit, and our guiding principles:

1. Align KM goals and strategies with the firm's goals and strategies.
2. Change as the needs of the firm and the needs of our clients change.
3. Promote quality, consistency, and efficiency of work product.
4. Provide the right information to the right people at the right time.

---

5. According to the 2014 ILTA KM Survey results, 46.7 percent of organizations reported that library services reported into KM departments. See the survey results in the July 2014 ILTA white paper, "Orchestrating Harmony through Data," http://www.iltanet.org/MainMenuCategory/Publications/WhitePapersandSurveys/Knowledge-Management-4.html.

5. People first, then process, then technology.
6. Communicate simply and often.

Throughout the rest of this section, you will see profiles of other firms' KM departments, including how they are structured, and you will gain valuable insights into how you may wish to structure your own KM department.

4.5.2 Levenfeld Pearlstein, LLP

Levenfeld Pearlstein (LP) is a Chicago-based general practice law firm of approximately 60 attorneys, who provide services ranging from corporate and securities to litigation to real estate to estates and trusts.[6] I interviewed Angela Hickey,[7] the firm's executive director, about their knowledge management efforts. Although it is smaller than most firms that engage in KM initiatives, LP and its people truly understand knowledge management, and they actually live and breathe it on a daily basis. That's because the firm's original managing partner, Bryan Schwartz, who is now the firm's chairperson, had a strong vision of a firm that is based on the concept of sharing knowledge, openness, and transparency.

Even though LP does not have a formal knowledge management department, it has one of the most mature KM attitudes that I have come across in my research. Knowledge management principles and ideas are a part of what the firm calls the LP Way—the firm's special way of handling both the business and practice of law. "For us," Hickey said, "knowledge management is not a support department, it is a way of doing business. It's a part of the culture of our firm and it's integrated into everyone's job." The LP Way is not just some slogan; it's a formal five-step process, the goal of which is the ultimate client experience. All employees—lawyers and administrative staff alike—are expected to honor the principles represented in the LP Way. In fact, to help protect and enhance the knowledge-sharing culture of the firm, the LP Way is discussed thoroughly with prospective new attorneys and staff members during the interview process. The firm wants to ensure that potential new hires value the same principles and ideas that have made the firm successful.

6. http://www.lplegal.com/.
7. http://www.lplegal.com/our-people/angela-m-hickey.

The firm's culture also manifests itself in tangible, useful knowledge management processes, procedures, and tools. One example that reflects the knowledge-sharing culture is the way the firm handles client contact information. All such contact information is stored in a customer relationship management system that is open to all attorneys. Thus, there is no concept of "my contacts," but rather all contacts are "firm contacts." The firm has a similar approach to form documents and requires that those resources be open and available to all lawyers.

The firm also has very robust SharePoint-based dashboards that display data such as timekeeper utilization summaries, top clients by hours worked, matter budgets, and matter financial information such as work-in-progress and accounts receivable. The dashboards also display firm-wide partner reports that show matter actual versus budget information and practice group reports that show individual attorney performance. These dashboards, and the decision to make so much information transparent and available, have had a great impact. Not only have they eliminated the inefficiency of creating and circulating multiple reports, but they also keep decision makers better informed of key data to help them make better decisions. They also enhance collaboration among attorneys, make everyone more accountable for their responsibilities, and greatly increase efficiency.

In addition to the firm-facing KM activities and technologies, LP has also delivered some impressive client-facing KM extranet tools. Applying the same principles of transparency and accountability as they do inside the firm, LP leveraged their SharePoint platform to provide their clients with valuable on-demand information. One example was the firm's Condo Extranet, which allowed its homeowner association clients to access data and case updates on the portal without the need to call a firm attorney and await a status letter. Clients love the extranet because it is faster, more efficient, and less costly. In fact, the firm has been able to use this positive client experience to change the way they charge for this type of work. Clients are no longer charged by the hour and are instead charged based on a flat fee structure, which the firm touts as a key differentiator when competing for business with other firms.

Another aspect of the LP Way that is closely related to knowledge management is the firm's focus on innovation, consistency, and process efficiency in the way they do their work. This is so important to the firm that they have a person dedicated to it—a manager of process improvement. In a nutshell, the scope of this role is to examine all of the firm's processes (the way they handle legal work); improve those processes to eliminate waste and unnecessary steps; and ensure the consistent execution of the improved process.

There are several examples of how the firm has improved processes, including when they revamped the way they create closing books for transactional matters.[8] The old procedure was costly, cumbersome, time-consuming, and wasteful. It involved printing reams of matter documents, sending them to a vendor, scanning the pages, assembling physical binders, sending them to the clients, and then physically storing them in the office. The whole procedure could take several days and cost up to $1,000. The LP team examined the process and figured out how to make it completely paperless—and save time and money to boot. In the end, the cost to the client was completely eliminated, the time to complete the task was reduced to less than 30 minutes, the need for physical storage was eliminated, and the process was more enjoyable for LP employees.

The changes that LP instituted through implementing knowledge management and process improvement, while beneficial to clients and the firm, have not been without challenges. As we will see more in Chapter 8, all change is difficult, even when that change results in improvements. But LP manages those changes by staying true to their culture. By remaining open and transparent, sharing knowledge freely, and communicating effectively, all LP employees gain a greater understanding of why changes are made. "While we are a smaller firm, our size is actually an advantage," Hickey said. "We can speak directly to every single person and understand them as individuals." For the same reasons, the firm also sees its smaller size as an advantage in executing KM initiatives. In the end, the firm's emphasis on communication—connecting with people—and its ability to do this effectively is a fundamental aspect of what helps knowledge management flourish.

8. http://www.lplegal.com/case-study-closing-book.

4.5.3 O'Melveny & Myers, LLP

O'Melveny & Myers is a large international law firm with approximately 800 attorneys in 16 offices.[9] The firm handles several practice areas that fall generally in the categories of litigation, transactions, and regulatory and government affairs.[10] I interviewed Jeffrey Rovner,[11] Managing Director for Information, to learn about KM at O'Melveny. Jeffrey has an interesting background, and his responsibilities are expansive. (Read Jeffrey's personal story about how he became involved in KM in Appendix B.) While the firm searches for a Director of KM, who will report to Jeffrey, he leads the efforts directly. In addition to his role as head of knowledge management, he also oversees the activities of information technology, the library, and records management. He is also a member of the firm's Technology Committee, Business Management Team, and he heads up the Innovation Committee. Jeffrey reports directly to the firm's Chief Operating Officer.

The firm's relatively small formal KM department started in 2003. "When all positions are filled, it consists of a director, a project manager, a project coordinator and a project specialist," Jeffrey said. "Closely affiliated with the formal KM team are several other colleagues: a professional support lawyer; six representatives from IT: three developers, two business analysts, and our head of training; two representatives from Library: the director and a library manager; one representative from Client Development." In addition to these members, Jeffrey also collaborates closely with all of the other functional departments and directly with the firm's partners. A simplified organization chart depicting how KM fits in at O'Melveny is shown in Figure 4.2.

Jeffrey also shared his KM department's vision and statement of principles. "Our KM vision is a paraphrase of Google's vision: To organize the firm's information and make it universally accessible and useful," Jeffrey said. "Of course, the 'universal' part is tempered by our need for security and confidentiality. I believe our holistic focus on information is made possible, in part, because my role permits me to orchestrate all of the firm's information functions."

9. http://www.omm.com/aboutus/overview/.
10. http://www.omm.com/practices/.
11. www.linkedin.com/in/jrovner.

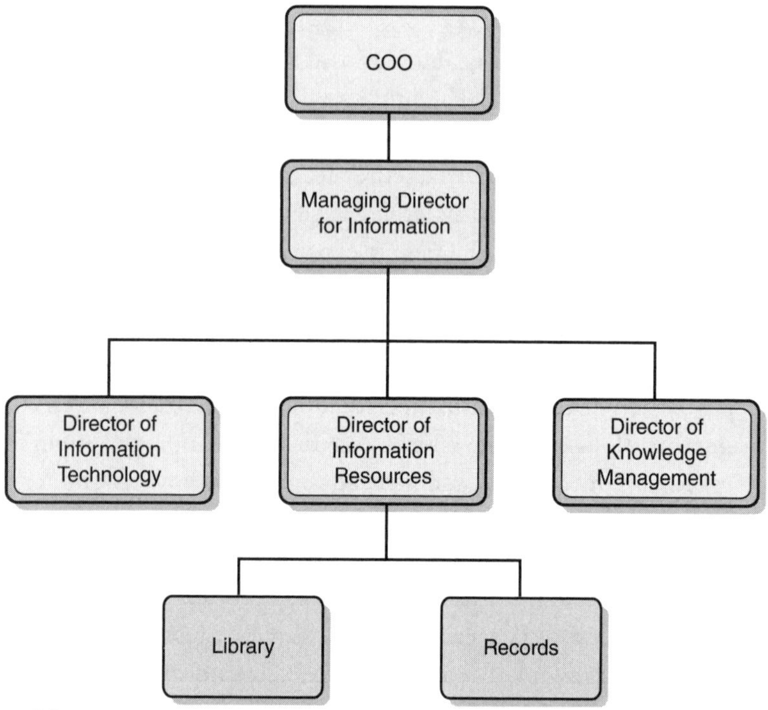

Figure 4.2
O'Melveny & Myers, LLP's knowledge management organizational structure.

O'Melveny's KM department principles are centered around the way they deliver services. This is done primarily through its firm intranet, called ommni. Read more about intranets in Chapter 9. The design of ommni is guided by the following principles:

1. Ommni should be a virtual embodiment of the firm in all of its complexity and depth. Ommni is not simply a collection of specific tools and content; instead, it is a more easily navigated representation of our entire firm.
2. Ommni should reflect and provide context for all of the client-related activity within our firm, automatically and in real time.
3. Ommni should be based on successful e-commerce principles, including the use of faceted search and the importance of delivering the "long tail" of content.

4. For the most part, ommni should provide useful tools, rather than end-to-end solutions.
5. What can be automated should be automated. With a little creativity, one can automate quite a bit.

In addition, Jeffrey notes, the KM team at O'Melveny is "guided by David Snowden's [original] three principles of knowledge exchange:[12] (1) Knowledge will only ever be volunteered, it cannot be conscripted. (2) We only know what we know when we need to know it. (3) We always know more than we can tell and we will always tell more than we can write down."[13]

4.5.4 Lawson Lundell LLP

Lawson Lundell is an example of a smaller law firm that, despite its size, has embraced the principles and ideas of knowledge management and benefited greatly from them. Lawson is a Western Canadian firm of approximately 115 attorneys in three offices that focuses on business law and provides a broad range of general practice services.[14]

The firm's knowledge management efforts started in 2008, when the firm formed a KM committee. Though the committee made progress, after about two years they realized that to take their efforts to the next level, they needed a full-time knowledge management lawyer. So, the firm brought on Euan Sinclair, who started in January 2011 as Director of Knowledge Management. Before taking on the lead KM role at Lawson, Sinclair was a practicing attorney for 12 years in his native Scotland. Immediately prior, he served as a PSL with the U.K. law firm Burness Paull, LLP.

Not surprisingly, because it's a smaller firm, the KM department at Lawson is small, with only one full-time employee—Sinclair. He reports to several different people and groups. Operationally, Sinclair reports to the KM committee, which meets monthly to address knowledge management issues. On financial issues and for performance reviews, he reports to the firm's executive director. The KM budget and strategy update is presented to the

12. Dave Snowden, "Volunteer not Conscript," Cognitive Edge Network, August 10, 2006, http://cognitive-edge.com/blog/entry/4524/volunteer-not-conscript.
13. The 3 Rules were updated to 7 Principles, http://cognitive-edge.com/blog/entry/5576/rendering-knowledge.
14. http://www.lawsonlundell.com.

executive committee annually. And on an ad hoc basis, Sinclair reports to the managing partner. (See Figure 4.3.)

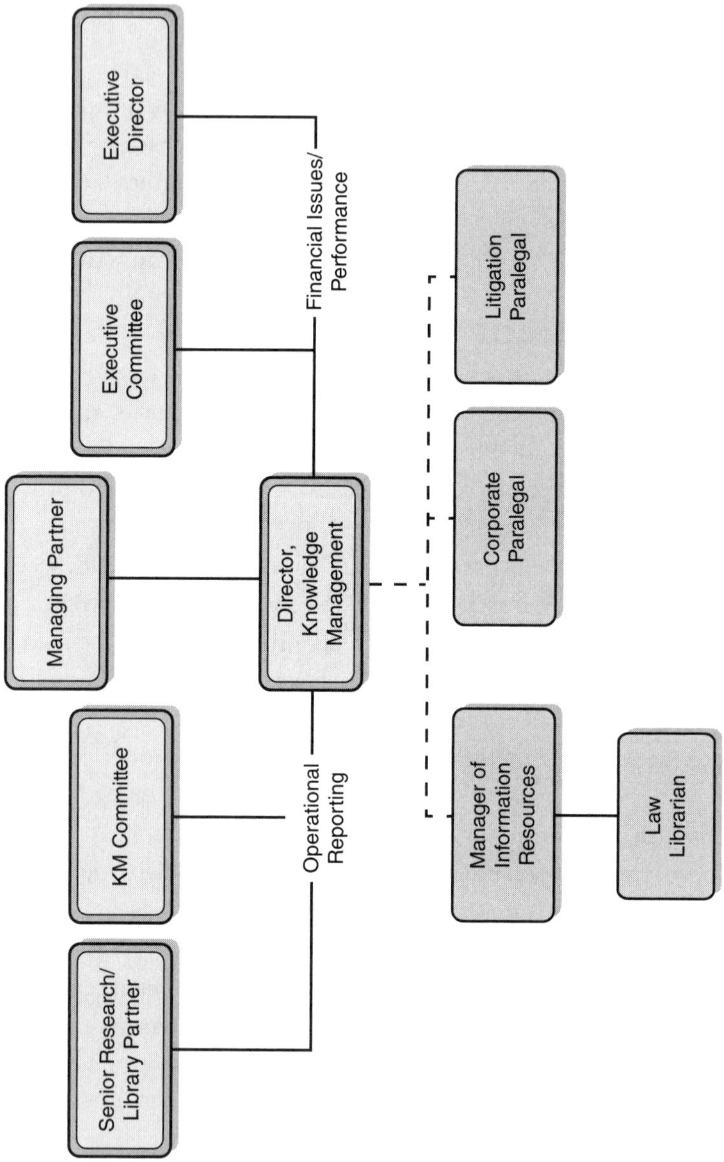

Figure 4.3
Lawson Lundell LLP's knowledge management organizational structure.

Because the KM group is small, Sinclair smartly leverages employees in other groups to participate in knowledge management projects and activities. For example, the firm repositioned a library manager role to become the manager of Information Resources. This newly minted role includes some KM responsibilities, such as the categorization and curation of a KM database that houses resources like precedent documents, boilerplate clauses, research, and closing books. In addition, Sinclair has the assistance of two paralegals—one from litigation and the other from corporate—when they have capacity to help, although their billable work for clients comes first. KM also collaborates with several other groups, such as Information Resources (formerly known as the Library), Information Technology, Business Development and Marketing, and various practice groups. These collaborations are common among firms with KM programs, and they are just as important with smaller firms as they are with larger firms.

Although Sinclair reports that the firm has no set knowledge management vision or mission statement or principles, he has personally evolved some over the years. He sees the KM group's vision as supporting Lawson Lundell lawyers to be more efficient in their practices by developing precedents and other resources, and to build and maintain an easily accessible repository of the firm's accumulated knowledge. In terms of the group's mission, Sinclair articulates it as "working proactively with practice groups to identify the areas where the scarce KM resources can be applied to best effect."

Sinclair has also developed a set of principles that guide his knowledge management efforts. These are sound concepts shared by many knowledge management professionals, as echoed throughout this book, but they take on particular meaning for smaller firms. The principles are as follows:

1. Don't try to "boil the ocean." In other words, don't try to do too much with the limited resources that you have. Every department in every firm has limited resources, and everyone must prioritize their projects and initiatives. This point addresses strategy (see Chapter 6), recognizing that choosing to focus on one thing means that you must make tradeoffs and not focus on other things. Choosing what not to do is often as important as choosing what to do.

2. Sinclair recommends "leveraging what we already have before we spend on technology." This is another sound piece of advice. With stretched budgets, it can be difficult to get approval for the latest and greatest technology. Although not necessarily the optimal choice, firms often can make do with the technology they have (e.g., Sinclair's use of the existing document management system), rather than spending money on new technologies that they may want.
3. "Build the culture first—people and process before technology." Again, this is sound advice for law firms and law departments of all sizes. Focusing on your organization's people—how they work, how they interact with each other, and how they are unique—will guide the choices you make about which processes and technology tools to implement. No matter how amazing the systems and tech tools you introduce, if you do not have the support of the people you are trying to help, then your efforts will likely fail.
4. Sinclair advises to use project management principles to keep KM projects on track. Most projects, especially those with any degree of complexity, need guidance. KM projects are no different. People on the outside (those who are not directly involved with the project) often see project management as an unnecessary layer of complexity and expense. Those who have attempted to complete projects on time and on budget without good project management, however, know that this invaluable component can be the difference between success and failure. See more about the importance of project management related to knowledge management efforts in Chapter 7, where I discuss the role of the KM Project Manager.

4.5.5 Debevoise & Plimpton, LLP

Debevoise & Plimpton is a New York–based law firm with approximately 650 lawyers throughout its eight offices worldwide.[15] Its practice is broad but focuses on corporate, litigation, and tax and employee benefits work. Debevoise began its knowledge management efforts more than a decade

15. http://www.debevoise.com/attorneys/.

ago, when they were carried out by a litigation counsel, supported by two staff members, and a corporate counsel, supported by two additional staff members. The firm saw the potential benefit of consolidating KM efforts with library operations, so they brought on Steve Lastres[16] to lead these merged groups. Steve has served as Director of Knowledge Management Service (KMS) since May 2005.

I know Steve, and I'm personally familiar with his operation at Debevoise, because I worked as his KM Manager for almost two years. With a master's degree in library science and a law degree, he has the right educational background to lead the department. Before joining Debevoise, he was library and records manager at Fulbright & Jaworski and library, records, and continuing legal education manager at Arnold & Porter. Steve is also a prolific writer and speaker on the topics of KM and law librarianship and has held leadership roles in the Association of Records Managers and Administrators (ARMA) International, the American Association of Law Libraries (AALL), and the International Legal Technology Association (ILTA). He was recently recognized as the 2014 ILTA Knowledge Management Professional of the Year and a FastCase 50 award winner, which recognizes the top 50 innovators, techies, visionaries, and leaders. In addition, he was an ILTA 2013 Publication Award Winner for Best Member-Contributed White Paper, entitled "Knowledge Management: A Strategic Role Change for Legal Information Professionals."[17]

Debevoise's KM department is one of the more mature and well-developed among U.S.-based law firms. The department's 20 members focus on delivering excellent service to the firm's more than 650 lawyers, and their vision is to "help lawyers work better, smarter, faster and cheaper, producing uniform, high quality, cost-effective work product, at anytime, anywhere in the world."

Reporting to the firm's CEO, Steve has direct access to the highest levels of firm management, an important factor among the most successful KM departments. Operationally, he is guided by a KM Task Force, which is made up of the firm's Presiding Partner, Head of the Corporate Department,

16. http://www.linkedin.com/in/stevelastres.
17. Steve Lastres, "Knowledge Management: A Strategic Role Change for Legal Information Professionals," http://epubs.iltanet.org/i/87421/32.

and various Practice Group Chairs. The KM group at Debevoise consists of a manager, who reports to Steve and leads a group of four KM analysts, two of whom have law degrees. The group also has one KM Counsel and two practice support lawyers, who work out of the firm's London office. In addition, the firm has two SharePoint and KM developers, who work on KM projects and report into the IT department. (See Figure 4.4.)

Library research is led by a senior research manager, who reports to the KMS Director and is supported by nine research librarians. The Electronic Resource Management (ERM) group supports all of the Library infrastructure, including the integrated library software platform, with an ERM manager and three analysts.

Like many law firms, Debevoise started focusing on legal project management; they are actively seeking a legal project manager. Additionally, they recently added a second Manager of Pricing to support client pricing models.

Although it is quite well-developed, the KMS department cannot do all of its work alone. They work closely with various other groups at the firm, including the IT department for SharePoint development and the Marketing department for business development purposes. They have also recently begun to work with the Accounting department, which is piloting the use of business intelligence software.

The KMS department's strategy focuses on high-quality content, collaboration, and access to knowledge resources. As stated by Steve, the KM group seeks to:

- Pursue a practice-driven content development approach, working directly with practice groups and integrating ongoing KM support with each group.
- Mobilize existing practicing lawyers in content creation efforts, with coordination by a small core practice support group.
- Coordinate and more closely integrate library and KM efforts and projects.
- Implement centralized access to comprehensive, integrated internal and external knowledge resources, fully searchable, with a clear and logical taxonomy.

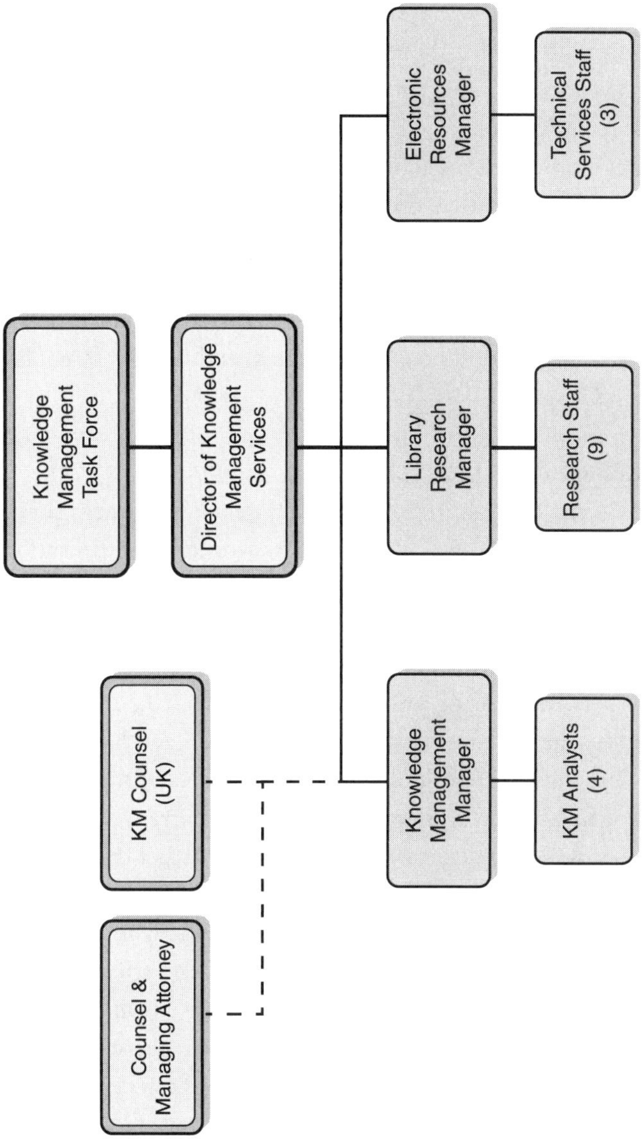

Figure 4.4
Debevoise & Plimpton's knowledge management services organization chart.

The Debevoise KMS department is always trying to improve the resources and quality that it delivers. As a part of those ongoing efforts, they are currently considering a migration from SharePoint 2010 to SharePoint 2013 as the platform for their firm-wide intranet. They recently deployed the iManage document management system (DMS) to integrate it with their electronic records repository. To help their lawyers find important precedent documents more quickly and easily, KMS will launch an enterprise search system and work product retrieval system. Finally, Lastres and his team are continuing the deployment of their social media platform, which they use for lawyer collaboration, business development, and project management. Read more about document management systems, enterprise search systems, enterprise social networking systems, and other KM-enabling technologies in Chapter 9.

4.5.6 Bradford & Barthel, LLP

Bradford & Barthel is a firm of approximately 95 attorneys spread across 13 offices in California. Well known for its workers' compensation defense practice, the firm also includes lawyers who specialize in subrogation, general civil litigation, appellate, and sports law, among other practice areas.[18] Bradford's knowledge management efforts are headed up by Eric Hunter, who serves as Director of Knowledge, Technology & Innovation Strategies.[19] Hunter has been with the firm since 2005 and has served in other roles, such as Financial Business Intelligence Analyst, Project Manager, and Director of KM, which was combined with his current position.

At fewer than 100 attorneys, Bradford & Barthel is a relatively small firm, but it has embraced knowledge management in a big way. The firm exemplifies that even smaller law firms can benefit from knowledge management programs and initiatives. Bradford's KM efforts began around 2009, after Hunter attended the ILTA Conference. Having previously been involved with project management and having held a role as a business analyst, Hunter saw parallels between what he had been doing in those roles and what he saw other firms were doing in knowledge management. He

18. http://www.bradfordbarthel.com/.
19. Hunter was awarded the 2010 International Legal Technology Association (ILTA) Knowledge Management Champion—Distinguished Peer Award and is the author of *The Sherlock Syndrome: Strategic Success through Big Data and the Darwinian Disruption* (London, UK: Ark Group Publishing), 2015. www.linkedin.com/pub/eric-hunter/3/521/498.

discussed it with his firm, and they decided to formalize their knowledge management efforts. Hunter became director of knowledge management, and two years later, the firm combined the KM role with technology and innovation strategies. Combining such roles is more common in smaller firms than at larger firms, where technology and KM tend to be separate departments, and their leaders tend to have peer relationships.

One of the primary drivers that led to the formation of the KM group was the realization that it was a complement to the other efforts (e.g., project management, business analysis, etc.) that they had adopted to make their work more efficient and profitable. "Workers' compensation law is a very high-volume and low-profit-margin practice area," said Hunter. "So, any steps the firm could take to make the work more efficient could have a dramatic effect on profitability." Connecting the lawyers to their own collective work product and to their fellow lawyers and clients were considered key ways to help increase efficiency and drive profitability.

Hunter reports to a group of senior partners, the senior management team, and board members. One difference between his KM department and those of some of the larger firms profiled here is the number of people dedicated to KM efforts. Whereas some of the larger firms have dozens of employees dedicated to KM efforts, Bradford has only six, including him. It should be noted, however, that the firm has combined KM, technology, and other areas into the department, so all of the teams' activities might not be considered knowledge management. In addition to Hunter, the team consists of a project manager, a business intelligence analyst, a KM analyst, a network engineer, and a business process analyst. (See Figure 4.5.) This combination has worked well for the firm, as the team is tight-knit and collaborative. In addition, many of the team members are cross-functional. For example, the project manager doubles as the assistant program manager, and the network engineer and business process analyst also take on traditional IT help desk duties, when needed.

Another uncommon aspect of Bradford & Barthel's approach to knowledge management is its openness to using cloud-based technologies to facilitate the management of documents and collaboration among lawyers and clients. Although the firm is not using cloud technologies exclusively (they still use on-premises servers for some applications, like financial reporting

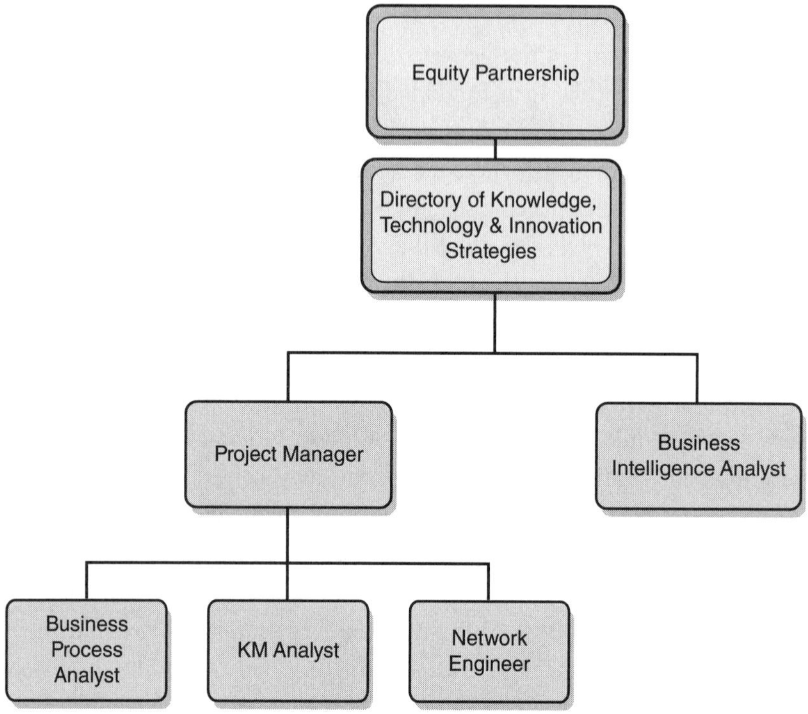

Figure 4.5
Bradford & Barthel's knowledge management department organization chart.

and billing), they have been using Google's suite of enterprise products, such as Docs, Spreadsheets, Presentations, and Gmail, for a few years. The Google suite of products is mainly used for collaboration in management, process teams, change management teams, and client collaboration. The firm also uses Microsoft Office applications, such as Word, when needed (mainly for secretarial and administrative staff) for its more robust document-formatting capabilities. Hunter and his team promote the use of Google Sites, which enables sharing of web-based content in what many would equate to a more traditional intranet platform. Finally, the firm has adopted the use of Google+ for social networking both inside and outside the firm.

Given the firm's openness to—and reliance on—consumer-based technologies, it's not surprising that their strategy includes "evolving the firm in tandem with global social consumer knowledge management." From a process-improvement perspective, Hunter says their focus is on "implementing firm-wide workflow modeling through spherical analysis[20] and process innovation, leveraging multiple collaboration points." The firm is also focusing on strategic pricing using predictive analytics. Overall, Hunter says, the KM department seeks to "foster a culture of creativity, trust, initiative, intuition, failure, success, and continual reinvention."

4.5.7 Bracewell & Giuliani, LLP

Sean Luman[21] is Senior Director, Knowledge Management at Bracewell & Giuliani, LLP, an international law firm with 485 lawyers in the United States, Dubai, and London. The firm serves Fortune 500 companies, major financial institutions, leading private investment funds, governmental entities, and individuals concentrated in the energy, technology, and financial services sectors worldwide.[22] The Knowledge Management group at Bracewell started in 2009 and is one of four teams under the Information Management department. The other three groups are User Services, Network/Infrastructure, and E-Practice.

Sean is a technologist with a business background and a degree in management and marketing. This gives him the ability to really connect with the other members of the Information Management groups in ways that KM leaders at other firms may lack. He considers himself an information management liaison among technology, financial, business development/marketing, and attorneys. "I have always interacted with the attorneys, both directly and through management," said Sean. "I'm a self-proclaimed marketer of technology, research, database design, records information management, litigation support, and systems integrations (data management, document management, financial, human resource/payroll, contact relationship management, competitive and internal research intelligence)."

20. Hunter describes the term "spherical analysis" (a term coined by the firm and its subsidiary, Spherical Models, LLC) as "shifting traditional linear organizational structures and workflow to a team-based process environment, with no static steps involved in business-driven initiatives."
21. http://www.linkedin.com/pub/sean-luman/10/232/355.
22. http://www.bracewellgiuliani.com/about.

Sean has a healthy perspective on the role of a KM leader. Liaison and marketer are two critical roles that a leader must play to make KM successful in any organization. The ability to speak the languages of KM, technology, and the law—and sometimes play the role of interpreter—is extremely valuable when you are trying to help people with varying backgrounds understand the value of knowledge management. See Chapter 7 for more on the role of a KM leader.

There are approximately 20 members in Bracewell's KM department. Sean reports to the Chief Information Officer and has dotted-line reporting to the Chief Financial Officer, Chief Operating Officer, Chief Human Resources Officer, Chief of Staff, and Managing Partner. In addition to his Senior Director role, he is also a member of the Technology Committee, Knowledge Resources Committee, and Information Governance and Records Management Steering Committee.

The KM department is divided into three main teams: Knowledge Resources, Information Governance and Records Management, and Technology. (See Figure 4.6.) The members of the KM department frequently collaborate with the firm's business units (including Operations, Marketing/Business Development, Information Technology, Finance/Accounting, and Human Resources), practice and office heads, and Office of the General Counsel.

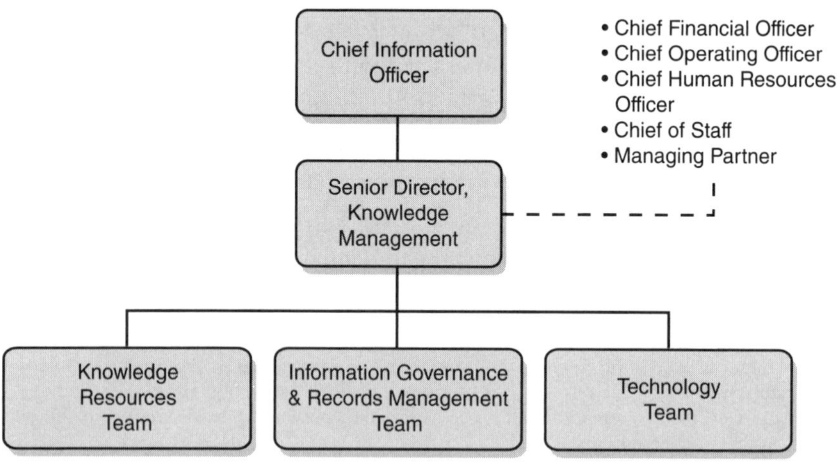

Figure 4.6
Bracewell & Giuliani's knowledge management department structure.

In the Knowledge Resources team, there are three research librarians and one acquisition librarian. There are also three administrative assistants/analysts who manage physical library materials throughout the firm and assist with managing vendor relationships, for example, with accounts payable management, budgeting, cancellations, reconciliation, and on-site and remote training opportunities. Librarians also manage a SharePoint intranet team site that contains links to specific practice-related resources and contact information, training materials, a password management application, and an online usage analysis system.

The Information Governance and Records Management team includes analysts who manage the firm's physical files. This team includes one full-time employee and individuals provided by the facilities management service at each office. In the future, this team will be led by a director and will also have individuals who manage litigation holds, ethical walls, and records management software, including management of documents and e-mail, as well as the traditional physical files.

The Technology team includes several web developers, SharePoint content analysts, database administrators, and individual department support staff, who assist with services related to various administrative departments, such as technology, financial, and business development/marketing.

4.6 The Role of Libraries and Librarians in Knowledge Management

You probably noticed that many of the law firms profiled here (and in Appendix A) include library groups (sometimes called research groups) in their knowledge management departments. Those that do not directly include these groups in KM often have structures that facilitate the collaboration of KM and library groups. There are several good reasons for this collaboration. One reason is that the skills of research librarians are often very similar to the skills of various members of a KM department. Organizing information, creating taxonomies (or classification systems), and helping lawyers find relevant content are all skills shared by both groups of professionals. Because of these similarities, some organizations merge the groups, while in others, knowledge management departments subsume libraries.

Another reason for this situation is that the nature of libraries is changing. There are still many libraries with stacks of hard-copy books, but the emerging (and continuing) trend among libraries—especially among law firm libraries—is a move away from the traditional "library as a place" to a more resource-focused, "library as a service center." This is not to say that many law firms and law departments have gone completely bookless. To the contrary, physical books are all around us. However, starting several years ago, particular hard-copy resources, such as court reporters, bound state and federal statutes, and even treatises, began to vanish from library bookshelves.

I was personally involved with a massive purge of old hard-copy library books when the law firm at which I worked at the time relocated and drastically scaled down the footprint of the library. The architectural plans for the new library space called for the reduction of close to half of the shelving that was available in the old space. Because part of my KM role was to manage the library, I knew this was the right thing to do. Many old hard-copy books were simply not being used, because attorneys were accessing the content online. Nevertheless, some attorneys wanted to hang on to the hard-copy books just in case. In the end, when reality took hold and it was clear that there would simply be no space for books that were not actually being used, the purge went forward. Not surprisingly, nobody missed the books that were cleared out, because their content was available online.

Although some libraries (the physical structures) may be going the way of the dodo, some *librarians* are well-suited for certain functions in KM, because many of the skills they possess are directly transferable to knowledge management. As you will see in Chapter 7, when we discuss the various roles involved in KM, the role of assisting lawyers in finding internal resources and collective knowledge is one that many research librarians can fill well. Because they are adept at legal research (typically focusing on external resources) and usually have good substantive knowledge of various areas of the law, research librarians can often excel when focusing their research skills on internal content, especially when armed with quality technology tools, such as enterprise search systems.

For other librarians, they are seeing the proverbial writing on the wall. They feel that the traditional role of the librarian, in some ways, is quickly becoming extinct and being replaced by knowledge management activities. Many of the KM professionals with whom I worked over the years were former librarians who hold Master of Library and Information Science (MLIS) degrees. In recent years, when I have sought to fill various roles in my KM departments, there has never been a shortage of applicants with MLIS degrees and/or library experience. Many are seeking to pivot in their own careers, and they point to advances in technology that seem to obviate the need for some of the services that had traditionally been provided by librarians.

Lawyers have also witnessed how technology has changed not only the way they practice, but also their needs when it comes to seeking assistance for legal research. Any lawyer who has been practicing for more than 15 years or so will recall learning how to find case law in reporters. Years ago, most legal treatises and other books were only available in hard copy; electronic versions were uncommon. The advent of online legal research providers like LexisNexis and Westlaw ushered in the age of virtual research, often completely obviating a trip to the law library and, for some attorneys, a consultation with a research librarian. Although I do not advocate eschewing the services of librarians, and in fact I relied on them as a practicing lawyer, the fact is that many librarian functions have been replaced by technology tools.

Leveraging the library staff is also a good way to bootstrap KM efforts when there is little or no budget to bring on dedicated knowledge management personnel. In my personal experience, and based on my observations at knowledge management and library conferences, I find that librarians are not only willing to assist with KM initiatives, but many welcome—and even pursue—the opportunity. In fact, in smaller law firms and law departments, the library staff often initiates KM efforts, such as organizing model documents or developing intranets.

Jean O'Grady, Director of Research Services and Libraries at DLA Piper, and Chair of the Private Law Libraries Special Interest Section of the American Association of Law Libraries,[23] understands this shift in the nature of law libraries. She announced in 2013 that the Private Law Libraries Board

23. http://www.aallnet.org/sections/pll/Leadership/Current-PLL-Officers.html.

sought to examine the merits of renaming the group. She stated that the "use of the word 'libraries' reveals nothing specific about we do. PLL members provide a wide array of services, including 'Competitive Intelligence, Business Intelligence, Knowledge Management, records, docket, web development, and other emerging digital roles.'" O'Grady noted that librarian roles have "radically changed, reflecting seismic shifts in the legal industry. 'Librarian' and 'libraries' fail to convey how our new responsibilities and skills serve the goals of our law firm or corporate employers and clients."[24]

As we have seen in some of the KM department profiles, library integration with KM is common. In addition to the examples noted previously, this is the case at Stikeman Elliott, LLP, where April Brousseau[25] was formerly Director of Knowledge Management & Library. Part of the reason for the tight bond with library services is that KM is "a one-stop shop for all of your resource and research needs in practice," Brousseau said. "Though [librarians] provide traditional library services (reference, resource management, media monitoring, and current awareness) they also provide support to KM." Here are a few of the ways that the library staff supports KM at Stikeman:

- Creation and maintenance of various resource and information repositories:
    a. A directory of externally published precedents made available through the library catalog
    b. Reference requests repository (an ongoing process of moving such requests out of e-mail and into a more easily searchable location)
    c. A repository of frequently requested documents (primarily includes consultative reports and case law)
    d. A fully searchable collection of the tables of contents of all major titles to the library catalog records
    e. Lists of key titles by practice area and legal topic made available and searchable through library catalog

24. Michael Ginsborg, October 13, 2013, http://firmerground.wordpress.com/2013/10/30/renaming-the-private-law-libraries-special-interest-section-pll-sis-of-the-american-association-of-law-libraries-aall/.
25. Brousseau currently serves as Interim Head of Knowledge Systems at Norton Rose Fulbright, https://www.linkedin.com/profile/view?id=57105128.

f. An index of catalog materials that lawyers receive from external legal education seminars to make them more widely available via a sign out (borrowing) procedure

- Research and content support:
  a. Provide search support for our knowledge management collection (internally created work product). Not only do librarians help attorneys find external content, like case law, legislation, and commentary, they also assist with finding precedents and other internal, previous work product documents that attorneys can use to help with their current matters.
  b. Work with the members of the KM team on updating major publications through legislative tracking and monitoring
  c. Deliver content to the firm's intranet through various practice group and our legal resources pages
  d. Work closely with the marketing department, providing competitive and business intelligence research via a series of templates. This allows any member of the team to answer a request from marketing using a consistent research methodology and final product.
- New developments/Current awareness:
  a. Library members are responsible for the posting to the Stikeman blogs. Though largely a data entry task, it requires knowledge of HTML, and the staff finds and creates all the links to legislation, case law, and other commentary referenced in the postings.
  b. Provide a customized new-development tracking service for lawyers and clients. This involves tracking proposed legislative changes as well as case law updates and sending daily alerts.

Brousseau sees even more potential for the collaboration between librarians and the knowledge management group. "I would like to see librarians fully integrated into various practice groups in a similar way that practice support/KM lawyers often are," said Brousseau. "They could provide in-depth research while also developing specific expertise in particular areas."

There is even the potential for librarians to collaborate with other administrative functions beyond what is traditionally considered to be within the scope of knowledge management. Data analytics is one area. Brousseau's library group has started down this path with the frequent reviews of particular pages and modules accessed in their externally provided resources, so that they can see what their lawyers are looking for and identify ways to get it to them faster and easier. "In the future, I would like to see us use those kinds of data analytics, combined with analytics from our search engine, to help identify what kind of templates we should be creating and collecting," Brousseau said. There are several other fields where Brousseau sees potential to leverage the skills abilities of the library group: electronic discovery (since searching and organizing electronic documents is an essential part of a librarian's role), budgeting initiatives (as librarians can apply their skills to review and organize data into phases and tasks), and taxonomy or classification management, since structuring data and information around practice areas, matter types, and industries is a common skill of trained librarians.

You can see how progressive, forward-thinking knowledge management professionals, like Brousseau, look at things differently. They don't restrict themselves—or the field of knowledge management—to the bounds of what KM once was (e.g., the identify–capture–disseminate–reuse model). They seek out ways to apply the principles and ideas of knowledge management to help lawyers in the practice—and business—of law, whether that is within their scope or not. And perhaps most importantly, they collaborate with others to address the things that will have the most significant positive impact to help their organizations achieve their goals.

4.7 Key Points

- The structure of knowledge management departments can be diverse and vary greatly depending on several factors, including the size of the firm or law department, the age and maturity of the KM program, and the individuals who lead KM efforts.
- The most significant factor that will dictate how a KM department operates (and whether it is successful) is the firm or organizational culture. Understanding the culture will help you decide how to approach your KM efforts.

- Although knowledge management is more common among larger firms, even smaller firms can benefit from KM initiatives and practices. Some smaller firms have had great success implementing KM efforts and programs.
- You should not seek to replicate the KM efforts or structures at other firms or law departments, because each organization is unique. However, you can draw inspiration from other firms to help guide your thinking about what might work in your organization.
- The nature of law libraries is changing; libraries and librarians are commonly part of modern KM departments, and they can be valuable assets to KM programs.

Chapter 5

Your KM Mission and Vision: Why Are You Doing This?

> Any kind of vision needs people.
>
> —Nobu Matsuhisa, chef and restaurateur

5.1 Chapter Preview and Target Audience

Chapter preview:

1. You'll learn why it is important to understand and be able to articulate why you are pursuing knowledge management in your organization.
2. You'll learn about KM vision and mission statements and understand their purpose.
3. We'll explore examples of vision and mission statements that will guide you in creating appropriate vision and mission statements for your organization.

Target audience:
Chapter 5 will be of interest to Lawyer Leaders and Administrative Leaders. Lawyer Leaders may want to skim the sections that list examples of KM visions and missions, while Administrative Leaders may want to spend more time reviewing them and thinking about how they might influence the development of your organization's vision and mission.

Why should a law firm or law department engage in knowledge management initiatives or programs? What is the purpose? Addressing the "why" and understanding the purpose are crucial to success in any endeavor, including knowledge management. This is obvious, right? Then why do so many people skip this critical step?

When you start KM initiatives—or any other initiatives for that matter—without first understanding why you are doing so, you will start down a path of an undisciplined pursuit of many things. Some of those things may turn out to be good and appropriate for your organization. Some may benefit the organization. But many will be diversions resulting in wasted time and effort, and they may ultimately cause your efforts to fail in the eyes of important stakeholders. If you don't know the purpose of your actions—why you are doing this—how will you know if you have succeeded? More importantly, if you don't know why you're doing it, and you cannot articulate it to the stakeholders within your organization, then chances are that you will be unable to garner the support required for a successful knowledge management program. As Simon Sinek, author of *Start with Why*, says: "People don't buy what you do; they buy why you do it."[1]

Before beginning on a knowledge management journey within your organization, I recommend that you act like a toddler: keep asking "why?" Challenge yourself to get down to the essence of why you want to pursue a knowledge management program or initiative and articulate it. Only by digging deep and repeatedly asking "why?" will you get to the heart of the matter and have a complete understanding of why you should pursue knowledge management and find the true purpose.

Clearly articulating that purpose—why you are doing this—will help members of your organization understand what you are doing and how you are doing it. Sharing that purpose will help you garner support for your initiatives and programs. Formulating mission and vision statements can help you communicate your purpose, not only to your KM team, but also to the entire organization.

1. Simon Sinek, https://www.startwithwhy.com/.

5.2 What Is a KM Mission? What Is a KM Vision?

When most people talk about vision and mission statements, they are referring to those of a company, rather than a department or group within a company. But departments and groups within organizations can—and I believe should—have clearly articulated visions and missions. This is becoming increasingly common among various departments and groups in many industries, including the legal profession. Law firm and law department knowledge management groups are no exception.

Some organizations have been slow to adopt mission or vision statements, in part, because the value of these statements has been questioned. Some have criticized them as being useless, meaningless, and full of fluff. Although some such declarations are in fact simply designed to fill an otherwise blank space in an annual report, others are valuable, because they guide, inspire, educate, and motivate members of groups and the customers or clients they serve.

As noted by Susan Manch and Michelle Nash in their book *Learning from Law Firm Leaders*, when referring to law firm efforts:

> So-called vision statements became very popular among law firm marketing gurus in the 1990s, but too often the statements are more about marketing than they are about strategy. They sound good and make the firm sound good, yet the actual day-to-day actions of firm members and the direction of the firm's business do not fully align with the tenets of the vision statement. Too often they are vague and jargonistic and do not report to internal or external stakeholders what the firm will do, what value it brings to the market, and how that value may be measured.[2]

2. Susan G. Manch and Michelle C. Nash, *Learning from Law Firm Leaders* (Washington, DC: American Bar Association, 2012).

5.3 What Is a Mission Statement?

Remember, a mission statement is not a declaration of what you do. It is a statement of "the purpose of an organization or company—the reason for this company's existence. A mission statement provides framework and context to help guide the company's strategies and actions by spelling out the company's overall goal."[3]

Several examples of mission statements can be found online. When formulating your own KM mission statement, it can be helpful to look at the mission statements from outside the legal industry. This may help you better understand the nature of a mission statement that fits the KM team at your law firm or legal department and avoid the trap of relying on jargon or something that lacks true meaning for your organization.

Put another way, a mission statement is:

> a written declaration of an organization's core purpose and focus that normally remains unchanged over time. Properly crafted mission statements (1) serve as filters to separate what is important from what is not, (2) clearly state which markets will be served and how, and (3) communicate a sense of intended direction to the entire organization.[4]

Probably the most well-known mission statement is Google's: "to organize the world's information and make it universally accessible and useful."[5] A version of Google's mission isn't a bad way to describe what some law firm or law department KM missions fundamentally are. In fact, Jeffrey Rovner, of O'Melveny & Myers, has adopted that very approach (see Chapter 4).

David Gurteen, a well-known knowledge management consultant, notes that mission statements are too often designed to be more like marketing statements, when they should really motivate and inspire the people who actually do the work in question. And when it comes to KM missions, those words should inspire all employees, because knowledge management

3. http://www.businessnewsdaily.com/3783-mission-statement.html.
4. http://www.businessdictionary.com/definition/mission-statement.html.
5. http://www.google.com/about/company/.

is everyone's responsibility. The mission statement should be written "to inspire and focus people to better work together, share knowledge, and learn from each other to achieve their objectives," Gurteen says.[6] He suggests that mission statements should be concise, clear, focused, and tie into the strategic objectives of the organization. All good advice.

5.4 What Is a Vision Statement?

Some say that a vision is a statement of aspiration or ambition. For example, Microsoft's original vision in 1977 was "A computer on every desk and in every home."[7] Simply put, a vision statement is "an aspirational description of what an organization would like to achieve or accomplish in the mid-term or long-term future. It is intended to serve as a clear guide for choosing current and future courses of action."[8] "Ranging from one line to several paragraphs, a vision statement identifies what the company would like to achieve or accomplish. A good vision statement provides the inspiration for the daily operations of a business and molds its strategic decisions."[9]

A sign of growing maturity of KM in the legal industry may be the number of firms that have formalized their KM programs and efforts. Since 2008, the International Legal Technology Association (ILTA) has asked some form of the following question: Does your organization have a formally articulated strategic plan or vision? In 2008, 42 percent of all respondents (and 52 percent of large firms) claimed to have a formally articulated strategy or vision. Although we might expect these numbers to rise in later years, they have actually fluctuated. In 2010, only 34 percent of law firms and departments reported having a formally articulated KM strategic plan or vision. By 2012, that number increased to 41 percent. The results from the 2014 survey seemed to head in an unexpected direction, indicating that only

6. David Gurteen, KM Missions, http://www.ikmagazine.com/display.asp?articleid=3dd7bfb0-d468-4bc6-91a8-b4cd6ffc8da2.
7. http://www.achievement.org/autodoc/page/gat0int-1.
8. http://www.businessdictionary.com/definition/vision-statement.html.
9. http://www.businessnewsdaily.com/3882-vision-statement.html.

32 percent of the 110 respondents had a formally articulated KM strategic plan or vision (although 33 percent had one in development).

5.5 Examples of KM Mission and Vision Statements

My firm's knowledge management department has developed a mission statement, a vision statement, and a set of guiding principles, all of which we publish on our firm's intranet. Publishing this information for the entire firm to see helps everyone understand our goals, what we can offer, and how we can help.

Our mission—or the reason the department exists—is, fundamentally, to help the firm succeed. So, we formulated our mission statement to reflect that, and we state it in a way that reflects the firm's overall goal of being the world's premier labor and employment law firm. Thus, our knowledge management department mission statement is: "Help Ogletree Deakins be the world's premier labor and employment law firm by being the world's premier knowledge-sharing law firm." This statement may seem a bit simplistic, but it is important to remember that a mission statement is not a plan, or strategy, to accomplish the goal. Rather, it is designed as a statement to encapsulate the goal itself.

We have also formulated a vision statement. Although it is somewhat similar to a mission statement, and still not as detailed as a strategy, a vision statement puts a little more meat on the bones and provides an indication of what we want to accomplish. Because we believe that knowledge management is fundamentally about connections (see Chapter 1), we have shaped our vision statement around that concept.

My firm's knowledge management vision is to improve the practice of law and business of the firm by:

1. Connecting our people with each other and our clients
2. Connecting our people with information and our collective knowledge
3. Developing innovative processes, procedures, and systems to make those connections and promote knowledge sharing

In addition to mission and vision statements, you may find it of value to articulate some principles that guide your thinking and actions around your knowledge management activities. These guiding principles tend to be general statements about what you believe to be important to the success of your efforts. They need not be KM-specific, but they should be relatively high-level ideals that keep the knowledge management team focused and communicate to the rest of the department and firm what you value as a knowledge-sharing organization. These guiding principles should also reflect how you and your firm envision what knowledge management is about and what being a knowledge-sharing organization means.

My firm's knowledge management department guiding principles are as follows:

1. Align knowledge management goals and strategies with the firm's goals and strategies.
2. Change as the needs of the firm and the needs of our clients change.
3. Promote quality, consistency, and efficiency of work product.
4. Provide the right information to the right people at the right time.
5. People first, then process, then technology.
6. Communicate simply and often.

Collections of knowledge management mission and vision statements can be found online. In his Knoco Stories blog, Nick Milton, a well-known knowledge management consultant, has collected[10] several vision statements, including one from Paul, Hastings, Janofsky & Walker, LLP, which reads: "The knowledge management vision within the firm is to enable professionals to acquire knowledge and synthesize data faster and easier."

Some of the KM mission and vision statements shared previously and in the personal stories in Appendix B are worth taking another look at in the context of this topic. Here are some of those vision and mission statements:

---

10. 15 Example Knowledge Management Visions, http://www.nickmilton.com/2011/12/15-example-knowledge-management-visions.html

- "To organize the firm's information and make it universally accessible and useful." O'Melveny & Myers, LLP, knowledge management vision
- "Help lawyers work better, smarter, faster and cheaper, producing uniform, high quality, cost-effective work product, at anytime, anywhere in the world." Debevoise & Plimpton, LLP, knowledge management vision
- "The overall purpose of our knowledge and PSL activities is to contribute directly to improvements in (1) divisional and firm-wide profit margins (2) quality of work and service delivery, and (3) the firm's risk profile. . . . This is consistent with the firm's purpose: Enabling our clients and people to succeed and flourish." Addleshaw Goddard, LLP, knowledge management vision
- "Improving efficiency by reducing the need to rediscover knowledge. Leveraging Foley & Lardner's collective knowledge through systems and processes to support and facilitate the identification, capture, dissemination, and use of the Firm's knowledge to meet our business objectives." Foley & Lardner, LLP, knowledge management vision
- "Focus on Knowledge Management as a core competence in order to succeed in the next decade by providing our clients and lawyers with the content and process that maximize our ability to (1) provide greater efficiency and process improvements for monitoring and effectively managing legal matters; (2) access, utilize and integrate the knowledge bases existing within and outside of the Firm; (3) develop and utilize best practices; and (4) foster collaboration with clients." Foley & Lardner, LLP, knowledge management mission
- "Littler firmly believes that the traditional law firm model is imperiled. It's threatened by dramatic changes in the market including the rise of alternative legal service providers, changing demands and expectations of clients, and significant advances in technology. While knowledge management is not the panacea for fixing the legal business model, it is clearly one of the major components for successfully reinventing how legal services should be delivered more efficiently." Littler Mendelson, P.C., knowledge management vision
- "Our mission is to support attorney collaboration, strengthen relationships with clients, and improve business process streamlining." Fox Rothschild knowledge management mission

In addition to these KM mission and vision statements, the 2012 and 2014 ILTA Knowledge Management Surveys provide a look into some other law firms' KM visions and mission statements. The survey question simply asked "What is your KM vision or mission statement?" The answers were not presented in a way that indicated whether they were vision statements or mission statements. And one might argue that some of the responses look more like descriptions of KM or even department slogans. Regardless, the responses are interesting and valuable to give us some additional insight into what some law firm KM departments see as their raison d'être.

Some KM vision and mission statements from the 2012 and 2014 ILTA KM Surveys are as follows:

- "Improving efficiency by reducing the need to rediscover knowledge. Leveraging the firm's collective knowledge through systems and processes to support and facilitate the identification, dissemination, and use of knowledge to meet business objectives."
- "Supporting the firm's value advantage"
- "To connect those who know with those who need to know in order to simplify the complexity of work."
- "To harmonize Global Law Services Group & Knowledge Management activities; allowing for regional needs that are also collaborative across the enterprise."
- "To provide knowledge and research services; internal and external information and knowledge; and solutions to help our people provide a high-quality, efficient service to clients and to grow the business."
- "Providing lawyers with easy access to the practice tools and resources they need to develop business and provide valued client service, supporting quality, excellence, and risk management"
- "To manage data and information in order to make meaningful contributions to: [improving firm cohesiveness, competitiveness, profitability, work practices, employee lifestyles, and expanding firm expertise.]"
- "At our firm, KM has far less to do with managing knowledge, and far more to do with leveraging, building, and creating new and better knowledge. KM brings together the many components of our organization to ensure that we all work optimally together for the firm's unified

objectives. KM exists to: help our lawyers add more value (through an enhanced client experience) and provide better guidance to their clients; help our lawyers manage their practices more effectively, accurately, and efficiently; and help us operate more profitably."

- "Deliver more value to clients by putting the collective experience and expertise of all firm attorneys and other professionals at the fingertips of each attorney."
- "KM is a permanent, strategic project management-based operation geared to virtually capture and deliver the best knowledge resources and services, external and internal, to practitioners firm wide by establishing, nurturing and facilitating relationships between knowledge seekers and knowledge providers."
- "To leverage internal work product for client services, lawyer efficiency and lawyer training."
- "To provide access to key knowledge, advice and information to all offices to support the advice we give our clients."
- "To provide lawyers with easy access to practice tools and resources to enable them to develop and share expertise, provide excellent client service and work efficiently."
- "Develop the people, processes and technological infrastructure to allow information (both explicit and tacit) to flow freely across the organization in a way that creates and preserves valuable options for our businesses."
- "Connecting people, reusing/increasing efficiency of/automating work-product creation and other knowledge, and providing knowledge regarding administrative procedures (to minimize time on non-billable work)"
- "Build and sustain a KM culture that connects those who know with those who need to know in order to provide accurate, responsible, timely legal support to our clients."
- "KM enables the firm to deliver more value to clients by putting the collective experience and expertise of all attorneys at the fingertips of each attorney."
- "Simplicity and value"

- "Promote efficient delivery of top-quality legal services."
- "Know where to go for indispensable legal knowledge."
- "To foster a culture of collaboration and seamless sharing of ideas and information across the firm; KM offerings will reduce the need to 'reinvent the wheel' and increase the satisfaction of our workforce by freeing our professionals to focus on the highest-value substantive challenges and opportunities."
- "Present an environment for information-sharing and collaboration that promotes an efficient means for delivering quality work, with a goal of improving value to clients and leveraging our investment in technology."
- "Just a click away"

When developing your own knowledge management mission and vision statements, you may feel tempted to simply replicate one that you have read here. Although your statement will undoubtedly have some similarities to some of the examples, you should resist the urge to take the shortcut and simply copy. Go through the exercise of asking "why?" Every organization is different, and each will have different reasons for starting a KM program. Contemplate the purpose of your endeavor. Figure out why you are doing this, and articulate it clearly and in a way that resonates with your people and fits your culture. Share it and be guided by it.

5.6 Key Points

- Understanding why your organization is engaging in KM initiatives is important to KM success.
- Being able to clearly articulate the purpose—why you are engaging in KM—will help members of your organization understand what you are doing and how you are doing it, and will help you garner support for your initiatives and programs.
- Formulating mission and vision statements can help you communicate your purpose, not only to your KM team but also to the entire organization.

- Taking the time to think through your organization's particular circumstances and objectives will help you formulate meaningful vision and mission statements that will help guide your KM efforts.
- It is okay to be guided by the vision and mission statements of other organizations, but resist the urge to simply copy them, because your organization is unique and requires unique vision and mission statements.

Chapter 6

Plan Your Attack: Knowledge Management Strategy

A strategy is just a plan.

—Unknown

Everybody has a plan until they get punched in the mouth.

—Mike Tyson

6.1 Chapter Preview and Target Audience

Chapter preview:

1. You'll learn what a knowledge management strategy is.
2. You'll learn the importance of having a knowledge management strategy and ensuring that it is appropriate for your organization and not simply a generic strategy.
3. You'll learn how to formulate or refresh your knowledge management strategy by examining the current state of your KM program, the desired future state, and the actions you need to take to get there.
4. We'll explore some useful tools that can help in formulating your KM strategy.
5. We'll explore how quick-win projects can give your KM program a boost, raise awareness about your efforts, and increase credibility among the leaders in your organization.

Target audience:
Chapter 6 will be of interest to Lawyer Leaders and Administrative Leaders. Administrative Leaders will want to read this chapter thoroughly, because formulating a KM strategy is a fundamental step in a successful KM program. Lawyer Leaders should pay close attention to Sections 6.2 and 6.3, which address what a KM strategy is and why it is important. Although less critical, Lawyer Leaders may also be interested in Section 6.4, which addresses how to formulate a KM strategy in detail.

6.2 What Is a Knowledge Management Strategy?

Armed with mission and vision statements, you now need a knowledge management strategy to implement them. But what is a strategy? Simply put, a strategy is a plan. It's a high-level plan to achieve overall goals or objectives. Your KM strategy, therefore, is your plan to achieve your organization's KM goals or objectives. Put another way, your KM strategy is *your* plan to achieve *your* organization's goals using KM principles and initiatives.

It is important to note the personal nature of that statement—*your* plan to achieve *your* organization's KM goals or objectives. Do not get caught up in a game of copycat when it comes to pursuing a KM strategy. Just because one firm is focusing on a particular KM strategy does not necessarily mean that it is right for your firm. There are many factors at play—difference of firm goals, demographics, KM maturity level—that will all shape the way you approach your KM strategy.

KM strategies are unique like snowflakes; although they may look similar, especially from afar, no two are identical. This makes sense, because no two law firms or legal departments are identical. Even though many share similar business goals, target clients, and other characteristics, they are not identical and inevitably will be at different levels of KM maturity at different times. For example, a firm that is in the beginning stages of forming a KM group will necessarily have a different KM strategy than a firm that has had an established KM group for several years.

KM strategies are, by their nature, dynamic and finite. If all goes well (according to plan), a strategy will be executed and completed at some point.

In other words, the plan will lead to the achievement of the articulated goals and objectives. At that time, a new KM strategy, with new goals and objectives, will probably need to be formulated. Alternatively, if the plan does not go as expected, or if outside forces come into play, the strategy may need to be revised or refreshed along the way.

6.3 The Purpose of Creating a Knowledge Management Strategy

"If you don't know exactly where you're going, how will you know when you get there?"[1] A KM strategy is important because it clearly states to all involved what you plan to do, when, and how. This is not to say that all of the minute details need to be articulated. Remember, a strategy is a high-level plan. It creates and articulates expectations. This is the first step in managing the expectations of a group of people (lawyers) who sometimes have a reputation for being quite demanding.

From the KM professional's perspective, a KM strategy is important and valuable, because as much as it articulates to your stakeholders what your organization plans to accomplish, it also articulates what you have decided *not* to do (or not to do at the moment). Consciously deciding what to omit from your plan is important, because there are always many more things you *can* do than you *should* do. As Steve Jobs said, shortly after his return to Apple in 1997, when he decided to reduce the number of products the company would offer, "Deciding what not to do is as important as deciding what to do. That's true for companies, and it's true for products."[2] It's also true for your KM initiatives. Everything matters, but everything doesn't matter equally.

This is particularly important, because at many law firms KM professionals (and most other administrative staff members) receive requests from various lawyers, all with their own needs and desires, and usually all with a sense of great urgency. The pecking order at many law firms (especially small to midsized firms) is (1) partners, (2) associates, and (3) everyone

1. Steve Maraboli, http://www.stevemaraboli.com/.
2. Walter Isaacson, *Steve Jobs* (New York: Simon & Schuster, 2011), 336.

else, so administrative staff often feel like they have multiple bosses. Even if there is a clear reporting structure from an administrative standpoint, staff members often feel like they have to cater to the requests of all lawyers as soon as they are asked. The expectation is that the administrative staff is there to assist lawyers. Although this expectation is almost universally true, often there is no framework for vetting and prioritizing requests. This can result in multiple conflicting projects for which there are typically no budgets. When those requests start coming in and stacking up, the demand on resources (both human and capital) can become overtaxed, and delays in delivery become inevitable. I have heard this complaint from many of my peers in various law firms. It is a common problem, but one that can be managed, in part, by articulating a strategy.

If lawyers at your firm have a tendency to make requests directly to lower-level staff members (those who typically execute much of the work), and those requests are not communicated to the senior managers, then this can result in duplication of effort and inefficiency. Take, for example, the situation where two litigation attorneys from different practice areas, both unbeknownst to each other, reach out to two different administrative staff members asking for similar work. Perhaps they both want to start collecting information about expert witnesses in a database (a common KM activity). These sorts of projects seem straightforward and easy to accomplish. So, staff members may be inclined to just perform the projects as a one-off, just to get them done, often without even mentioning it to their managers.

Of course, such projects are usually far less straightforward than they appear. They often involve not just the initial setup and design of a database, for example, but also the ongoing maintenance of the data. If both staff members agree to do the work, you can see how the initial quickie project has already resulted in duplicative effort and has also created the expectation that someone will keep the data updated. This can create further issues, for example, if the KM leader had already planned to create a firm-wide expert witness database later in the year. In this example, it is easy to see that if the individual staffers and attorneys had been informed about the broader plan, which included efforts to address how to manage expert witness information, then it could have prevented a lot of duplicative effort.

A clearly articulated strategy keeps all stakeholders informed so that they know the goals and planned accomplishments of the larger group. It keeps team members focused on those goals so that they do not deviate from the plan and become sidetracked with projects that can simultaneously compromise the goals and undermine the organization's confidence in the knowledge management group. Perhaps most important, the lack of a clearly articulated strategy diminishes the ability of the KM team to support the organization and accomplish its broader goals.

Other reasons to create a strategy include increasing awareness for KM efforts, building support for your initiatives, measuring the effectiveness of your program, and adding legitimacy to your efforts by declaring what you plan to do and when. Lawyers will understand that this is not just another flighty idea coming from some administrative department. The strategy clarifies the purpose of your actions and demonstrates how they will benefit the organization. Communicating the strategy to the lawyers in your firm or law department makes them aware of your efforts. It can build excitement, interest, and support. Once a strategy has been declared, it is easy to tell whether the plan has been accomplished. Along the path of executing your strategy, you can use it as an excuse to report on—and thereby promote—your efforts.

As mentioned in Chapter 5, the number of law firms and law departments that have formally articulated KM strategic plans or visions has increased over the years. Indeed, 27 percent of ILTA KM Survey respondents identified "developing a formal KM strategy" as a primary focus for the calendar year 2010. Although the same question was not included in the 2012 ILTA KM Survey, anecdotal evidence from presentations and comments made at various conferences and KM group meetings[3] suggests that articulating a KM strategy remained a focus of attention. By 2014, the ILTA surveys showed that 33 percent of respondents were in the development phase when it came to a formal, articulated KM strategy, plan, or vision. In addition,

3. E.g., ILTA 2011 Annual Conference, "Creating an Optimal KM Value Strategy," http://2011conference.iltanet.org/MainMenu/Downloads (alternate title: How to Formulate or Refresh Your KM Value Strategy, http://ilta.ebiz.uapps.net/productfiles/productfiles/695896/KMPG5.pdf).

25 percent of respondents cited "undefined scope/function" of KM as one of the top three KM challenges in 2014.

At ILTA's Annual Conference in 2011, I moderated a discussion entitled "How to Formulate or Refresh Your KM Value Strategy."[4] As a part of an interactive audience poll during the presentation, only 17.6 percent of respondents had a formal, written KM strategy at their firm or law department; 55.9 percent did not have one, and 17.6 percent were working on a KM strategy. Of course, at least some of the audience members presumably attended this session to learn about KM strategy formulation, so the relatively low number of respondents who already had a strategy in place was not surprising. More troublesome is that only 41.2 percent of respondents in the audience said that their firms or law departments had an overarching business strategy that had been conveyed to the administrative side of the organization. The remaining 58.8 percent of respondents' organizations either did not have one or the respondent was not aware of such a business strategy.

All of this feedback makes it clear that formulating a KM strategy is no simple task. As we shall see, it is imperative that a firm's or law department's KM strategy be linked to, and support, the organization's overall business strategy. Although this may seem obvious, it is not uncommon for KM professionals to get caught up in the shiny new software product that promises KM nirvana without assessing if such a solution would further the business goals of the organization.

6.4 Formulating a Knowledge Management Strategy

Now that we understand some good reasons to have a KM strategy, let's examine how you go about formulating one. When formulating a KM strategy, it is helpful to think in terms of a KM maturity model or progression model. Many KM pundits have developed such models, and many of these models are very good and useful. I am particularly fond of the work of Carla O'Dell and Cindy Hubert, which is on the APQC website[5] and in

4. The panel included John Gillies, Director of Practice Support at Cassels Brock & Blackwell, LLP; Steve Lastres, Director of Knowledge Management Services at Debevoise & Plimpton, LLP; and Sally Gonzalez, then Senior Director of HBR Consulting.
5. http://www.apqc.org/.

their book *The New Edge in Knowledge: How Knowledge Management Is Changing the Way We Do Business*.[6]

When it comes to KM maturity or progression models (or any models for that matter), it's important to keep a few things in mind. First, models are examples. They are general suggestions about how to do something in a nonspecific situation, not under a set of real-world circumstances. Second, models are meant as guides rather than instructions that should be followed precisely with the expectation that things will turn out in a particular way. As the common disclaimer goes: Your results may vary. Just as a lawyer would never use a template or model document without adjusting it to apply to the facts of a particular case, you should not apply a model to your KM situation without considering your particular facts. Finally, given these points, you should take from the following model (or any model) only what you find of value and use it for your particular purposes. Your situation is unique, your organization's situation is unique. As George Box said, "Essentially, all models are wrong, but some are useful."

The KM Maturity/Progression Model in Figure 6.1 is one that I find useful when thinking about how to approach knowledge management and a KM strategy. It assumes a scenario in which there are no formal KM initiatives and no one in the organization is in a dedicated KM role. This model assumes a midsize to large law firm environment, but it could be adapted to a corporate law department or other similar organization. Again, this model is provided, not as a set of instructions to follow, but rather for context when considering developing or refreshing your KM strategy. In the wise words of Bruce Lee: "Absorb what is useful, discard what is useless, and add what is specifically your own."

Let's look at the various parts of the model, keeping in mind that you may wish to choose certain parts and exclude others. You may also wish to consider various parts out of order, rather than in the relatively linear fashion in which they are presented. In fact, I would expect that most readers would do just that. For simplicity, however, we'll address them in order.

6. Carla O'Dell and Cindy Hubert, *The New Edge in Knowledge: How Knowledge Management Is Changing the Way We Do Business* (Hoboken, NJ: John Wiley & Sons, Inc., 2011).

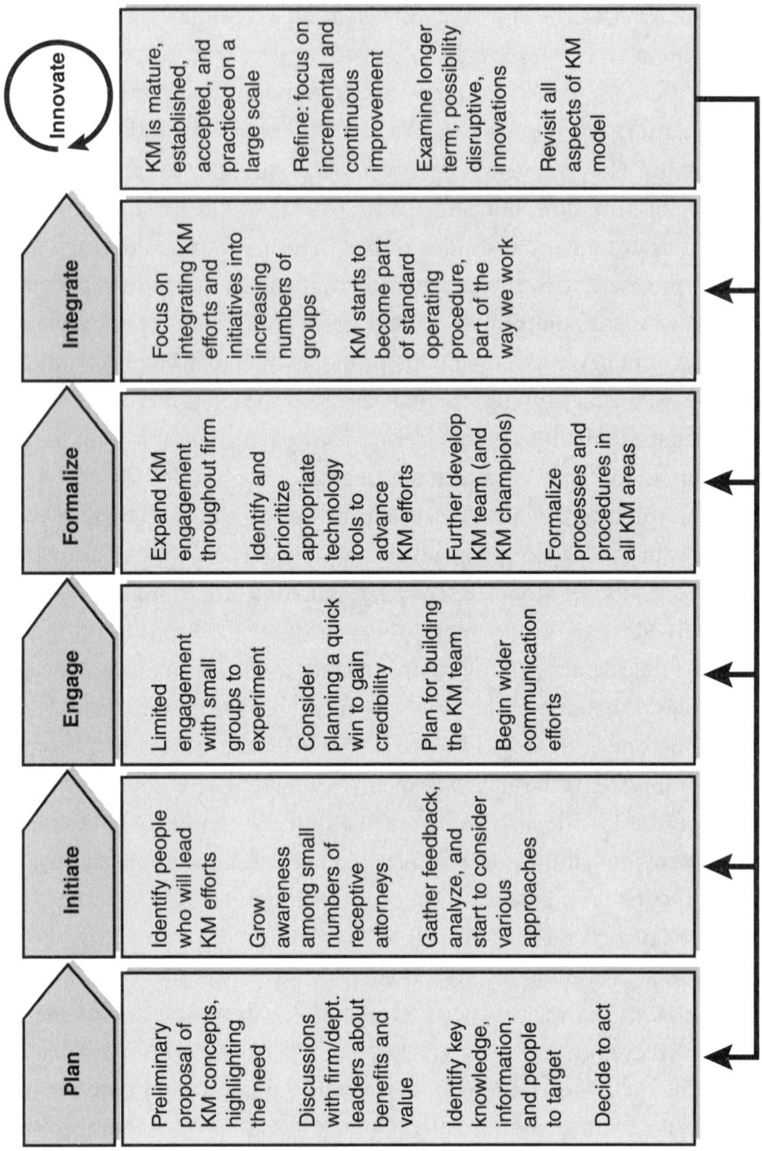

Figure 6.1 A KM maturity/progression model.

6.4.1 Plan

If you're convinced that your organization should develop a formal KM program, then someone (perhaps you!) needs to take the bold step of proposing that you do so. It might turn out very well, as it did for me several years ago.[7] I hope that having read this book will prepare you to do so. This planning step is not common in many similar KM models, but I include it in mine because of my experience starting KM programs. Thinking about and planning how you will make your KM pitch can make or break the effort. You'll need to figure out whom to approach and how. You may wish to do some reconnaissance work and casually investigate the challenges that members of your firm are facing—without mentioning the K word. Have discussions with attorneys and key administrators and ask them about their pain points. Think about how KM efforts and activities could help. When you have assessed the lay of the land, you'll have a better sense about whom you should approach and how. When you get the green light, you'll be ready for the initiation phase.

6.4.2 Initiate

The speed with which you progress along the steps of the KM model will vary depending on many factors. The time you have to commit to these activities (presumably, you already have responsibilities in your firm that take up most, if not all, of your time), your access to various attorneys and others for feedback, and the amount of assistance you can get from others will all be factors. This initiation phase should be one of identification, discussion, and analysis. You should start to identify people who are open-minded to KM efforts. Perhaps you identified some of these people in the planning stage, or perhaps the managing partner (or whoever authorized you to proceed) provided some suggestions. In any event, you'll want to identify attorneys and key administrators who will likely be open to your efforts.

When you have identified these open-minded people, you should start to open up about your efforts. Engage them in conversations about KM, and begin to gather feedback about their thoughts and ideas. (Remember the approaches to communicating KM in meaningful, non-jargonistic ways; see Chapter 1.) This approach has the dual effect of growing awareness of your efforts and setting the stage to gather information and insights. You will likely find that many of the people you speak with have good ideas about what they would like to see happen from a KM perspective. Take it

7. See the story about how I started my KM career in the Introduction.

all in, but don't make any promises about taking any action at this time. You may find it helpful to describe your efforts as exploratory, in order to manage expectations. Remember, this is the information-gathering and analysis phase, not the action phase.

6.4.3 Engage

Once you've done your preliminary work, you may be ready to start doing something more substantive. Here, in the engagement stage, you should consider making your KM efforts official. Revisit the firm leader(s) to whom you pitched your KM vision, report your preliminary findings, and get approval to make your KM efforts part of your job description. At first, you may only be able to justify devoting a small portion of your time to these new efforts. Much will depend on what you've discovered so far and other factors, such as the interest that has been generated by your preliminary discussions with various attorneys and others. It is quite possible that your work up to this point will have unearthed pent-up ideas and demand for action. That's great! But don't bite off more than you can chew.

With this newfound support and enthusiasm, you should focus on laying the groundwork for your future endeavors. I would suggest that your efforts should remain mostly low-key. Now is the time to think about your staffing needs—building your KM team. Consider engagement with a small practice group that has a high likelihood of acceptance of KM ideas (use the contacts you made in previous stages). Think about whether there is an opportunity for a quick KM win (see the KM Alerts case study in Section 6.4.10). Start to plan how you will communicate your KM efforts on a wider scale.

6.4.4 Formalize

At this stage, your organization understands the value of, and has committed to, knowledge management. This does not mean that every attorney and other employee fully understands and values KM, but your efforts have reached critical mass. Now you have expanded KM engagement throughout the firm. You're spreading the good word of KM at practice group meetings and among the other administrative departments. Firm leadership has even started talking about your KM efforts. Attorneys with whom you've never spoken may be reaching out to you and your team for help with problems that they believe may be solved with knowledge management. Demand for KM services and solutions is a good problem to have (it's better than the alternative), but this means that you will need to start prioritizing your efforts. You cannot do everything, and you certainly cannot do it all at once. See more about a prioritization method in Section 6.4.8.

This is also the stage at which you should further develop your KM team and find your additional KM champions. Building the right team with the right people will truly be the key to KM success. Read more about KM teams in Chapter 7. It is also important to find people outside of the KM department who are proponents of your work. These are your best and most vocal customers—KM champions. They are the ones who inherently get KM and its value. You'll know them when you see them, because they will say things like, "I've been waiting so long for the firm to do something like this."

Finally, this is the stage where you should start to examine various processes and procedures in your firm and look for ways to improve them. You'll likely find that things are not being done as efficiently and effectively as possible. It may not be clear who set up certain procedures and why. You may have to hunt people down to help you figure things out. You may find that the people who established ways of doing things are no longer with the firm, and because KM efforts were previously lacking, there probably won't be a record of what was done, by whom, and why. Formalizing these efforts will lay the groundwork for further efficiencies in the future.

6.4.5 Integrate

During this phase, you should focus on integrating KM efforts and initiatives into increasing numbers of groups. You will already have made some progress with early adopters in the firm, and slowly, more employees will begin to come around and adopt the approaches that you have set out. If you have developed an intranet, for example, you should start to see increased adoption and indications of acceptance of self-service (fewer e-mails asking where to find certain resources, for example). Don't take this as a sign that you're finished, however. You must continue to communicate and educate colleagues about the resources, tools, and approaches you have developed. Don't get discouraged by the large number of employees who seem to have no understanding of even the basics of KM and the resources you have developed, despite your tireless efforts. Remember the rule of seven touches—the sales theory that it takes at least seven interactions with a sales lead before that lead becomes a customer. Similarly, it will take multiple interactions with the people in your organization to reach them. Be persistent. Also remember that perspectives differ. You live and breathe this stuff, whereas others are focused on various things that are important to them. You must see things from their perspective to find ways that you can integrate KM into the way they do their work on a daily basis. If you can help and make it easier to do their work, you will soon have additional KM converts.

6.4.6 Integration Example

Things aren't all doom and gloom. During this phase, KM starts to become part of employees' standard operating procedure. It becomes part of the flow of how people work. A good example of the integration of KM into a law firm's way of doing business centers around the life cycle of a matter or engagement with a client.

At the beginning of a matter, most firms collect information about the client and matter to aid in various aspects of the matter as it progresses toward completion. All too often, however, lawyers are rushed; they scramble to get a matter opened as soon as possible so that they can begin work immediately. There is good reason for this sense of urgency, but too often it results in lack of certain upfront work that could benefit the lawyer and the firm, and make future work more efficient.

In many firms, the only requirements to accept a new client and begin work on a matter are a conflicts check to ensure that representation of the client would not create an ethical or business conflict due to the current representation of other clients and the establishment of a billing account (usually represented by a unique client-matter number in the accounting system). There are good reasons for taking these steps before starting the work. However, a law firm that has integrated KM efforts into its everyday activities would not likely stop there. Here are just a few additional things that such an organization might do upon (or shortly after) opening a new matter (this list is not exhaustive; you may think of others):

- Run a business background check on the client (could reveal potential solvency issues that could lead to nonpayment of legal bills)
- Set up news and legal alerts on the client and adverse parties to the matter (keeps attorneys abreast of the client's business developments, could reveal additional business opportunities with the client or strategic opportunities related to the matter)
- Add the client's key contact information to the firm's client relationship management system (useful for marketing to the client in the future and for other lawyers in the firm to cross-sell legal services beyond the nature of the current matter)
- Search the matter database for colleagues with experience in similar matters or in industries in which the client operates (this can guide decisions on matter staffing and identify those who you wish to consult for advice about the matter or marketing)
- Run a competitive intelligence check on the opposing law firm (could reveal strengths or weaknesses in opposing counsel that could affect strategy for handling the matter)
- Run a background check on opposing parties (could reveal insights into the party's motivation for initiating an action)
- Create an extranet site for the matter (facilitates collaboration with the client and makes management of the matter more efficient)
- Create a budget and matter plan for the matter (clarifies the scope of the representation, manages the client's expectations, and guides all members of the matter team about the goals and progress of the matter; also facilitates easier onboarding when others join the matter team)

Some of these activities can, and should, be done at various times throughout the life cycle of a matter—not necessarily at the beginning. The most important thing is to build this behavior into the way people work—to integrate KM into everyday workflows, or as Carla O'Dell and Cindy Hubert say, to put knowledge where people will trip over it.[8]

8. O'Dell and Hubert, *The New Edge in Knowledge*, 128.

6.4.7 Innovate

When your organization has reached the Innovate stage, your KM program is mature, established, and accepted throughout. Your KM initiatives are practiced on a large scale, and KM practices are fully woven into the fabric of your firm. Knowledge management is a part of how your lawyers and administrative employees work on a daily basis: Collaboration is common, the use of KM technologies is second nature, people are leveraging existing work product to gain efficiencies, and employees are connecting with knowledgeable colleagues to develop business opportunities.

This is the stage in the KM model where you seek to refine what you have established. Focus on incremental and continuous improvements in this work to extract even more return on your KM investments. To make even greater gains, you should start to think critically about what you have done and explore opportunities to leapfrog those accomplishments. Remember that what got you to this level won't necessarily get you to the next level. As I tell my team, "nothing is sacred." Just because something works, or has worked in the past and is popular, doesn't mean that it can't be replaced with something better and more useful. Don't be afraid to consider disruptive innovations. Just as smart companies, like Apple, are willing to develop new products that they know will kill the market for their own profitable products, you must be willing to find innovative ways to bring more value to your organization despite your past successes. To do this, you must revisit all aspects of the KM model and look for opportunities to apply new ideas to solve new and existing problems.

6.4.8 Where You Are and Where You Want to Be

As mentioned previously, how you formulate your KM strategy will depend on where your organization is in its KM journey. We have seen that your KM strategy needs to be tailored to your organization and that you should not just look at what other firms or law departments have done. So how do you decide what to do?

Answering that question will require some analysis, some collaboration, and some imagination. You will need to determine where you are today, where you want to be, and how you will get there. Put another way, as articulated by Oz Benamram[9] and Sally Gonzalez in their ILTA White Paper article, "Forming a KM Strategy for Your Firm," you must perform a current-state analysis, form the vision of the future state of your KM environment, and engage in high-level planning that describes how you will make the transition from the current state to the future state.[10]

A law firm or law department that is just starting out with a formal KM program will have a different strategy than one that has been at it for awhile. One of the first questions you must ask yourself is: "Where are we?" In other words, what is the current state of knowledge management in your organization? If you are a typical law firm without a formal KM program, you may realize that although it is unstructured, many people have been engaging in KM-type activities for years. It's likely that some attorneys have been amassing and reusing collections of documents in some repository. Perhaps a small group of attorneys has agreed to share and reuse those documents to help ensure consistency of the work product they produce.

On the other hand, maybe your firm or department is a little more advanced. Perhaps someone at some point decided that he or she needed some technology tools to help manage things. A typical scenario is that someone set up a database, a collaboration site such as a wiki, or maybe an intranet that started out as someone's pet project. Such efforts, if not well-planned and supported by the organization, typically start with great excitement and promise, but then they fade out when the reality kicks in, because it takes time, effort, and discipline to make it work. This common scenario is usually the result of putting tactics before strategy, of chasing the new, shiny thing that is marketed by some vendor who promises to provide the only KM system you will ever need. Beware of those who claim to be selling a KM system. As discussed more in Chapter 9, knowledge management is not about software or technology.

9. Oz Benamram is Chief Knowledge Officer of White & Case, LLP, and he was awarded the 2012 International Legal Technology Association (ILTA) Knowledge Management Champion—Distinguished Peer Award.
10. Oz Benamram and Sally Gonzalez, "Forming a KM Strategy for Your Firm," ILTA Knowledge Management White Paper, June 2011, http://read.uberflip.com/i/34417/20.

Perhaps your organization is at an even more advanced level of knowledge management. Maybe you have people who have actual KM roles and focus their time on KM initiatives and activities. If you're at this level, you've had some success with your KM efforts. Whatever the case, you should start by understanding and recording where you are. A useful tool to help with the assessment of your current state is a radar chart (also known as a spider web chart). With this tool, you choose the factors you want to measure and assign each one a value (e.g., 1 to 5, with 5 indicating highest). Plotting the strength of each component of your KM program can give you a succinct, one-glance view of where you are and where you want to be. It's a simple tool, but it can help clarify things, and going through the exercise will help you get a better understanding of your approach. (See Figure 6.2.)

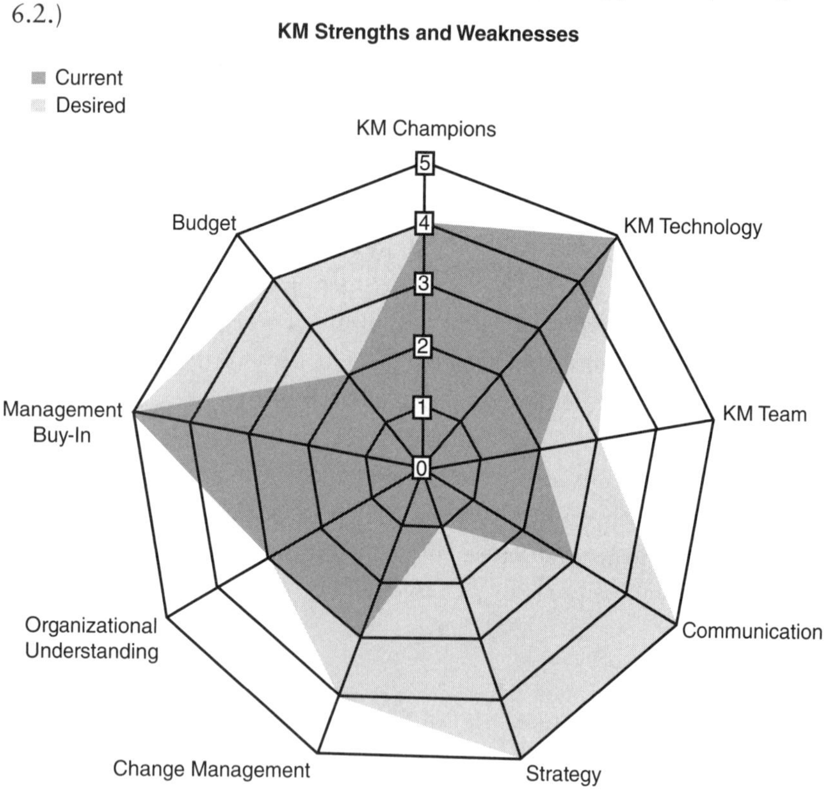

Figure 6.2

A radar chart can aid in the assessment of the current and desired states of your KM program or initiatives.

The desired future state of KM in your organization does not materialize by haphazardly selecting and completing projects. It requires you to determine which projects to do and when. In short, it requires prioritization. The article mentioned earlier by Oz Benamram and Sally Gonzalez articulates an approach to prioritizing your KM efforts to build your strategy. The exercise involves evaluating the relative value to the organization and the effort to complete multiple projects. The projects are plotted on a two-by-two matrix, which makes it easier to compare. When visualized in this way, it becomes very clear which projects are of the highest value and the easiest to implement. (See Figure 6.3.) The projects in the upper half of the matrix are the most valuable to the organization, so you should generally focus on them. Those of the highest value and the easiest to implement (upper right quadrant) should be targeted first. Those of low value and great difficulty should be avoided (lower left quadrant). The lower right quadrant should not be completely ignored, but choose from this group wisely. A project that is extremely easy to implement and just below the middle of the value line, for example, may be a quick win worth pursuing. Quick wins have another sort of value that make them desirable: They can help your KM program gain attention and credibility.

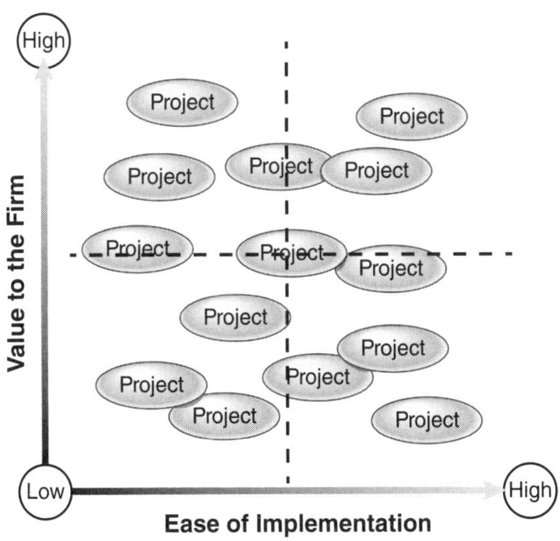

Figure 6.3

Oz Benamram's and Sally Gonzalez's matrix to visualize the value and ease of implementation of projects can help when developing your KM strategy.

6.4.9 Quick Wins Can Boost KM Programs

Your KM strategy will not always take a linear path. You may find that there is value to taking on a quick-win project, even though other higher-value projects are under consideration. I am not suggesting that you take on a project that is of low value just because it would be quick (easy to implement). Low-value projects, even if they are easy to implement, are generally to be avoided. But projects that are of some value and very easy to implement (i.e., quick wins) should be considered under the right circumstances. One scenario when you might consider a quick win is when your efforts are doubted or under heavy scrutiny by particular lawyers or groups within your organization. Perhaps individual, influential lawyers just don't seem to get KM, or pockets of KM resistance have developed in your firm. There may be some value in accomplishing a quick win to show them what you can do and to gain some credibility (and maybe even some KM converts).

6.4.10 Case Study: A Quick Win with KM Alerts

One such quick win came when I first started out in knowledge management at the law firm where I had been practicing as a litigation attorney for several years. My preliminary strategy included building awareness and understanding about the nature of KM and communicating the potential benefits. I had been making the rounds, telling attorneys about KM, and explaining the benefits. I booked time on practice group meeting agendas and at quarterly partner meetings. I presented my pitches and told the attorneys how our new KM initiatives were going to really improve the practice and business of law. A few attorneys got the idea, but frankly, most of them brushed it off as some abstract fad that would, in their opinion, soon fade away. To them KM seemed good in concept, but where were the tangible benefits? I could practically hear them saying, "What's in it for me?" and "Why should I care?"

It wasn't until I focused on "more show than tell" that the message really hit home for many attorneys. I needed to demonstrate a tangible way that my KM efforts would have a positive impact on the attorneys' lives. That demonstration came in the form of what I called KM Alerts, an automated system that alerted attorneys when their clients were named as defendants in newly filed actions. This all started when a very senior partner sent me an e-mail with a simple question: "You're reviewing these CNS e-mails and letting us know if there is anything that needs our attention, right?"

The e-mails to which the attorney was referring were part of a subscription service from a company called Courthouse News Service (CNS). Subscribers received daily e-mails that listed the newly filed actions in particular jurisdictions. For the benefit of those who are unfamiliar with civil litigation procedure, let me explain the value of such a service. In most jurisdictions, litigants are required to file an action (a.k.a. lawsuit or proceeding) with the court before serving papers (e.g., summons and complaint) on the defendant. In many jurisdictions, for example, papers typically must be served within 120 days of filing. Because service of papers is usually the first notice to a defendant that an action has been commenced (courts don't typically advise defendants of the filing), keeping tabs, via CNS alerts or other means, on newly filed actions gives an attorney the advanced notice of a lawsuit against a client. This is a window of time to advise the client that there is a threat of a pending lawsuit. This may not only help a defendant prepare for the action, but it gives an attorney a way to demonstrate that he or she is looking out for the client ("I noticed that an action has been filed against you, so let's discuss your options."). That's the good news.

The challenge was that CNS e-mail reports are long and filled with dozens of newly filed cases, and it was time consuming to review them every day. On top of that, the e-mails were structured such that each only contained newly filed actions from a particular jurisdiction. Because my firm represented clients in various locations, we had to subscribe to multiple e-mails to cover them all. In total, the firm received 14 CNS e-mails each day, and each one potentially listed dozens of newly filed actions. The sheer volume of information in those e-mails was almost impossible for one person to process; hence the question from the senior partner hoping that the KM department was doing it.

The KM department was not doing it. And my guess was that without a very large staff, which I did not have, it would be impossible. But to make sure I was right, I gave it the old college try. For one day, I did nothing but review CNS e-mails and alerted attorneys when I saw a newly filed action against one of their clients. On that day, there was an average of 12 newly filed cases listed in each of the 14 CNS e-mails. That's 168 cases to review.

The information to review for each case was not overwhelming: the court, plaintiff's name, plaintiff's attorney, defendant's name, and a brief description of the cause of action. The process was straight-forward: I focused on the defendants' names; if a listed defendant was a client of the firm, I determined who was the relationship attorney for that client and forwarded the e-mail to him or her, pointing out the action.

A few minutes into the process, I realized that it was going to be a long day. First, I realized that some actions named more than one defendant, which was a common occurrence. So, although there were only 168 actions to review, the work was greater, because each defendant had to be reviewed. Second, I quickly realized that, for the most part, despite having practiced law at this firm for several years, I was unsure whether most of the defendants listed were clients of the firm. I needed some mechanism to find out. That turned out to be a clunky, slow, and difficult-to-use database. Because I wasn't sure if a particular listed defendant was a client, even when I got a hit in the client database, I did not know who the relationship attorney for the client was. To find out, I had to look up the client name in yet another clunky, slow, and difficult-to-navigate database. Finally, the easy part was to forward the e-mail to the relationship attorney.

As you can imagine, the whole process was not only time consuming, but it was extremely monotonous and boring. About an hour into it, I knew that it was not sustainable. At my pace, I would never get through a fraction of the work (I estimated it would take about 10 hours per day), and even if I could, they couldn't pay me enough to do it. I immediately knew that the process had to be automated. A computer could do this work in seconds, it wouldn't get bored, wouldn't make mistakes, and wouldn't be earning a salary.

Because I had no computer programming skills, I sketched out the workflow and requirements and brought them to a coder in our IT department. In less than two days' time, with software that the firm already owned, he was able to replicate the work that I had tried to do manually. The system ingested all of the CNS e-mails and scanned them for client names, which were supplied by the client database. If there was a match, the system looked up the relationship attorney for the client in another database. In a final step, the system generated and sent an e-mail to the relationship attorney, highlighting the client name and informing him or her of the newly filed action. The KM Alerts System was born.

Attorneys loved the system because they no longer had to review the lengthy CNS e-mails, but they received immediate notification if any of their clients were being sued. It enabled them to be proactive with their clients and tell them when they were named as a defendant in a new action. This was valuable actionable information that attorneys could use to strengthen client relationships and to bring in business. Shortly after rolling out the KM Alerts System, I received feedback from several attorneys, who told me that they were able to use the information they received to win new business. From a KM perspective, this was the epitome of "getting the right information to the right people at the right time" and demonstrated that KM was not just some theoretical exercise but that it could have a positive effect on the bottom line of the business. It was also a valuable quick win that helped our credibility so that people would pay attention to future KM efforts and even start to think about how else knowledge management could help the business of the firm.

6.5 Refreshing Your KM Strategy

As mentioned at the outset, a KM strategy is dynamic and finite. At some point, you will have accomplished the goals you set forth in your strategy statement. Maybe part of your strategy was to build your KM team, and now it operates like a well-oiled machine. Now you need to focus on other things, perhaps optimizing or expanding the functions of certain team members. Even if everything went according to plan, other things may have changed in your organization that will cause you to take a hard look at things. Did your firm expand or contract? Did you open offices in new locations? Was there a change in leadership? What if the new leaders are not as KM friendly as the previous leaders—how will you help them understand the value of KM? What if there is a repeat of the global economic crisis? What do you do next? You reset and refresh your strategy. Countless changes could have an impact on how to refresh your KM strategy. Essentially, you'll have to start over and make a new KM strategy. Use the tools and approaches you learned in this chapter to guide your thinking. Ask yourself again: Where are you and where do you want to be? Both answers will be different than they were the first time around.

6.6 Key Points

- A KM strategy is a high-level plan that is designed to achieve overall KM goals or objectives.
- Formulating a KM strategy that is unique to your organization is a fundamental part of building a KM program.
- Your KM strategy should not focus just on what you plan *to* do but should also address what you have chosen *not* to do. Clearly articulating the plan will help everyone in your organization understand why you will take some actions and avoid others.
- When formulating or refreshing a KM strategy, you should determine your current state, where you want your KM program to be in the future, and the steps you will take to get there.
- Using tools such as a KM maturity model, strengths and weakness analysis chart, and a priority matrix will help you work through developing your KM strategy.
- Pursuing easy-to-accomplish quick-win projects (even if they are of moderate value) can sometimes boost the credibility of and excitement about your KM efforts, resulting in increased support.
- Because they are dynamic and finite, you will need to refresh KM strategies over time. Simply start the strategy formulation process over, examining your current state, desired future state, and the actions needed to get there.

Chapter 7

Building Your Knowledge Management Team

Never make the mistake of thinking you know everything about anything.

—Unknown

7.1 Chapter Preview and Target Audience

Chapter preview:

1. You'll learn how to get started in a knowledge management career.
2. You'll learn the types of people who lead legal KM efforts and how to find a KM leader.
3. You'll learn about the various roles involved in successful KM departments.

Target audience:
The bulk of Chapter 7 will be of primary concern to Administrative Leaders who are interested in building a team that will make up the KM department. Sections 7.2 and 7.3 will be of particular interest to readers who are seeking to break into a KM career. Lawyer Leaders will benefit from a cursory review of the entire chapter, but those who are planning to hire a KM leader will want to spend time on Sections 7.4 through 7.10, which are all

about finding the right person to lead KM efforts. The remaining sections get into some detail about various roles within a typical KM department and may guide your thinking about how to build your team.

The makeup of KM teams is different at various law firms and law departments. Unlike more established functions like human resources or marketing, KM departments tend to be quite diverse. Who should lead? Who are the key players and supporting staff members? To whom should the KM department report? This chapter will discuss several organizational models and recommend models for various types of law firms and other legal organizations. We will also examine common roles involved in KM departments.

When I transitioned from practicing lawyer and took on the role of Chief Knowledge Officer (CKO) at my previous law firm in 2005, most of the practicing lawyers didn't know what to make of it. Many of them made jokes about my title, having never heard of it before (e.g., "So now when I have a question, I come to you because you have all the knowledge, right?"). Others questioned why I would want to derail my legal career with such nonsense, expecting the role to disappear in a few months. And still others were happy that I somehow figured out how to get out of the litigation rat race but still use my law degree and experience as a practicing attorney (and some of them asked how they could do the same).

Establishing a KM department is not an easy task. Among the difficulties is ensuring that everyone understands the role of the KM department and the people in it.[1] It's important to be clear that the creation of a KM department does not mean to imply that all of the firm's knowledge resides in the department or with the members of the department. Rather, the department is established to formulate the strategy, promote KM concepts and principles, and execute programs and initiatives that support the strategy and principles. Just as an Innovation Office or Chief Innovation Officer (CINO) is not the only group or person in an organization responsible for innovative ideas, knowledge sharing and the development of a KM culture is not the exclusive domain of a KM department or CKO. Knowledge management is everyone's responsibility, and it needs to be a part of how everyone works.

1. For advice on communicating KM to busy lawyers, see Chapter 1.

We discussed several examples of KM departments in Chapter 4. There are similarities among them, but there are no identical structures. This is because knowledge management and the needs that KM fulfills are different at various firms and organizations. I have yet to find a standardized model for a KM department. Nor have I found anyone who recommends such a standardized model, because most KM professionals who have observed knowledge management in multiple organizations realize that it is not practical. When it comes to knowledge management, one size simply does not fit all. Your KM department needs will vary depending on, among other things, the size of your firm, the type and scope of the practice of your firm, the other functions that are currently being handled by existing departments, and the people within your firm.

There is great diversity in the makeup of law firm KM departments partly because KM is a relative latecomer in the game. Most people cannot think of a time when there was no accounting or human resources department at their firms. Some who have been practicing law long enough will remember that a marketing department was not always present, but that quickly changed in the last 30 years or so. But even though knowledge management, as a discipline, has been around since the 1980s, law firms were slow to catch on and adopt it.

Because building a KM team means finding the right people to fill the right roles, and because over the years I have been asked by many people how to get started in knowledge management, I want to address that topic here. In addition to what you read in this chapter, you can consult Appendix B to read about how several other KM professionals got started in their KM careers.

7.2 How to Get Started in a Knowledge Management Career

The way people get involved in legal KM careers today is quite different from the way they did it 15 to 20 years ago, when legal KM was in its infancy. Back then, there were very few established KM programs at law firms and law departments. There were few opportunities to find available

KM positions. Many of those who started KM careers at that time created their own job descriptions and later realized that there was a discipline called knowledge management that seemed very much like what they were doing.

Take, for example, one of the pioneers of legal knowledge management, Jeffrey Rovner, the Managing Director for Information at O'Melveny & Myers, LLP. Rovner's KM story started in the early 1990s, before he even knew of the term "knowledge management," when he was a young partner at Morrison & Foerster. He sought to automate some of the more tedious aspects of practicing municipal bond financing law, so he learned how to create databases and form documents that helped his personal efficiency. He also acted as a mentor to associates, who needed to learn municipal bond financing, by gathering the fundamental elements of the practice and packaging them into training courses. This had the dual benefit of bringing young associates up to speed faster and helping him complete his own legal work more quickly and efficiently. In 1996, armed with this experience and the desire to improve the practice of law with similar approaches, Rovner joined the Brobeck firm as Of Counsel and Director of Practice Development for the Business & Technology Group. In this role, he developed the firm's intranet, BrobeckNet, which was a great success. Ironically, it was only when he was asked to speak at a conference about BrobeckNet that he realized what he was doing for the firm had a name: knowledge management. I encourage you to read the rest of Jeffrey's story in Appendix B. Jeffrey had the benefit, and challenge, of writing his own job description and of developing his firm's KM program from scratch, at a time when there were few examples from which to draw inspiration.

Getting started in legal knowledge management today is a different story. Many firms have established KM programs, and many more are investigating and experimenting with developing programs. There are several excellent KM conferences, such as those produced by the International Legal Technology Association (ILTA), the ARK Group, KMWorld, APQC, and others, where KM professionals share their experiences and help their fellow legal professionals. And there is no shortage of blogs and online communities where those interested in KM can learn from their peers.[2]

2. For a list of knowledge management blogs and other similar resources, visit my website, www.LawyerKM.com.

The paths to a KM career are varied and often unintentional. Later in the book, you'll have the opportunity to read about how several KM professionals got their starts. For example, Rick Krzyminski found his way to KM in the mid-1990s because of his desire to help lawyers work more efficiently by organizing information on a firm intranet. Milena Higgins, on the other hand, is a physicist by training who stumbled into legal KM after stints as a science advisor at an intellectual property law firm and as chief scientist in the legal department of an international products conglomerate.

Over time, patterns of development of legal KM programs have emerged. However, there is still no industry standard for the makeup of legal industry KM departments, in the same way as such standards have developed for human resources, business development, or technology departments. Just as the whole of KM remains in flux, so does the makeup of KM department structures. However, some roles and functions have begun to emerge and are common, as we will see later in this chapter.

7.3 What Type of Person Is Right for Knowledge Management?

No single type of person is right for knowledge management. Although the majority in the industry have backgrounds as lawyers or have previous experience in law firms, this is not essential. Many have come from previous positions in libraries, technology, business, and various other industries. Increasingly, we are seeing KM roles filled by those with backgrounds in project management and even data science. Having team members with diverse backgrounds to assist in your KM efforts is important. In this way, building a KM team is not all that different from building other teams within your organization. Various members of the team will have assorted strengths, skills, and specialties. A strong understanding of the KM mission, belief in the purpose, and a willingness to walk the talk of KM are essential. Every member of the team must be committed to the fundamental principles of KM and promoting it within the organization. In short, every member of a KM team must be a KM champion. With this need for diversity, but common cause in mind, let's explore some of the common players on a KM team.

7.4 The KM Leader

The leader of a KM department can go by different titles: Chief Knowledge Officer (CKO), Director of Knowledge Management, Head of KM, Head of Know-How, etc. For convenience, I'll typically refer to the leader of KM as the CKO or KM leader. Whatever you call this person, he or she is (at least) responsible for the KM team, strategy, initiatives, culture, and deliverables. And just as there is no agreed-upon definition of KM, other than what was noted previously, there is also no agreed-upon scope of what falls under the CKO's purview. This often depends on the CKO's background. Is she a practicing lawyer who has taken on this additional responsibility? Is he a former practicing lawyer who has decided to leave the practice of law for greener pastures? Does she have a technology background? Is he a librarian? Does she have a degree in business administration? Law firm CKOs come in many shapes and sizes. Some colleges and universities now offer course work (and even degrees and certificates) in knowledge management, but professionals with such credentials in law firms are rare.

The ILTA Knowledge Management Peer Group has been surveying its members biennially since 2008 and has captured some metrics about who leads KM at law firms and law departments. ILTA asked its members about the background of the primary person managing KM efforts or projects on a day-to-day basis. As KM becomes more common and mature at law firms and in legal departments, the role of KM leader is increasingly being filled by former practicing lawyers. In 2008, the survey results showed that the KM leader was most often—26 percent of the time—a nonpracticing lawyer. In subsequent years, that number grew to 31 percent in 2010 and to 43 percent in 2012. In 2014, it inexplicably dipped to 32 percent. Surprisingly, the other common KM leader backgrounds also dipped (IT Specialist to 10 percent and Librarian to 17 percent) or remained the same (Practicing Lawyer at 8 percent). Although the survey results do not explain the cause of the dip in nonpracticing lawyers leading KM in 2014, I suspect that the raw numbers did not decrease from previous years, as the number of respondents in 2012 was relatively low. In addition, with the increasing numbers of KM programs at law firms that did not previously have them, it is likely that the leadership roles were taken on by existing employees with other responsibilities. In 2014, for the first time, the survey results revealed that a significant number of organizations (11 percent) described their KM leaders as having a background in project management.

This upward trend of placing nonpracticing attorneys in the KM leadership roles is not surprising. It is an indication of the growing importance of the role and the recognition that a deep understanding of the practice of law *and* business of law is an important factor in successful KM programs. This is not to say, however, that all law firm or law department KM leaders must be lawyers or that nonlawyers cannot do the job effectively.

During the same period, from 2008 to 2014, the percentage of law firms or departments with *practicing* lawyers leading KM efforts has diminished. In 2008, 14 percent of organizations had practicing attorneys in this role, but by 2010, the number had fallen to 12 percent. By 2012, it dropped to only 8 percent and remained at that level in 2014. This is even further evidence that law firms and departments are recognizing the role of knowledge management as a significant and legitimate function. No longer is KM just something that a busy lawyer can do in his or her spare time. "Practicing lawyers are either too busy billing or not equipped to manage or lead," said Ron Friedmann,[3] a consultant with Fireman & Company, a legal industry–focused management consulting firm. Just like IT, HR, and marketing, KM requires someone who is focused on KM full time, especially in larger firms and law departments. The most successful law firm KM programs have several, and sometimes dozens of, people who are dedicated to KM efforts.

Significantly, it is becoming rare for the head of an IT department to lead KM efforts. In 2008, 11 percent of organizations had IT Directors leading KM, but those numbers dropped to 6 percent in 2010, 7 percent in 2012, and to less than 3 percent in 2014. Again, this points to the increasing legitimacy of the role of KM and the understanding that KM efforts are not synonymous with technology. Firms are realizing that they need a full-time KM champion, not just someone who spends part of his or her time on it.

3. http://www.linkedin.com/in/ronfriedmann.

7.5 What Do You Call the KM Leader?

As mentioned previously, the KM leader goes by many names, and in some situations, it is a matter of semantics. For example, in some organizations few, if any, chief titles are used, in which case "director" is more common. Regardless of the title, the seniority level of the KM leader often indicates how seriously a law firm or legal department takes knowledge management and can also be a view into the level of KM maturity at the organization. The ILTA KM surveys give us some insight into what organizations have called the head of KM over the years.

The ILTA KM surveys have consistently asked respondents to "Identify the category of title into which the person responsible for KM falls." Across all four survey years, the most common title was Director of Knowledge Management or some variation thereof. It was used by 34 percent of organizations in 2008, 24 percent in 2010, 37 percent in 2012, and 28 percent in 2014. Another common title for the head of KM role, although lesser used than Director, is KM Manager or some variation thereof. That title was used by 11 percent of organizations in 2008, 14 percent in 2010, and 9 percent in 2012. In 2014, that percentage dipped to 2.3 percent, probably because of the increasing number of other various titles, which were grouped differently in the 2014 survey results.

Perhaps the most significant development in KM titles is the rise of the use of Chief Knowledge Officer or an equivalent. Although the use of the CKO title seemed to be relatively flat in 2008 and 2010, at 9 percent and 8 percent, respectively, it increased to 15 percent in 2012 and dipped slightly to 14 percent in 2014. In addition to the survey evidence, the increasing popularity of the CKO title has been shown anecdotally, with my observance of no fewer than three law firms seeking people to fill the role during the time I have been writing this book.

7.6 Reporting Lines: To Whom Does the KM Leader Report?

For knowledge management to be effective, access to law firm leadership is important. The more direct access, the better. As we have seen, KM organizations vary greatly from firm to firm, and KM leadership differs as well. Thus, as you would expect, the reporting lines of KM leaders is a mixed bag. However, there are some commonalities, especially among firms that have more mature KM programs. The ILTA KM Survey results have given us a look into KM reporting lines over the years and how the trend is pointing to more direct access to law firm leadership. Although the three surveys, from 2008 to 2012, articulated and classified the questions and answers slightly differently over the years, the trend is clear: More KM leaders and departments are reporting directly to senior firm management. In 2008, for example, a total of 55 percent of KM leaders reported to the top administrator (i.e., 25 percent reported to the managing partner or administrative partner, and 30 percent reported to the executive director or chief administrative officer) at their firms. By 2010, the percentage of KM leaders who reported to senior firm management increased to 58 percent, and by 2012, that number was 61 percent (comprising 25 percent reporting to senior administrative management and 36 percent reporting to senior legal management).[4] By 2014, a majority of KM leaders (53 percent) still reported to senior management, but the split between senior administrative management (34 percent) and senior legal management (19 percent) reversed from 2012.

Many factors can impact the decision about reporting lines: the maturity of the firm's KM program, the size of the firm, and the structure of the firm management. Some firms have the head of KM reporting to the CIO or head of technology, but this trend is decreasing. The ILTA KM surveys show that in 2008, 23 percent of KM leaders reported to the head of technology. This increased in 2010 to 32 percent, but by 2012, the trend had reversed and the percentage of KM departments reporting to IT dropped to 22 percent. In 2014, it dropped further to 19 percent.

I applaud this trend, because I consider it inadvisable for the KM leader to report to the CIO or head of technology. The primary reason for advising against this practice is that KM is not about technology; in fact, it is more about people and processes than it is about technology. Just as every

4. The 2010 ILTA KM Survey allowed the combined answer "senior management of the firm," while the 2012 Survey broke this answer into two categories: senior administrative management (25 percent) and senior legal management (36 percent).

other administrative department relies on technology and collaborates with members of technology departments, KM needs to do the same (perhaps more than others, depending on your KM initiatives). But structuring KM to report to IT is as suitable as having HR, Marketing, or Accounting report to IT. It is easy to see that all of those departments are heavily dependent on technology, but few, if any, would report into IT, because technology is only an enabler of what they do and the services they provide to a firm. Similarly, technology is an enabler for KM. Read more about the relationship between KM and technology in Chapter 9. At the firms where I have served in knowledge management roles, the head of KM has always had a peer relationship with the head of IT. This arrangement has worked well.

7.7 What Does the KM Leader Do?

A KM leader wears many hats: liaison, translator, simplifier, marketer, promoter, cheerleader, evangelist, change maker/manager, technologist, advocate, etc. The National Aeronautics and Space Administration (NASA) describes the CKO position as:

> [having] two important advocacy roles: facilitator and champion. The CKO should leverage, nurture, and highlight formal and informal work happening across the agency and serves as a conduit between the workforce and leadership to ensure the workforce has the tools and resources necessary to meet NASA's most pressing knowledge challenges.[5]

Authors Michael Earl and Ian Scott wrote (not of legal industry KM leaders, but in general) that, "The best CKOs fulfill four roles: entrepreneur (willing to champion risky new initiatives); consultant (able to match new ideas with business needs); technologist (fully IT-literate); and environmentalist (able to design settings and processes to maximize knowledge)."[6] Sim-

5. http://km.nasa.gov/about/.
6. Michael Earl and Ian Scott, "The Role of the Chief Knowledge Officer," National Post Online, July 24, 2001, http://www.providersedge.com/docs/leadership_articles/the_role_of_the_cko.pdf.

ilarly, in the legal industry, you will note the importance of understanding the business of law, especially in the entrepreneur and consultant roles.

Just as no practicing lawyer can be an expert in all areas of law practiced by a particular firm or that may be addressed by a particular in-house law department, a KM leader need not be an expert in all such areas. He or she should, however, have a strong grasp of the fundamentals. Law school and practice in a law firm can prepare someone for this, but it is not required to be a KM leader. Law firm or law department experience in a nonpracticing role can also be adequate preparation. However, based on the ranks of current KM leaders in major law firms today, it is clear, although perhaps unfair, that breaking into the legal KM industry will typically be much easier for the Juris Doctors among us. The bottom line is that some subject matter expertise, or at least familiarity with the business and practice of law, will go a long way in gaining credibility among the lawyers in your organization.

This book is not about organizational management, but it is important to note that the CKO or KM leader is also a team manager and must therefore possess management skills, like any other person in such a leadership role. The exception is the KM leader who is the KM department of one. This is not the norm among law firms, but it is not an uncommon phenomenon—usually of smaller organizations or those just starting out in KM. Even the KM leader without a team to lead must be an organizational leader and must be able to collaborate with his or her peers in other administrative departments, as collaboration between and among those groups is essential to the success of KM efforts in any organization.

The scope of the KM leader's position often depends on his or her background. I personally have been in law firm environments where the head of KM also oversaw the Litigation Support Department and the Library. Where the head of KM has a technology background, it is not uncommon for application development to be included in the scope of the job. Professional development, while sometimes a separate group, is commonly included in KM from an administrative perspective, especially where the KM leader is a lawyer. In contrast to other industries, it is less common in the legal industry for training to fall within the scope of KM, as that function is typically the responsibility of the IT department. Nevertheless, specific training on knowledge management–related tools and topics is frequently the domain of the knowledge management department.

7.8 Selecting a KM Leader

Organizations seeking to find the right KM leader are encouraged to look beyond a candidate's current role. Do not assume that any particular background would make a good foundation for a new role as KM leader. Just because someone is a lawyer, technologist, librarian, or other role commonly associated with legal industry KM does not mean that he or she will be an effective KM leader. I do not mean to imply that an understanding and familiarity with the legal industry is not beneficial. As mentioned previously, these are very important traits of a successful legal KM leader. Although a law degree is certainly not a prerequisite, the ability to understand the needs of practicing lawyers and the ability to communicate effectively with them is paramount. In short, the KM leader must understand the practice of law and the business of law, and specifically, he or she must understand the practice and business of his or her particular organization.

When seeking to fill the KM leader role, organizations often encounter the build-or-buy dilemma. The phrase "build or buy" is borrowed from when organizations must decide how they will fulfill the requirements for a needed technology solution: Should they try to build the solution using in-house software developers, or should they try to find an off-the-shelf software solution that will meet their needs. The former may be difficult, or impossible, to do with current internal resources, but the latter may be expensive and riskier, as the product is not fully known until it is acquired and tested in the specific firm environment.

When seeking a KM leader, law firms and in-house legal departments often face a similar choice—grow or hire. And as with the software dilemma, the right choice will depend on several factors: Are there appropriate candidates with the skills and clout currently within the organization who can fill the role? Can those candidates build and maintain the appropriate excitement and momentum to kick-start and drive the KM program to make it a success? Is the culture of your organization one that values the insider view, or do employees give more credence to messages coming from outsiders who are perceived as industry experts?

Whoever you select to lead knowledge management efforts should:

- Have a deep understanding of knowledge management and its principles
- Have a solid understanding of the legal industry
- Have a solid understanding of, or quickly learn about, your organization, its strategies, and its goals for the future
- Understand your organization's culture and the importance of leveraging that culture to achieve KM goals
- Have a solid understanding of current technologies and how they can help accomplish KM objectives
- Be an excellent communicator and have the ability to present ideas persuasively to executive-level leadership
- Be able to articulate the value of knowledge management to the organization's leaders and obtain their support and buy-in
- Be well-versed in project management and process improvement concepts
- Be enthusiastic, motivated, and passionate, yet patient and tolerant
- Have an entrepreneurial, innovative mindset and a willingness to be experimental
- Embrace and seek out change and see it as an opportunity to advance
- Be able to guide and mentor a knowledge management staff
- Command the respect of your attorneys and senior leaders

Not long ago, there wasn't much of a choice. Most, if not all, KM leaders were developed in-house, usually from the ranks of technologists, information professionals, or lawyers who sought to do something more interesting, productive, and fulfilling with their legal experience. The good news is now that the legal KM industry has been developing and expanding quite steadily for a couple of decades or more, many qualified experts in the field can move laterally and fill these roles.

7.9 Knowledge Management Task Force/Committee

Before a KM department or group is established, a firm or law department may wish to convene a KM task force or committee to help develop the initial goals of forming the department. If your organization decides to do so, the task force should be made up of a diverse population, including practice area leaders who not only have a fundamental understanding of the value of knowledge management, but who also have the political clout within your organization to convince the decision makers to take the necessary steps to make your KM goals a reality. The group should also include appropriate administrative personnel, perhaps from technology, information management, or paralegal roles. It is also a good idea to broadly communicate the initiative in your organization, because it is not uncommon (especially in large organizations) that someone or some group is already thinking along the same lines. You may find that some practice group, for example, has already designated a lawyer or paralegal as a part-time knowledge manager. You will want to consider any such like-minded people or groups in your task force, because it will help your efforts gain momentum.

Members of the committee or task force should learn what they can about KM and the value it offers to law firms and legal departments. I recommend this book as a good start, but there are many other resources, such as blogs (see my website, www.LawyerKM.com, for a list), conferences, such as those produced by the International Legal Technology Association and the ARK Group, and online webinars produced by these and other groups.

If the goal of the committee or task force is solely to establish a KM group or department, then it may be disbanded in relatively short order, when its mission has been accomplished. But you may consider maintaining it as a standing committee to liaise between and among the KM department and practice groups, other administrative departments, and senior organizational leadership. This approach can help support and promote the KM department and give it a voice in the organization at large. This is especially recommended at law firms or law departments where the inherent support or enthusiasm for KM efforts is not strong, where KM is underappreciated, or where there is a general lack of understanding about knowledge management.

7.10 Knowledge Management Partner/Sponsor

Your law firm or legal department may consider designating a KM partner in addition to, or in place of, a KM task force or committee. The KM partner should be a highly respected, senior-level attorney who has influence at the highest levels of the organization's senior management. If the firm has also established a KM committee, the KM partner may act as co-chair, along with the KM department leader. In either event, the KM partner acts as sponsor, promoter, and champion, not just of knowledge management initiatives and efforts, but also of the KM department itself.

7.11 Practice/Professional Support Lawyers

Practice Support Lawyers (also known as Professional Support Lawyers or PSLs) can be a key component to an effective KM program and department. PSLs are popular at law firms in the United Kingdom, Australia, and Canada. For example, see the KM department description in Appendix A of Addleshaw Goddard, a U.K.-based firm, which employs about 20 PSLs. Such large PSL groups are not uncommon among U.K.-based firms. Although they are not as popular in the United States, some U.S.-based firms have begun to employ PSLs as KM departments mature and evolve.

Also known as KM Counsel, KM Attorneys, or the like, PSLs are non-practicing lawyers who support a firm's practicing lawyers by offering high-level, substantive, practice-area-related assistance with legal matters. That's a pretty broad description of what a PSL does, but that is because, like KM itself, the role of a PSL can be quite diverse. There is no standard job description for a PSL, and the roles of PSLs have evolved over time. Likewise, the functions and duties of PSLs within a firm can change as a firm's KM program matures and develops. I will spend a good bit of time on this topic, because I believe that PSLs are among the key roles in legal knowledge management.

One of the primary functions of any PSL—or anyone involved in knowledge management—is to promote knowledge sharing as a philosophy. Every member of your KM group or department should promote KM principles, but PSLs have a unique opportunity to do so because of their access to the practicing attorneys at your firm. Because PSLs will likely have daily direct interaction with many of your organization's practicing attorneys, they have multiple opportunities to spread the good word of KM. Singing the praises of knowledge management doesn't need to be blatant or an in-your-face hard sell. The product (or service, in this case) can be the promotion. When a PSL can deliver excellent results quickly, then practicing lawyers will take note.

Because PSLs are most effective when they can assist lawyers from a substantive legal perspective, it is best to match PSLs with practice groups. In fact, PSLs are often embedded into practice groups and focus all (or a majority) of their efforts on the work of specific practice groups. This can be an effective approach, because the members of the practice group feel that they have a dedicated, personal KM representative who is looking out for their interests. It helps to build trust between the PSL and the practicing attorneys in that practice group. If your KM program is mature enough, and the firm has committed to providing enough resources, there may be one (or more) PSL for each practice group (or at least the major practice groups). This situation, however, is rare. More likely, each PSL will be assigned to several practice areas.

PSLs also help practicing lawyers locate existing firm work product that they can use for their current matters. If the firm has a document management system—or better yet, an enterprise search system—PSLs can assist attorneys with formulating search queries to find the work product they need. The same goes for locating other attorneys in the firm with experience with particular legal issues or with adversaries. It is not uncommon for PSLs to intercept firm-wide e-mails from attorneys asking for such assistance. Most lawyers are familiar with these e-mails, which I call "PTI e-mails," because they are often prefaced with "pardon the interruption." PSLs can respond to these e-mails, not only with the specific answers, but also with instructions about how to find these answers in the future. I call this the "give them a fish and teach them how to fish" approach (see Chapter 8). This is a subtle way to promote KM in the firm. The PSL immediately shows his or her value by providing an answer and provides long-term value by teaching the attorney how to self-sufficiently get the answer in the future.

Another important PSL activity is one of the most fundamental functions in knowledge management: knowledge sharing in the form of training. Most law firms and legal departments provide an employee training function (some are actually part of knowledge management departments), but training attorneys has historically been a challenging undertaking. Whether it's because attorneys claim to be too busy or whether they feel that they just don't need it, getting lawyers to attend training sessions is difficult. This problem not only results in undertrained lawyers, but it can also affect a law firm's ability to generate revenue, as evidenced by at least one story that created a sensation in recent years. Casey Flaherty, an attorney at Kia Motors America, Inc., developed a basic technology competency audit that he administers to his outside law firms.[7] Flaherty reported that lawyers have not done very well on the audit, and he reduces their rates until they pass a subsequent audit. Although some have criticized the audit's tasks (e.g., formatting a motion in Word, preparing motion exhibits in PDF, and creating an arbitration exhibit index in Excel) as things that paralegals or secretaries rather than attorneys should be doing, the point is that clients are demanding that lawyers possess certain skills that allow them to operate more efficiently. This is where PSLs can fill a gap.

Having PSLs take on the attorney training role has, in my experience, been very effective. There are two main reasons for the success of this approach: (1) the receptiveness of the practicing attorneys and (2) the practical perspective of the PSLs. As unfair as it may be, lawyers tend to be more receptive to learning from other lawyers rather than from nonlawyers. When lawyers are advised of training opportunities that are conducted by members of the training department, they often assume that the training is not applicable to them or that it is just for staff members. In contrast, when their peers are conducting seminars or training sessions, they tend to tune in. This behavior is natural, as people tend to relate to and connect more with their peers. In addition, because PSLs are lawyers (many of whom have practiced), they understand the perspective of their fellow lawyers. They know what parts of the training will resonate with them and can use this perspective to deliver

7. D. Casey Flaherty, "Could You Pass This In-house Counsel's Tech Test?", *ABA Journal*, July 17, 2013, http://www.abajournal.com/legalrebels/article/could_you_pass_this_in-house_counsels_tech_test.

a meaningful and highly relevant training curriculum. Unlike a nonlawyer trainer, who may emphasize points with generic examples, a PSL can tailor her examples to the specific practice area of the attorneys she is addressing. Not only does this help the lawyer better understand the lesson from a very practical perspective, but it also reinforces the lawyer's continued receptiveness to the training.

Other common PSL functions are creating and updating high-quality sample and template documents that are made available for practicing lawyers to use. The value is clear: Practicing lawyers can reuse such documents rather than creating them from scratch, which saves time, money, and ensures consistency and quality of work product. Because a qualified lawyer (the PSL) is responsible for ensuring that the documents are up to date and accurate, practicing lawyers who rely on them can use them confidently. Depending on the size of your PSL staff, expecting PSLs to create and maintain a large number of these manually curated sample and template documents may be unreasonable. There may simply be too many documents for them to keep up to date. Trying to maintain a collection of manually vetted documents has been cited as contributing to the downfall of many KM efforts in the past. The key is to avoid this trap by understanding that you cannot (nor should you try to) make samples or templates for every conceivable situation. Be highly selective with the documents that PSLs create and maintain. Maintaining this collection is most important, and that means ensuring that it does not grow out of control and unwieldy. Losing control of such a collection is a sure way to fail at this KM effort.

Sometimes a PSL's role with respect to a collection of sample and template documents can be one of *management* rather than creation and maintenance. This approach is especially effective if there is only a small number of PSLs on staff. Under this model, the KM department recruits practicing attorneys to create the documents and adds them to the vetted collection. One benefit to this approach is that the responsibility for maintaining the documents is distributed over a greater number of people, so that the whole burden does not fall on a few PSLs, which can easily become out of control. Another benefit is that the responsibility for creating documents can be assigned to the most qualified attorneys. PSLs, no matter how well qualified, cannot be experts in all areas of law that the firm handles. Thus, a practicing attorney who is a subject matter expert in a particular area of law is often the better choice for creating a sample or template document. That subject matter expert probably has already created the appropriate documents, and they simply need to be identified and added to the collection.

When employing this multiattorney approach, the PSL takes on a role of collection management, rather than one of creator. As a manager, the PSL coordinates the efforts of the attorney contributors, tracks down those who fail to deliver documents as promised, and sets periodic reminders for the contributors to review the documents to ensure they remain current or in compliance with appropriate laws and rules. The success and viability of the attorney-contributor approach depends on several factors, not the least of which is the firm's culture and willingness of the practicing attorneys who are asked to participate. Senior management support will be essential. Having endorsement from firm leadership on this type of project helps convince reluctant attorneys that this valuable endeavor is worth dedicating time that would otherwise be billable.

The contributions of PSLs should not be limited to substantive legal assistance or training. In fact, limiting their role to these areas ignores a great opportunity to tap the potential value of PSLs, especially those who have practiced law. Specifically, PSLs can make valuable contributions to projects involving attorney and client-facing applications, such as intranets, extranets, or various other applications. Their perspective is important, because they know what practicing attorneys want to see and what information is important to them. From an extranet and client-facing application perspective, they can opine about what clients want to see.

I personally have the good fortune to have two PSLs (we call them KM Counsel) on my KM team who were former practicing attorneys at our firm, one of whom, Evan Shenkman, tells his personal KM story in Appendix B. Because our KM Counsel have experience at our firm as practicing lawyers, they have the unique insight into the culture, practices, likes, and dislikes of their fellow lawyers. Another benefit is that they know—and have practiced with—those fellow lawyers. Their existing relationships come with a built-in level of trust and respect, which gets imputed to the KM department as a whole, because they interact with the firm's attorneys on a daily basis, unlike some other KM personnel. In short, the value of a

PSL—whether they have practiced at the firm where they serve in a KM role or elsewhere—can be great. You should not restrict a PSL's activities to what some may consider to be customary PSL work. By doing so, you may be missing a good opportunity.

Another PSL function, although not as common as some of the standard functions mentioned previously, is the creation of substantive legal news and updates. Some PSLs create these materials for consumption by attorneys within the organization, and some also publish these materials to clients. This function is less common among PSLs than some of the other activities, because they are often handled by others members of a law firm. Publishing substantive legal updates to clients—something that is commonly done today via blog posts—is often performed by members of the marketing department. Like KM roles, roles in law firm marketing departments are often populated by former practicing attorneys. At other firms, these materials are created by practicing attorneys. It is not uncommon for partners to enlist the help of associates to draft these articles or blog posts, make revisions, and publish the work with a shared byline.

7.12 Knowledge Management Analysts and Coordinators

Knowledge management analysts (sometimes called specialists) and coordinators are the front-line soldiers of your team who execute strategies developed by senior management. Although they are not as common as analysts and coordinators in other fields, KM analysts and coordinators are among the more common roles in KM departments, and their job descriptions tend to be better established than some other KM positions. Thus, it is relatively easy to get a sense of what they do on a daily basis.

As with all KM team members, the roles of analysts and coordinators vary from organization to organization and also change over time depending on the maturity of your KM program and your current initiatives. The roles may also vary depending on the structure of your KM team. As mentioned, my KM team consists of multiple groups, two of which have analysts and coordinators: KM Firm Solutions and KM Client Solutions. As the group names imply, one focuses on internal-facing KM efforts and the other on external-facing efforts.

Some of the common activities of analysts and coordinators in the KM Firm Solutions group (or similar groups elsewhere) are as follows:

- Helping to develop the structure and architecture of the intranet
- Creating training programs
- Training new employees on the use of the intranet (this may include new attorneys and/or administrative personnel)
- Developing applications and databases to help make administrative work more efficient
- Analyzing administrative functions and tasks to identify opportunities for efficiency
- Creating and maintaining intranet pages, such as office, administrative department, and practice group pages
- Training intranet content owners to maintain their pages
- Working with application developers to communicate specifications for custom intranet and other application development
- Participating in build versus buy analyses to determine whether to buy third-party software or create internal software applications to meet KM application needs
- Updating news and information pages (if working under a centralized distribution model)
- Assisting content owners when updating news and information pages (if working under a decentralized distribution model)
- Ensuring that others are adhering to firm and intranet standards and style guides (if working under a decentralized distribution model)
- Helping client teams collaborate by, among other things, creating client-specific intranet pages
- Testing and quality checking updates to intranet pages

The analysts and coordinators in the KM Client Solutions group (or similar groups elsewhere) are concerned with client-facing tasks, such as the following:

- Setting up extranet sites for clients
- Developing and maintaining various client-facing applications

- Setting up e-rooms or document-sharing and collaboration sites
- Working with attorneys to gather requirements and specifications for client-facing applications
- Helping to create client-facing applications
- Maintaining client access to extranet sites and other client-facing technology applications
- Populating content on client extranet sites
- Working with attorneys and clients to develop periodic reports on matters
- Assisting attorneys with client billing reports and invoicing issues
- Assisting attorneys and others with the setup and maintenance of electronic billing software
- Performing data analyses and assisting with requests for proposal (RFPs) and pitch materials to help attorneys win new business
- Creating matter-related databases
- Assisting attorneys, paralegals, and staff members with client-facing technologies
- Participating in build versus buy analyses to determine whether to buy third-party software or create internal software applications to meet KM application needs
- Assisting with compliance with client engagement agreements
- Creating and maintaining process documents
- Testing applications to ensure proper functionality

A review of some descriptions of KM analyst and coordinator roles in LinkedIn profiles gives a good view into the types of activities they perform (some are paraphrased):

- One KM analyst at a large firm listed the following:
    a. Define, analyze and write specifications for KM solutions
    b. Test, document, and train attorneys and staff when new KM products or functionality are introduced
    c. Work closely with application developers and end users during projects to ensure success and completion of work

- Another KM analyst listed these activities:
  a. Develop and implement matter management best practices, procedures, tools and techniques that ensure client matters are executed in the most efficient, cost-effective manner, and within budget
  b. Provide business analysis/solutions to law department and practice groups
  c. Update knowledge repositories and other internally developed repositories and tool kits

In reality, the tasks of KM analysts and coordinators can and will vary widely depending on the current focus of KM efforts. One of the core functions of knowledge management—to make work more efficient—can manifest in many and various ways. Thus, the tasks required to achieve that efficiency will be different. This variety is one thing that makes the work of KM analysts and coordinators interesting, challenging, and rewarding. As one KM coordinator expressed, "No two assignments are alike, and some require more time than others." And another said, "The tasks I perform vary greatly from day to day."

7.13 Knowledge Management Project Manager

Knowledge management departments, especially those that are more mature and well-defined, tend to be among the most active and prolific groups in a law firm or legal department. They are constantly active in application development, whether intranets/portals, databases, content collections, extranets, or other client-facing applications. Although KM is not all about technology, we constantly use technology tools to create the products and services that deliver the value and benefits of knowledge management to our organizations and clients. Delivering these products and services is accomplished by defining, scoping, planning, and executing projects. A project manager is responsible for seeing such projects through to completion.

When I refer to KM Project Managers and KM Project Management, I am not referring to Legal Project Managers or Legal Project Management

(LPM). That discipline, which is related to but different from KM, is discussed in Chapter 10. Here, I am referring to a professional in the field of project management, who ensures that projects are delivered in a structured, planned, and orderly fashion, on time and within budget. Project management is a common discipline in many industries from construction to software development. Although it is not as common in the legal industry (but this is changing), some law firms and legal departments employ project managers. They are sometimes part of IT departments or members of independent project management offices (PMOs). The latter are becoming more popular in recent years, but PMOs are still relatively infrequently found in the legal industry.

Even though project management and project managers are not exactly common and are arguably underutilized in the legal profession, both are critical to successful KM initiatives. This is not an exaggeration. If you want a KM project to succeed, first ensure that someone is responsible for managing the project and seeing it through to completion. Anyone who has failed to deliver a project on time, and within scope and budget, will surely agree with this statement. Too often in the lean, thinly staffed legal services industry, we are pressured to do more with less. This attitude is not unique to the law, but in an industry where for decades lawyers have done things their own way, it is often suggested that we don't really need particular expertise to get the job done. Devoting time, let alone a full-time employee, to managing projects is a foreign concept to many lawyers. In the law, there has often been an attitude of "just get going and get to work!" rather than one of "take adequate time to plan and get it right" and the recognition that this planning and managing is, in fact, part of the work. Those who have been through a project where you "just got going and got to work" realize that planning and managing is not merely *part* of the work, it is a *critical part* of the work that can make or break a project.

A good project manager is like an orchestra conductor. He or she coordinates the actions of many players, all of whom have expertise in their own specialty. Individually, each member of the orchestra plays an instrument and has a particular job (i.e., playing the right notes, at the right time, to contribute to the overall performance). Each musician may have a good idea about how the performance should sound, as a whole, but they need guidance as a group. The conductor, like the project manager, follows the sheet music (the plan) to guide all of the various players so they are all contributing their portion of the music (work) at the right time. As with an orchestra playing a complex musical composition, any complex project requires someone to guide all of the team members so that each does what they are supposed to do when they are supposed to do it. Your project management needs will vary depending on the number and complexity of projects that you have going on at any particular time. You may not need a full-time project manager who spends all of his or her time on a single project, but you will need a dedicated project manager who is fully responsible for delivering the completed the project.

I have been involved with many KM projects, big and small. Some have had no project managers, some have had internal shared project managers, and others had dedicated project managers from third-party consultants. As you can imagine, the results of the projects without project managers ranged from successful to a complete disaster to needing to hit the reset button and start over. Neither of the latter two situations is desirable. I am not suggesting that every project that operates without a project manager is destined to fail, but going down that unmanaged path greatly increases the chances of failure. Project managers who are shared among other internal departments, like those who report to a PMO, and are assigned to multiple, diverse projects can work out well, if their workloads are balanced. Like any other employee, if a project manager has too much on his or her plate and is spread too thinly, the work on all projects can suffer. The workload needs to be balanced so that a project manager can focus enough time on each project for which he or she is responsible.

My best experiences have been on projects where a dedicated project manager has focused most, if not all, of his time on my KM department's projects. In my particular situation, the project manager was from a third-party consultancy and acted like an adjunct member of the KM department. This would have worked equally as well (maybe even better) if the project manager were an actual member of my department. But whether the project manager is a third-party consultant or an employee of the department, it's crucial that the project manager be dedicated to the KM projects and commit adequate time and effort to them.

Among other things, the project manager is responsible for creating and maintaining the project plan. A project plan is just what it sounds like: a detailed list of the steps it takes to get from the start of the project to completion (hopefully on time, within scope, and within budget). Once the plan is created and shared with the team, everyone knows exactly what is expected of them. Tasks are assigned to individuals and given due dates. Good project managers don't just assume that team members have read and are working on the upcoming tasks; they preemptively check in and inquire about the progress *before* the scheduled end date. Ensuring that tasks are moving along at the pace they should be can prevent team members from waiting until the last minute, which frequently results in missed deadlines. Regularly scheduled touch-point meetings with the entire project team are useful in this regard. During these meetings, not only will the project manager review the tasks that were scheduled to have been completed, but he or she will cover those tasks that are to be completed in the coming days, weeks, or months. This preemptive highlighting of upcoming work gives team members an opportunity to voice any concerns about their ability to complete the work in a timely manner.

One of the main reasons that having a dedicated project manager leads to success more often than not is that the project manager keeps the team *focused*. Focus is as much about doing what one should be doing as it is about *not* doing what one should not be doing. In a law firm environment, where so many bosses can compete for attention and resources, getting sidetracked can be a big problem. For example, if an influential partner reaches out to a team member (say, an application developer) for assistance with a pet project, then the developer may feel great pressure to say yes, even though committing to the partner's project will take him away from the project on which he should be focusing. The project manager can assist the team member and intervene with the partner, explaining that the application developer is fully occupied with another high-priority project. Although it is never easy to tell partners that they cannot have the assistance they are requesting, the project manager (perhaps with the assistance of the head of KM) can legitimately and convincingly explain that the application developer's attention and focus cannot be detracted from the current project.

In summary, you should always seek to include the expertise of a project manager on your KM projects. Although some (those who have limited experience) may argue that adding yet another resource to the project would be overkill, too expensive, or slow the project down, those who know better would not agree to undertake a project without a project manager. There is no better way to ensure project failure than to do just that.

7.14 Application Developers

Application developers (also known as coders or programmers) are members of the team who focus on developing, customizing, and configuring the software that enables an organization to execute its KM initiatives. In short, they create the software tools that employees use to access the information they need to do their jobs efficiently and effectively.

Historically, application developers have been (and most of the time still are) members of technology departments. Some firms, however, have shifted the reporting lines of developers into KM departments, because they often work so closely with other KM team members. Regardless of the reporting lines, developers frequently work closely with KM analysts, coordinators, and project managers to bring to life the applications that the KM team designs. Because they work so closely together, it is important to ensure that the lines of communication among these team members are open. It is not uncommon during the course of a KM project for developers and the KM team to meet several times per week, if not daily.

7.15 Knowledge Management Network

Members of what I like to call a Knowledge Management Network are not really members of the KM department. Rather, they are like KM liaisons—employees of the firm, outside of the KM department, who act as champions and help promote and facilitate all aspects of KM throughout the organization. In some ways, the KM Network is like an auxiliary police force—members of the community who you can count on to help out with the work of the main force. They are not fully trained, or experts, but they are well-versed enough to help the rest of the community with knowledge management efforts.

A KM Network is more appropriate for larger law firms or law departments, especially those that have multiple offices,or many practice groups. KM Network members can be instrumental in directing colleagues to KM tools and resources. For example, it is common in larger, multioffice firms for lawyers to e-mail members of particular offices asking for assistance with finding resources related to that jurisdiction. Attorneys making such requests often fail to include the KM staff on the e-mails. A local KM Network member in the office (who is on the local e-mail distribution list) can step in to remind the requestor of various resources (e.g., search tools, document collections, databases, etc.) or people (e.g., subject area experts, PSLs) who can assist with the request. Thus, a primary goal of establishing a KM Network is to help keep KM principles, tools, resources, and people in mind when the members of the KM department are not aware of the need. In addition, KM Network members can report back to the KM department if they see the need for training or KM promotion. They expand the reach of the KM department and assist by keeping their eyes out for opportunities to advance the organization's KM efforts.

It should be noted that the formation of a KM Network should not obviate efforts to spread KM ideas and principles across all members of your organization. Remember that a fully mature KM organization is one in which all employees understand and value knowledge management.

7.16 Key Points

- Just as the organizational structures of KM departments differ among organizations, the makeup of KM teams is different at various law firms and law departments.
- Getting started in a KM career may not be as straightforward as some other professions, but several resources can help you along the way,

and the KM community is filled with helpful people who are willing to share information and advice.

- No specific type of person is right for knowledge management. Having team members with diverse backgrounds is beneficial. Experience in a law firm or legal department is a plus but not always necessary. That said, it is often desirable for the KM leader to have a legal background.
- The KM leader is a critical member of the team and should be selected carefully. The KM leader plays many roles, including liaison, translator, simplifier, marketer, promoter, cheerleader, evangelist, change maker/manager, technologist, and advocate. The scope of the KM department will often depend on the KM leader's background.
- Creating a KM task force or committee can help guide the KM department in achieving its goals. Supporting the KM team with a sponsor who is a high-ranking member of the law firm or law department can be extremely beneficial.
- Practice/Professional Support Lawyers (PSLs) are valuable members of a KM team, because as fellow lawyers, they command respect from their peers. Their perspective allows them to provide several functions, including research support, training, model document creation and management, application development assistance, and creation of substantive legal news and updates.
- The roles of KM analysts and coordinators tend to vary among organizations and also change over time depending on the maturity of KM programs and current initiatives.
- It is useful to employ a dedicated project manager and an application developer staff if the KM department is creating and maintaining technology tools, such as intranets, extranets, and other applications.
- A KM network is a group of people outside of the KM department who act as KM champions and help promote and facilitate all aspects of KM throughout the organization.

Chapter 8

KM Tactics: Executing Your Knowledge Management Plan

Action is the foundational key to all success.

—Pablo Picasso

Everyone who's ever taken a shower has an idea. It's the person who gets out of the shower, dries off and does something about it who makes a difference.

—Nolan Bushnell

8.1 Chapter Preview and Target Audience

Chapter preview:

1. You'll learn how the U.S. Army JAG Corps developed their knowledge management efforts and turned them into an award-winning KM program.
2. You'll learn the basics of change management and see examples of how taking a structured approach to introducing change to your organization can help minimize the impact of a potentially difficult situation.
3. We'll explore the importance of building a knowledge-sharing culture and how taking deliberate steps to do so will help ensure knowledge management success.

Target audience:
This chapter will mainly be of interest to Administrative Leaders who will be responsible for executing a KM strategy. It contains case studies that show the value of particular tactics and lists several ideas that you may want to incorporate at your firm or law department. It also provides an overview of change management. Lawyer Leaders will want to review the case studies (Sections 8.2 and 8.5) and the sections on change management (Sections 8.3 and 8.4), as this topic is a vital part of any KM effort.

Ideas are worth nothing unless they are executed. I can't help you execute your ideas, but I hope I can help motivate you to do so.

In previous chapters, we discussed the what, why, and who of knowledge management. We examined what KM is about, why KM is important, and who can help make it a success. So, now that you are convinced that KM is a worthwhile endeavor, let's get to the heart of the topic. How do you take action? What KM initiatives and activities should you undertake? How do you promote a KM program in your law firm or organization? We will start this chapter with a case study about a very large organization that is known not only for its strategy but also for its execution: the U.S. Army.

8.2 Case Study: The U.S. Army JAG Corps: Building a Law Department Knowledge Management Program

The U.S. Army Judge Advocate General's (JAG) Corps is the largest of the uniformed lawyer departments in the U.S. Armed Forces. It is made up of judge advocates, legal administrators, and military paralegals who, among other things, provide legal assistance to soldiers and adjudicate claims against the Army. It is also made up of approximately 2,000 uniformed lawyers, about 100 law office managers, and approximately 1,700 paralegals. In addition to the uniformed corps, there are more than 550 additional civilian attorneys and about 600 civilian paralegals. In all, there are about 5,000 total legal practitioners in the JAG Corps. Add to those numbers another 5,000 legal personnel in the Army Reserve and the National Guard, and a total of around 10,000 legal professionals are practicing law and supporting the legal practice in the Army JAG community.

Colonel Scott Reid (retired) was the first Chief Knowledge Officer of the JAG Corps from 2011 to 2014. In 2011, before becoming CKO, Reid was the Staff Judge Advocate at Fort Belvoir, Virginia, leading the installation's legal office. In the summer of 2011, Reid received a call from the Deputy Judge Advocate General (DJAG) of the Army, Major General Clyde Tate. Major Tate was not only a two-star general and the Army DJAG, but he was also the Chief Information Officer. In that capacity, General Tate had recently attended an International Legal Technology Association (ILTA) Conference; he came away from the event with the desire to pursue a knowledge management strategy for the JAG Corps. He had known Reid for years, and after a brief conversation between them, Tate confirmed his instinct that he wanted Reid to lead the KM charge.

Later that summer, Reid moved to the Pentagon and became the CKO of the Army JAG Corps, working in the Office of the Judge Advocate General. He then assembled his team of knowledge management counsel, six associate-level military attorneys who were assigned to a specific practice area (Administrative and Civil Law, Criminal Law, Legal Assistance, Claims, International and Operational Law, and Contract and Fiscal Law) and embedded in the policy proponent office for that practice area. The KM counsel duties included staff work, but their KM work took precedence and constituted the majority of their responsibilities. Additionally, Reid was given a senior legal administrator (i.e., law office manager) with a strong technical background.

With his KM team in place, Reid's next order of business was for the team to learn everything they could about knowledge management. He planned to spend his first 90 days learning what the job was. In addition to reading whatever he could find, Reid attended the ILTA Conference in August 2011 and attended all of the sessions that addressed KM strategy. He also spoke with many of the KM professionals who attended the conference (networking with peers is one of the best features of the conference). He found that while most of his new peers were dealing with KM in law firms and not large law departments, such as the JAG Corps, they shared common challenges, such as human resource and capital restraints, organizational buy-in, and change management, to name a few.

Having digested so much new information about knowledge management in a very short time, Reid and his team formulated the JAG Corps KM strategy. He obtained the approval of General Tate and, in October 2011, presented the KM strategy to 150 senior leaders of the active and reserve components of the JAG Corps at the JAG School's annual Worldwide Continuing Legal Education conference in Charlottesville, Virginia. Knowing that the strategy would not execute itself, he also asked his fellow officers for help and support.

Reid sought a clever and creative way to communicate his KM strategy and make it stick with the audience. Much like Chris Boyd's and Ron Friedmann's KM windmill concept,[1] Reid likened KM efforts to using a turbine to harness the energy of a raging river. Reid told me:

> We thought of information as a raging river that poured over the rocks and slipped through our fingers whenever we tried to capture it. We had to find a way to harness our information and turn it into knowledge power, the way a hydroelectric dam generates power from the raging river. We have all these practitioners doing highly effective and innovative things at military installations and in deployed environments worldwide, but we need to harness that activity into knowledge power for the entire Corps.

The JAG Corps' KM strategy had four elements. First, they sought to establish communities of practice, an enterprise social networking (ESN) effort for all practitioners of the JAG Corps. This was the most important aspect, or the "center of gravity," to use a military term of art. The second element was a document repository that put the most common, helpful documents and templates in one place so that they were searchable and retrievable. The third element was to establish an enterprise search capacity for the JAG intranet. The fourth and final element of the new KM strategy was to audit the various existing legal practice management software applications across the JAG Corps in order to identify redundancies, best practices, and opportunities for improvement.

1. http://iltanet.org/MainMenuCategory/Publications/WhitePapersandSurveys/KnowledgeManagementCollaborativeExpertise.txt.

This case study focuses on the first element and its importance to the JAG Corps KM program formulation. When setting out to execute the first element of the KM strategy, the communities of practice, or ESN element, it became clear that they had to consider the scope and size of the enterprise. Although Reid and his team were part of the Army JAG Corps, he realized that much of what the Army lawyers do was also done by Navy and Air Force JAG lawyers who had the same legal issues and challenges. For that reason, Reid wanted to make the communities of practice in the ESN available across all branches of the armed forces and not be limited only to the Army. All of the various military branches were under the same Department of Defense umbrella, so why not leverage the knowledge of one branch for the benefit of the others? "Our goal was to invite the Navy, Marines, and Air Force legal personnel into an 'unbranded' community of practice—so they didn't feel like they were guests in the Army JAG Corps' space—where they could ask questions and share information, work products, and lessons learned," Reid said.

Reid and his team built the six communities of practice (one for each legal practice area) in an internal military social media platform, called milBook, which is similar to consumer social networking sites like Facebook and LinkedIn. They also created a seventh community of practice called Leadership, Management, and Training, which provided a strategic communication platform for JAG Corps leadership, as well as a forum for law office management and training issues. These seven groups were collectively known as JAGConnect on milBook and were administered by the KM team. Reid kept the groups relatively low key at first, with the intention to market them to the Army, build them up, and reach a critical mass. Once there were a reasonable number of members who generated some valuable content, they started promoting the communities to other branches of the military. This gradual approach was important, because they didn't want new members arriving into the community if there was no content to view and nobody to interact with. "We weren't going to invite anyone into a store with empty shelves," Reid said.

The first milBook group, Legal Assistance, was developed as a pilot program from October 2011 to February 2012. Based on its success, General Tate approved the plan to expand the communities to all practice areas.

By the end of March 2012, Reid and his team launched the remaining six groups to a wider audience. They announced the initiative over the JAG Corps intranet on the daily announcements page, sent e-mails, and networked in any way they could, telling people about the new communities of practice and that they were ready for use. The new platforms were now ready and available to the approximately 10,000 members of the Army JAG community.

One surprising factor was that younger users, such as Millennials (a.k.a. the Millennial Generation or Generation Y, who were born between 1980 and 2000), were not always the most tech-savvy and proficient with the ESN communities. This finding is contrary to everything we hear about generational differences when it comes to technology. Young people, the digital natives who grew up online with MySpace and Facebook and text messaging, are supposed to take to ESN like fish to water. In reality, Reid found that he couldn't easily put users into generational boxes; he couldn't assume that all younger users would adapt quickly and that older users would invariably need more convincing and coaching. In fact, some of the most enthusiastic users were the more mature, experienced counsel who were ready to try new things and eager to share what they knew.

Reid realized that changing people's behavior, getting them to adapt to the new platform and to integrate milBook into their work habits, would require a calculated and concerted effort. He also saw value in starting with a grassroots approach, first targeting junior attorneys and junior paralegals and setting up introductory-level milBook classes at the JAG School in Charlottesville, Virginia. Reid and his team sought exposure for the ESN and KM efforts during continuing legal education (CLE) classes, at brown bag lunches, and by setting up demonstration kiosks at the school, handing out trifold pamphlets, and spreading the message by word of mouth.

The grassroots approach was effective with the younger demographic, but Reid felt that many midgrade and senior members of the JAG Corps needed to see evidence of leadership endorsement before getting fully involved. He prepared short, strategic communications for JAG Corps' senior leaders and asked them to promote knowledge management and the ESN communities of practice as they traveled around the world to various military installations and the legal offices there. In this way, the leaders had a script they could follow to communicate the message in a concise, consistent way. This approach also opened the opportunity to recognize certain JAG lawyers who made valuable contributions to the milBook communities, highlighting their efforts. These contributors were presented with Commander's Coins, small commemorative coins that displayed the JAG Corps crest, a reward for a job well done. This public praise by superiors sent the message that participation in the KM communities was visible to, and valued by, the JAG senior leadership.

All of these efforts—the training classes, kiosks, lectures at CLE courses, brown bag lunches, and personal recognition by senior leadership—were especially effective, and it showed. Community membership and usage of the milBook groups spiked after these events or when someone was publicly recognized for their good contributions. Another way Reid promoted the milBook communities was simply to send a private thank-you note via the messaging features of the platform. "If somebody took the time to write a very thoughtful answer to somebody's question or shared something particularly valuable, I would write them a direct note," Reid says. "I wanted to provide some personal feedback, especially when senior practitioners and subject matter experts took the time to contribute something in milBook."

Members of Reid's team would also post public thank-yous when others made good contributions or answered questions. This recognition is an important part of the social nature of such systems. Unlike synchronous communications, such as face-to-face or telephone discussions, you don't get immediate feedback in social networking platforms. Simple acknowledgments can go a long way toward encouraging people to use—and continue to use—these tools. That's why the Facebook "like" button exists. Members of Reid's team would also occasionally help the communities along. If someone posted a question, or needed help with a particular area of law, Reid's KM counsel would often either answer the question themselves or seek out a subject matter expert to contribute. This helped build the content on the platform and slowly helped users realize that it was a valuable source of reliable information. It also kept content fresh and provided answers more quickly.

All of the hard work that Reid and his team put into the milBook communities of practice paid off. Not only were the milBook communities a huge success within the various branches of the military, but the work was recognized by outside groups, as well. The JAG Corps was awarded the ILTA Innovative Law Department of the Year Award in 2012, the Law Technology News Innovation Award in 2013, and the American Counsel for Technology and Industry Advisory Council (ACT-IAC) Excellence.Gov Award (Digital Government) in 2014. Reid, in his own right, was named to Federal Computer Week's 2014 "Federal 100" list of leading influencers in federal information technology.

8.3 Change Management

As we just saw from the U.S. Army JAG Corps case study, when executing your KM plan, you will be making changes that impact the way people work. The changes will be good and will help lawyers work more efficiently and effectively. The end result will be better, more profitable work and more success for your organization. That's the good news. The bad news is that the changes will be painful for many of the people in your organization, and some will resist the changes, kicking and screaming like a toddler who refuses to eat his or her vegetables.

Dealing with the impacts of those inevitable changes falls under the discipline of change management. Like knowledge management, there is no agreed-upon definition of change management. However, for our purposes, we'll describe change management as "a systematic approach to dealing with change, both from the perspective of an organization and on the individual level."[2] There are other definitions, such as "an approach to transitioning individuals, teams, and organizations to a desired future state"[3] and "a set of basic tools or structures intended to keep any change effort under control,"[4] and those are good, too, but we'll keep it simple.

Some changes will affect certain people more than others, because you are asking more of them. For example, one of your KM initiatives may be

2. http://searchcio.techtarget.com/definition/change-management.
3. http://en.wikipedia.org/wiki/Change_management.
4. http://www.forbes.com/sites/johnkotter/2011/07/12/change-management-vs-change-leadership-whats-the-difference/.

to create a collection of model documents, checklists, and other practice resources. There is good reason for this initiative: Your lawyers can use the model documents to be more efficient and deliver more consistent, higher-quality work product to your clients. Many changes are implied by this plan. For example, when the plan is fully implemented, your lawyers may be expected to use these resources as a basis to create new work product. That may be an uncomfortable change for lawyers who are used to working in their own way or using their own personal collection of model documents that they have been using for years.

This was the experience that John Gillies had in 2001.[5] At the time, he and Joshua Fireman had been hired by McCarthy Tetrault to create a browser-based KM repository, designed to capture key matter documents. The documents were annotated by lawyers who worked on the matter, tagged, categorized, and made available to be searched. John was enamored with the new system they had created. He and Joshua assumed that if they just explained how it worked and how useful it would be, that lawyers would instantly be compelled to contribute their own documents, and it would be a huge success. John learned that this was not a fairytale example of "if you build it, they will come." As he told me, he soon came to realize that, "unless you have something that either directly improves lawyers' billings or clearly answers the question 'What's in it for me?,' adoption is going to be a huge challenge."

Accordingly, the KM team undertook an extensive campaign to provide hands-on, one-on-training on the KM system in the lawyers' offices. They prepared sample searches in advance that depended on the lawyers' personas (such as practice group, office location, associate versus partner, etc.). They would run these individualized canned searches to give an idea of the type of content available and then ask the lawyer being trained to identify recent matters that he or she had been involved in and run searches to pull up relevant content. They also scheduled short speaking slots at monthly practice group meetings to highlight recent submissions, thereby encouraging the lawyers to remember to use the KM system when starting a new matter. Furthermore, since the KM team members were included in practice

5. Read John Gillies's personal KM story in Appendix B.

group e-mail lists, when a lawyer from the practice or client group sent out a broadcast e-mail asking if anyone had experience with a particular matter, they would find relevant content from the KM system and forward it to the requesting lawyer, using "reply all" so that the other group members would be reminded of content that was available to them. In the end, the innovative tool that they built significantly transformed the way lawyers practiced, but not without considerable effort to manage the change that was to come.

Another example of the impact of changes—one that comes into play even earlier with similar projects—is if practicing attorneys are asked to contribute to the creation or review of a model document collection. This is not an insignificant change. They are being asked to take on work they may feel is inappropriate for them. Perhaps they feel that they are already too busy with billable client work. Maybe they feel that the work is beneath them, that someone of their level should not be bothered with such trivial work or menial tasks. Perhaps they are in favor of the concept, but they simply do not want to take on the extra responsibility. Or maybe they are insecure about having their work held out as the gold standard. These are just some of the challenges that come along with this sort of change. So, how do you and your organization deal with the challenges of these changes?

8.4 A Structured Approach to Managing Change

The key to dealing with changes—big or small—is to manage them effectively. You need a structured approach. Julia Montgomery, Senior Change Management Consultant with Traveling Coaches and 2012 ILTA Consultant of the Year, introduced me to a great resource for approaching changes called the ADKAR model.[6]

ADKAR stands for Awareness, Desire, Knowledge, Ability, and Reinforcement:

6. You can learn more about the ADKAR model by visiting www.change-management.com.

- Awareness of the need for change
- Desire to support and participate in the change
- Knowledge of how to change
- Ability to implement desired skills and behaviors
- Reinforcement to sustain the change[7]

I was reminded of the importance and potential impact of managing change in a structured manner on a recent flight. As the flight attendants passed by serving drinks, one said to the other, "I want to punch the person who decided to remove the ice bucket from the top of the cart. Now it takes three steps every time I serve a drink. It slows things down. It doesn't make any sense." The flight attendant was genuinely frustrated. She described to her colleague how she now had to bend over, pull the ice container out of the sliding drawer, scoop the ice into a cup, slide the ice container back, and then fill the cup with a beverage and hand it to a passenger. This true story is an example of the apparent failure to manage what surely seemed to be a simple change. I'll speculate a bit about this situation, since I am not privy to the details, and assume that the ice bucket location change was needed and not just arbitrary.

It appears that the need for this change was not communicated, so that the people it would affect (primarily, flight attendants) did not understand the nature of the change, why it was made, and the risks involved in not implementing the change. Nobody likely communicated to the flight attendants (at least not the one who I overheard complaining) why this change was necessary. In short, those impacted by the change were not made aware of the need for the change. The need may have been legitimate (maybe there were too many instances of buckets of ice being dumped on passengers' heads), but without making the flight attendants aware of the need, the airline was off to a bad start in managing this new way of doing things.

When someone is not made aware of the need for a change (especially one that makes one's work more difficult), it becomes more difficult to encourage the desire—or willingness—to support and participate in the change. If the flight attendant had been advised of the reasons behind the change, she

7. Jeffrey Hiatt, *ADKAR: A Model for Change in Business, Government and Our Community* (Loveland, CO: Prosci Learning Center Publications, 2006).

might not have felt such frustration. She might have thought, "Well, this new procedure is more time consuming, but it's better than the risk of dropping a bucket of ice on a passenger." So, you can see how awareness of the need for the change and one's desire or willingness to support it are connected.

Knowledge about the change and how to deal with it is the next step. Again, I am speculating based on what I overheard, but it seems unlikely that the flight attendant was trained or otherwise given the necessary information about how to deal with the new drawer-based ice containers. It's entirely possible that some tool or technique is intended to be used with the new ice containers. Perhaps the flight attendant was simply unaware that she was expected to remove the container from the drawer and affix it to the top of the service cart in a manner that makes it spill-proof, thus allowing her to dispense ice effectively the way she always did. Without the change maker communicating this important information to the flight attendants, they wouldn't necessarily know how to deal with the new equipment. Thus, transferring the appropriate knowledge about the change is a crucial aspect of managing the change.

The flight attendant's ability to take the knowledge about the changed ice container procedure and implement that change is the next step in the process. Let's assume that the Awareness, Desire, and Knowledge parts of the ADKAR model had actually been considered and followed (although I don't think they were). That doesn't necessarily mean that the flight attendants could actually implement the change effectively. They might be able to physically do the job, but could they do it efficiently? The flight attendant complained that the new equipment slowed down the drink service process. What would the impact be if the process was so slowed that the flight attendants could not complete the beverage service in a timely manner? Perhaps passengers would be prevented from accessing the aisle (and bathrooms), because the service cart is in the way for an extended period. Or maybe some passengers would not be offered a drink, because it simply takes too long to make it to all of the passengers. The impact might be not only flight attendant frustration but also passenger frustration, leading to complaints and possibly lost business. If, up until this point, you were thinking that a little employee frustration is not worth the time and effort of dealing with change management issues, surely you'll agree that the risk of losing business is a good reason to seriously consider it now.

Reinforcing a change, the final step in the ADKAR model, is about sustaining the new way of doing things through recognizing the benefits of the change on a personal level. In our flight attendant example, the benefit of the change may be the recognition that flight attendants are primarily there to ensure the safety of passengers. One might reason that although the ice container change makes it a little more challenging to dispense cool drinks, it also helps prevent accidents that could injure passengers. Recognizing that aspect of the change could be enough to make it more tolerable, or manageable, from the flight attendant's perspective.

This simple example, involving a seemingly minor change in a flight attendant's procedures, shows the importance of taking a structured approach when planning changes that can affect the way people do their jobs. You may have noticed that an underlying aspect of this structured approach is the importance of communication. When making changes, communication is the key. In fact, in my experience, *over*communication is the key. You should communicate early and often about your plans. Following is a case study that emphasizes the importance of communication when implementing a KM initiative.

8.5 Case Study: Managing Change in the Ways Lawyers Find Internal Work Product

When we set out to introduce an enterprise search system (ESS) at my firm, Ogletree Deakins, we knew that it would be a big change in the way our lawyers and staff members would go about finding the information they needed to do their work. Before our enterprise search project, users relied on the firm's document management system (DMS) to capture, store, and retrieve work product. This was effective for file management purposes (e.g., keeping a digital case file) but not optimal to locate model or precedent documents to apply to other matters for purposes of efficient work product generation (e.g., not reinventing the wheel). The main problem was that attorneys found the search function on the DMS difficult to use, and its results were inconsistent. If you have dealt with law firm DMSs, then you're likely aware of this problem. Although we knew that implementing the ESS would be a positive change, it would nonetheless be a different way of doing things, and it would therefore cause some stress for our users.

Knowing that people tend to be more comfortable with change when they know that it's coming and have plenty of time to mentally prepare, we adopted an "early and often" communication approach. We decided to overcommunicate our plans so the change seemed gradual and did not come as a shock to our lawyers and staff members. Several months before our planned launch date, we announced our plans on the intranet as follows: "The Knowledge Management and Technology Departments are working on a great new Google-like search engine, called ODSearch. You'll be able to use it to quickly find documents, firm subject matter experts, and matter information." The announcement went on to remind people of the recommended way of naming documents in the DMS. We focused on the DMS at this point in the change management plan, because the new enterprise search system would use the DMS as one of its main sources of content. Because this was the first time that most users had heard of the plan, one of the main goals of the announcement was simply to introduce the firm to the name ODSearch and to let everyone know that a plan was in the works. Planting this seed in users' minds was the first step in familiarizing our user base with this plan.

A few weeks later, we opened up a "pre-beta" version of ODSearch to a significant number of users. We invited our office administrators and senior management—approximately 80 people—to have an early look at the project and asked for their feedback, being careful to stress that ODSearch was still in the development phase. We wanted to make sure that this important group, who would hopefully become proponents of the tool and promote its use, realized that they had a voice and a true role in its development. This communication to office administrators and senior management was more detailed than the basic name-recognition announcement we made weeks before. We described the nature of the project and the reasons for what we were planning. The invitation included sections such as the following:

- What is ODSearch?
- Why should you care?

- How does it work?
- What should you do now (before the launch)?

Again, the purpose was not only to increase awareness but also to involve this important group in the process of developing and refining the product before making it available to the entire firm. We had also hoped that members of this group would eventually become product champions and enthusiastically promote ODSearch to others. This turned out to be a wise move, because several members of this group gave excellent feedback on the development and did become big proponents of the project, spreading the word to others. The pre-beta effort with office administrators and senior managers also included demonstrations of the new system followed by early access, so that they could actually use it and provide feedback. This was doubly beneficial. It gave us the critical feedback we needed to address development problems, and it eased a large part of the firm population into using the product, allowing them to become familiar with it before they were expected to use it.

The next major change management effort, approximately one month before the scheduled launch date, was to invite several attorneys to become members of a Secret Beta Testers Group. This is one of my favorite tactics, which I implement frequently.

I sent an e-mail, which included the "secret" branded logo (Figure 8.1), to an Undisclosed Recipient List. I advised the group: "We're in the final stages of development and we need people to test out the system to make sure it's working properly. I'd like to invite you to become a member of the Secret Beta Testers Group and give you early access so that you can try it out before anyone else."

Figure 8.1
ODSearch Secret Beta Testers Group logo.

The implication was that this group was limited and exclusive—they were getting VIP access. This is a play on what's called the "scarcity heuristic," which is used by marketers to generate interest in products based on the psychological basis that people tend to value things that are more difficult to acquire.[8] In reality, the undisclosed recipient list was really the all attorneys e-mail distribution list. All were welcome to join this exclusive group. And my plea to the members to keep the secret was also less than authentic; in fact, I wanted people talking about this group. As you may have experienced, the best way to get the word out about something is to ask people to keep it to themselves. The interest in joining the beta group was greater than I had expected. For purposes of managing feedback, we limited the group to 50 attorneys.

This Secret Beta Testers Group invitation served several purposes. First, even for those who did not accept the invitation, it was another communication about an impending change. It was one more reminder to expect a new tool—a way to spread the word so that lawyers would not be surprised on the official launch day. Second, along the same lines, this was one more opportunity to get some name recognition for the brand ODSearch. Third, we conducted demonstrations of ODSearch to the group, familiarizing them with the application. This reduced the number of attorneys we had to train during the official training period. Fourth, we received valuable feedback from these users, and we were able to adjust the application based on this feedback before the official launch. Finally, the invitation itself—even for those who declined—sent a valuable message to our lawyers: Their opinions were important.

Knowing that the vast majority of the firm now had several opportunities to at least hear about ODSearch, we were ready to announce the launch. We crafted a carefully worded firm-wide e-mail and an identical announcement on our intranet. We learned during the previews that the beta users often noted that the new search tool was in some ways like Google. We thought it was a good analogy with which most everyone was surely familiar, so we embraced the concept with the punchy opening line: "Today, we're

8. http://en.wikipedia.org/wiki/Scarcity_heuristic.

launching an amazing new tool called ODSearch. It's like Google for the Firm's collective knowledge."

The announcement included interface screenshots, concise descriptions of the functionality, beta user comments (e.g., "Unbelievably helpful"; "Very intuitive and user friendly"), tips on getting started, links to a digital quick reference card and a list of frequently asked questions, and a special e-mail address to reach someone for help using the application. We also scheduled seven 30-minute training webinars over the next seven business days. We staggered the times of the webinars to accommodate attendees in our several offices (43 at the time) across five time zones.

A week after the initial announcement, we took another step to ensure a smooth transition and to create additional excitement around the ODSearch launch. We designed a digital scavenger hunt and awarded an Apple iPad to two randomly selected attorneys who accurately completed the hunt. To be eligible to win, attorneys had to use ODSearch to find the answers to ten questions, all of which were designed to ensure that they used all of the main functions of the system. Here are the sorts of questions we asked:

1. How many documents (excluding e-mails) reference Acme Corporation of America?
2. Identify three attorneys who have experience with the Family and Medical Leave Act and who also speak Spanish.
3. How many age discrimination matters have we handled in the Software Publishers industry that mention the Hon. Michael J. Smith?

In addition to providing answers, attorneys also had to articulate how they arrived at their answers, indicating that they had used the search functions and/or applied filters. The scavenger hunt was designed so lawyers could spend a little time using and becoming familiar with the system. That way, when they needed it for their work, they would feel confident that they knew how to use it. The promotion was a huge success. We received many entries, and we announced the winners at our all-attorney retreat a few weeks later.

The scavenger hunt, like the Secret Beta Testers Group invitation, served many purposes, all of which were designed to manage the significant change that we had asked our users to endure: notification of the change, brand recognition, familiarization with the system, training, and consideration for the users. As you can see, communication about the change is at the heart of most, if not all, of these KM efforts.

Recognizing that change is not an event, but a process, we have never stopped communicating and providing training. We offer live ODSearch training sessions via webinar on a weekly basis. The training is designed for new attorneys, but the sessions are open to everyone at the firm. We also have recorded video training sessions available on our intranet and offer live just-in-time training opportunities whenever someone requests it.

In the end, the rollout of our enterprise search system went well. This positive change was embraced by the vast majority of the lawyers and staff members at the firm, and I believe the main reason for its success was the emphasis on communicating the nature of the change early and often.

8.6 Deliberate Knowledge Sharing

One fundamental category of KM activities is knowledge sharing; it also happens to be among the most challenging. Sharing tacit knowledge—that personal experience and knowledge that is inside of one's own head—is one of the most challenging aspects of knowledge sharing in any type of organization. It will not happen (at least not to a significant extent) on its own. Deliberate action is needed to ensure that knowledge is shared and that it does not escape forever when your knowledge assets—your most experienced lawyers and other employees—leave the firm through retirement or resignation.

So, what can you do to help get some of that valuable knowledge out of people's heads and spread it around your organization? Deliberate knowledge sharing involves *actively* seeking out the people and methods involved in sharing knowledge and experience throughout your organization. Some examples of deliberate knowledge sharing are interviewing your attorneys, developing in-house professional development training programs, holding regular group gatherings and meetings, and establishing mentoring programs.

8.6.1 Interview Your Most Knowledgeable Lawyers

One way to get the knowledge out of individuals' heads and make it available to the others at your firm is to interview your attorneys. This technique is surprisingly easy, and you may find that many of your lawyers are willing to participate. This is not to say that you should interview all of your attorneys. Rather, you should target those who have true depth of knowledge that would be helpful to a large number of other attorneys. It is especially valuable to interview those attorneys who you know are close to retirement age. Not only do they tend to have extensive amounts of experience, but you know with certainty that they will not be around for very much longer and be available for the quick phone call or discussion when you need to pick their brains. Therefore, you need to extract as much good knowledge from them as possible while you can. They are much more likely to sit down with you while they are actively practicing in your organization than when they are on a beach somewhere with drinks in their hands.

Finding the right interviewees is important. In some law firms, it may be obvious to everyone who is the appropriate lawyer to discuss particular topics. Elsewhere, it may take some investigation. Begin the process by talking to your lawyers and asking them who they would speak with if they had questions about a particular topic. You may find that there are several potential subject matter experts whom you want to interview. Once you have found the right expert, discuss with the prospective interviewee the idea of the project and why it is important. This important step will help you flesh out the questions and topics to discuss during the interview. Don't be surprised if your interviewees suggest topics and points that you didn't consider asking—they are the experts, after all.

Next, you should work with your interviewer to come up with a series of questions that probe the topic of the interviewee's expertise. These questions should be written out and shared with the interviewee well in advance of the recorded interview. Allow a period of time before the interview for your expert to think about the questions and offer any changes or additional topics that would add to the substance of the interview.

At the outset of the recorded interview, include an introduction so that the interviewee can describe his or her area of expertise and set the stage for what will be discussed. Don't assume that just because this interview is of a member of the firm that everyone will know and be familiar with him or her. This introduction is especially important at large, multioffice law firms. For those who do not know the interviewee, this background will also establish credibility.

The interviews don't need to be formal, but they should be well planned and recorded with video or audio. These days, such recordings can be done at very little expense. Although it is nice to have a high-quality video recording, you could use technology as common as a smartphone or web camera to do the job, too. There are several ways the interview can be conducted, but one effective method is to have the video camera positioned off at an angle but trained on the interviewee the entire time. The interviewee should face the interviewer, rather than looking into the camera. This encourages a more casual conversation that does not seem formal or forced, because the interviewee will not be looking directly at the camera.

Preparation is the key. In most cases, the interviewer should be an attorney who is familiar with the interviewee and his or her area of expertise. This will ensure that the expert is asked appropriate questions and that if the conversation goes off script, the interviewer is familiar enough with the topic to explore nuances in the subject area that may add value to the prescripted content.

Once you have conducted the interviews, you can leverage the content that you have generated in several ways. The video interviews should be housed in a central location, such as the firm's intranet. Lengthy videos can also be broken into smaller clips, which may encourage people to watch them during downtime or when they are looking for guidance on specific points made in the longer interview. It is also advisable to transcribe the text of the interviews so that people may choose to read the content, rather than watch or listen to it. Transcribing the interview also makes it easy to add it to document repositories, so that the content can be easily discovered with search engines. Finally, periodically highlighting particular interviews or the location of the collection of interviews will help remind lawyers of this valuable resource. This can be done via intranet or e-mail announcements.

8.6.2 Develop In-house Professional Development Programs

Professional development efforts are often within the domain of knowledge management, but they may be the responsibility of a separate group outside of the KM department. This is often the case at larger firms, where managing this effort is time consuming. Regardless of where the responsibility falls, promoting knowledge sharing via presentations and programs conducted by members of the firm can be very valuable.

Most law firms provide at least some form of professional development for lawyers. Some firms, like Drinker Biddle & Reath, take it very seriously. First-year associates there spend four months in training, working at a reduced salary, and they are not expected to—or allowed to—bill clients for work.[9]

Although there are many good third-party providers of professional development programming, there are certain additional benefits when in-house colleagues conduct the programs. First, in-house programs can be specifically tailored to your organization's lawyers and type of law they practice. Second, because in-house programs are conducted by trusted members of your organization, the interaction between the presenter and audience members tends to be more engaging and frank. Unlike with third-party providers, where lawyers might feel reluctant to ask sensitive questions or discuss real-life examples, these concerns are often quelled when the presenter is a coworker. Finally, engaging in-house resources for professional development presentations provides more opportunities to share knowledge and for easy follow-up. Presentations can be conducted almost anytime, such as during lunch meetings, practice group meetings, and attorney retreats. Furthermore, if lawyers have questions, following up with the presenters is easy, because they are members of the same organization.

These professional development efforts are a fantastic way to share and transfer knowledge between and among lawyers in your organization. In addition to the immediate benefit of lawyers learning and acquiring knowledge, when in-house lawyers conduct these programs, it helps to build familiarity among your lawyers and encourages future interaction.

9. David Segal, "What They Don't Teach Law Students: Lawyering," *The New York Times*, November 20, 2011, http://files.parsintl.com/eprints/71116.pdf.

8.6.3 Establish Regular Gatherings to Discuss Current Work

I commonly refer to lawyer gatherings as L.A. Law meetings, based on the popular 1980s television drama "L.A. Law," in which members of the firm would gather to discuss their matters and bounce ideas off of each other. For the television program, this was merely a plot device designed to move the story along, but in real life, such meetings are an opportunity to share and transfer knowledge. Quite simply, these gatherings entail getting together with colleagues (perhaps over lunch) to discuss work and share thoughts and ideas. At the first law firm where I practiced as a litigation associate, a group of about five or six attorneys would have lunch together in an empty conference room almost every day. It was a great way for a young lawyer to learn from some of the more experienced attorneys in a casual setting. In smaller firms, such gatherings may involve all attorneys, whereas in larger firms, these meetings often manifest themselves as practice group meetings.

8.6.4 Hold Matter-Reporting Meetings

These meetings are similar to L.A. Law meetings, but they are specifically designed to share with your colleagues the outcome of a particular matter or part of a matter. You might consider these meetings to be mini after-action reviews. Upon completion of a matter, there is greater context of the matter as a whole, so a group review can often be more meaningful and helpful to others. An attorney can review the entire matter, describe lessons learned, and talk about what went right and what went wrong. The review process may bring to light the need for changes in the way attorneys are handling cases or the need to alter office policies or procedures.

8.6.5 Establish Mentoring Programs

Formal mentoring programs, or even informal mentoring activities, are effective ways to ensure knowledge sharing in firms of all sizes. Mentors don't need to spend time teaching new lawyers black letter law, because they presumably learned that in law school. The true value of a mentor is to pass along the wisdom about the real *practice* of law. To be truly effective, mentoring must be intentional and purposeful. Inviting a mentee along to a client meeting, negotiation session, deposition, or other such activities is an easy way to help new lawyers learn the ropes and transfer knowledge.

8.6.6 Consider Environmental Factors

Because lawyers have a tendency to spend much of their time working autonomously, often behind closed office doors, and because the most effective knowledge sharing happens when people interact face to face, it is wise to consider ways to encourage interaction. Environmental factors can promote knowledge-sharing opportunities and enhance collaboration. One firm at which I worked, for example, created collaboration spaces to encourage knowledge sharing. These small rooms (similar to conference rooms but with a more casual feel) were reserved for internal meetings. There was also an attorney lounge where groups could gather and collaborate in an environment that was less restrictive than a traditional conference room. The lounge had comfortable chairs, a television, and a stock of snacks and drinks. It was an inviting space where people enjoyed spending time and working together.

Maximizing the use of space for knowledge-sharing opportunities can be challenging if your organization encourages a closed-door policy or allows employees to work from home. Although some may argue that they work better when they are left alone to concentrate, there are some tradeoffs with this approach. As Yahoo! CEO Marissa Mayer said in defense of her decision to ban employees from working from home, "People are more productive when they're alone, but they're more collaborative and innovative when they're together. Some of the best ideas come from pulling two different ideas together."[10]

Another progressive CEO, Tony Hsieh, of the online retailer Zappos, employs various environmental tactics to enhance collaboration and knowledge sharing. One such tactic is an open-office design in which all employees, including Hsieh, sit closely together in a nonhierarchical seating arrangement—no big corner offices there.[11] This (literally) removes the walls between employees and encourages interaction. Another Zappos tactic is to limit the ways employees enter and leave the building in order to maximize

10. Nicholas Carlson, "Marissa Mayer Defends Her Work from Home Ban," *Business Insider*, April 19, 2013, http://www.businessinsider.com/marissa-mayer-defends-her-work-from-home-ban-2013-4.
11. Aaron Taube, "Why Zappos CEO Tony Hsieh Sits at the Same Size Desk as His Call Center Employees," *Business Insider*, October 21, 2014, http://www.businessinsider.com/zappos-ceo-hsieh-sits-at-same-desk-as-call-center-workers-2014-10.

the interactions among employees. "[W]e do a lot to get people running into each other," Hsieh said. "At our office, for example, there are exits on all four sides of the building. We've locked them all except one. It's more inconvenient, but we prioritize collisions over convenience."[12]

These tactics might not work well with your organization's culture, but they may give you some ideas about how to use the environment of your workplace to encourage interaction and knowledge sharing.

8.7 Leveraging Activities and Converting Them into Knowledge-Sharing Opportunities

Unlike the active, deliberate knowledge-sharing activities described previously, leveraging other activities for knowledge sharing is opportunistic. It can also require more creative, out-of-the-box thinking. You may also find that the specific ideas for such knowledge sharing comes from the far corners of your organization and not necessarily from those employees who are charged with the responsibility of ensuring effective KM at your firm. One basic example of leveraging such activities would be to distribute to people inside your organization the articles, presentation materials, or blog posts that your attorneys create for marketing or client development purposes. This may seem simplistic, but how much time do your attorneys spend on your firm's website, where such articles and blog posts are typically published? Attorneys often are not even aware that their colleagues have published such materials. Reposting these materials on a firm intranet, for example, will expose members of your firm not only to new legal content but also to information about colleagues ("I didn't know Steve had experience with estate planning.").

12. Issie Lapowsky, "Tony Hsieh's Rule for Success: Maximize Serendipity," *Inc. Magazine*, January 25, 2013, http://www.inc.com/magazine/201302/rules-for-success/rule-2-tony-hsieh-maximize-serendipity.html.

8.8 Promoting Knowledge Management and a Knowledge-Sharing Culture

Just as an employee who aspires to advance his career should "dress for the job he wants, not for the job he has," the law firm that aspires to become an effective knowledge-sharing organization should dress the part and represent itself as such. This means taking active steps to not only dress the part but also play the part and act like a knowledge-sharing organization. As Aristotle said, "We are what we repeatedly do; excellence then, is not an act, but a habit."

Constant repetition, reminding, and promotion of the value of knowledge management is needed to help develop the culture of knowledge sharing and knowledge transfer in any organization. The "rule of seven touches" is the sales theory that it takes at least seven interactions with a sales lead before that lead becomes a customer. If you think about your own consumer buying habits, you'll agree that repeated exposure to a product or service is an important aspect in your decision to ultimately buy a product or service. How many times can you honestly say that you learned of a product or service and immediately bought it? The truth is that you need to be convinced that this product or service is right for you. It generally goes something like this: You first see an advertisement. Then you see a product in a store and take a look at it. Maybe you'll compare it to other similar products, check it out online, look for customer reviews, and ask friends for their opinions or about their experiences. Maybe eventually you decide to buy the product.

This rule of seven touches applies not only to sales people but also to promoting knowledge management (or any new idea). Unfortunately, this may be even more challenging when selling KM in law firms, because lawyers can be tough customers. Lawyers tend to be far more skeptical and risk averse than the average population (see Chapter 2). Thus, seven touches may not be enough.

Don't expect results overnight. Developing a knowledge-sharing culture takes time. An organization can impose rules and mandates about behaviors, but this does not mean that a culture shift has occurred. A culture shift comes when the members of a community behave in a particular way without being forced to do so. It happens when they *want to do it*. Jon R. Katzenbach, a founder and co-leader of the Katzenbach Center at Booz, which focuses on culture and leadership, believes there's no such thing as a culture turnaround and that "company culture changes very slowly, so efforts to do an about-face are inevitably a waste of time and energy."[13] One cannot simply declare that "as of tomorrow, we shall be a knowledge-sharing law firm." Cultural shifts take time; there is no knowledge management light switch. It is more helpful to think of a knowledge management culture shift as a spectrum rather than a switch. (See Figure 8.2.) This is not to say that a firm's culture cannot change, however. If your firm's culture is one of knowledge hoarding and internal competition, it can evolve and be shaped over time into a knowledge-sharing culture.

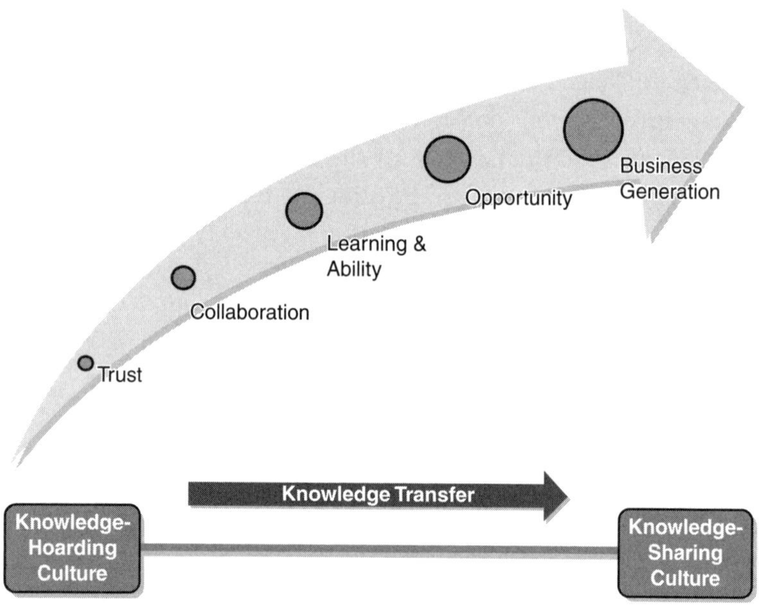

Figure 8.2
Knowledge-sharing spectrum.

13. Jon Katzenbach, "There's No Such Thing as a Culture Turnaround," *Harvard Business Review*, December 18, 2013, http://blogs.hbr.org/2013/12/theres-no-such-thing-as-a-culture-turnaround/.

When organizations see the value of embracing a knowledge-sharing attitude, they can change, even if they naturally tend to be closer to the knowledge-hoarding end of the spectrum. As mentioned previously, it's all about what the firm values. To help skeptics understand why knowledge sharing is valuable, it helps to understand what happens when people become more open to it.

Trust is a fundamental factor in developing a knowledge-sharing culture, but trust doesn't come easy to everyone. This is especially true of lawyers who all experienced the ultracompetitive nature of law school, where fellow students compete to score in the coveted top 10 percent of their class to help ensure optimal career opportunities. Add to this experience the fact that most lawyers tend to be more skeptical than the general population, and it's no surprise that, as Dr. Larry Richard has found, lawyers "tend to be slower to trust others."[14] Even though it can be difficult when lawyers seem hardwired to mistrust others, building trust among colleagues is an essential first step toward building a knowledge-sharing culture. The good news is that most lawyers who join a firm (as opposed to those who go it alone or who start their own firms where they rule) are at least somewhat predisposed to a team mentality and therefore may be more trusting than others within the legal profession. They were willing to join a firm—a team of colleagues—where they knew they would be expected to work together not only for their own benefit but also for the benefit of the entire team.

The more lawyers trust in the skills and abilities of their colleagues and coworkers, the more they will be willing to collaborate with them to accomplish shared goals. None of this comes easy, and lawyers are not likely to trust blindly. Just as trust builds over time, so does the willingness to collaborate and to allow someone else to take on responsibility and feel confident that things will be handled properly and effectively. With increased collaboration, people learn more about each other and become more familiar and comfortable with the idea of working together. Moreover, they learn not just about their colleagues' skills and abilities but also about their business goals and strategies. In addition to improving the quality of the team's work

14. Larry Richard, "The Lawyer Personality: Why Lawyers Are Skeptical," LawyerBrain blog, February 11, 2013, http://www.lawyerbrainblog.com/2013/02/the-lawyer-personality-why-lawyers-are-skeptical/.

through greater collaboration and cooperation, it can also lead to increased business generation, for example, in the form of cross-selling legal services to existing clients.

So, how can you promote knowledge management and help move your firm along the spectrum toward knowledge-sharing nirvana? There are several methods and approaches. First and foremost, your knowledge management initiatives must add value; they must be important, worthwhile, and useful. If your KM efforts do not add value, then they are not worthy of promotion in the first place. Do not encourage behavior or KM activities that do not add value. What adds value depends on what the firm values, and this should be clear to you if you know and understand the firm's overall strategy. Focusing your KM efforts to align with your organization's strategy will help ensure success of your KM initiatives. See Chapter 6 for a discussion of aligning your KM strategy with your firm's strategy.

Here are some general approaches that can help develop a knowledge-sharing culture:

1. *Decide that knowledge sharing is important to your firm.* This is not an individual decision, but rather a collective decision that's made among senior leadership. Agreement among senior leaders and the act of affirmatively declaring that KM is important gives KM the official stamp of approval. Some firms go so far as to clearly state in their strategic plans that knowledge sharing and collaboration are fundamental to firm success. This type of commitment is a great way to begin to infuse knowledge management into the firm's culture.
2. *Communicate why knowledge sharing is important.* Members of the KM department should constantly communicate why knowledge management is important, but it is just as important—perhaps more important—that firm leaders outside of the KM department communicate the same message. As mentioned earlier, having others promote your cause can be even more persuasive than self-promotion.
3. *Recruit others—knowledge champions—to help you spread the word.* Don't just rely on members of the KM department and senior leaders to spread the word about KM. When a KM team member provides excellent service to a customer (i.e., a lawyer at your firm or

law department) who expresses appreciation for the efforts, don't be reluctant to ask him or her to tell others about the experience. A simple laudatory e-mail to his or her colleagues can go a long way, not only to promote KM but also to bolster the feeling that the firm embraces and values knowledge-sharing activities.

4. *Start communicating the knowledge-sharing message early—during interviews and even in job postings.* Encourage your outside recruiters and HR department to describe to prospective new attorneys and lateral hires the importance of the KM culture at your firm. New employees will enter the firm with the right mindset and be predisposed to support the knowledge-sharing culture.
5. *Make knowledge-sharing activities a measurable part of all employee performance evaluations.* Consider offering billable hour credit for KM activities, such as creating model documents, conducting internal training programs, contributing to discussion boards or wikis, and other activities.

8.8.1 Never Just Give Someone a Fish[15]

> Give a man a fish and you feed him for a day. Teach a man to fish and you feed him for a lifetime.
>
> —Chinese proverb

Knowledge management professionals need to encourage sharing and the dissemination of knowledge throughout their organizations. This can be difficult, and it can be even more difficult to encourage others to do the same. Even firms with wonderful technology tools and resources can have difficulty effectively reaching some members of the firm.

KM professionals tend to be the go-to people in law firms. Probably second only to the help desk, people come to KM professionals for answers. This is especially true of firms that include practice support lawyers among their KM ranks. Responding to the myriad of questions and requests for

15. Some of this section was previously published in my blog, LawyerKM, in the post entitled "Promoting Knowledge Management: Never Just Give Someone a Fish," February 10, 2013, http://j.mp/LawyerKM-Fish.

assistance can be a great opportunity to not only respond to lawyer's needs but also to promote the KM way of doing things. When KM professionals are asked to assist, for example, with locating some internal resource or model document, it is important that they not only answer the question but also provide a description of how they answered it and provide a reference to the resource. In other words, don't just give someone a fish, but also teach them how to fish.

Take this opportunity, use it to your advantage, and do it regularly. Never squander a teachable moment. Never waste an opportunity to teach someone how to be a more efficient and effective lawyer or staff member. Integrate the spirit of teaching into everything you do; make it a part of your standard operating procedure, a part of who you are as a KM professional. Make it a habit. Always be ready to teach someone how to fish. Here are a few examples of how to do just that:

1. For people in roles that require them to respond to requests for research assistance (e.g., professional support lawyer, paralegal, reference librarian, etc.), in addition to providing the research result requested (the fish), they should also include a reference and link to the resource from which they obtained the result (the skill). Lawyers often seek this sort of assistance because they are not sure where to look for the content in the first place. Armed with the knowledge about how to obtain the materials, the lawyer may choose the self-service option in the future. I am not suggesting that you adopt a go-find-it-yourself attitude, but giving people self-service tools is always a nice option. It is often faster, easier, and less costly than requesting the assistance of someone else.
2. Even if there is no opportunity to provide a requesting attorney with some directly relevant information, as in the previous example, there may be an opportunity to provide some tangentially related information that can be helpful in the future. For example, if a lawyer is requesting help finding preexisting work product related to 50-state surveys for a particular employment law topic, in addition to delivering the specific result, you may also point out the firm's KM collection of other 50-state surveys and a list of third-party resources that have

similar collections, because the requesting attorney might not have known about these resources.

3. A third way to teach people how to fish when responding to their inquiries is unrelated to their request. I call this the e-mail signature approach. (See Figure 8.3.) This involves appending a "did you know?" type of footer to your e-mail messages. Regardless of the communication, you are always promoting some KM tool or concept. For example, just above your standard e-mail signature, but below a line dividing it from the main part of the e-mail, add something like, "Did you know you can find model documents using the firm's enterprise search engine [link to resource]?" or "Find contacts for business development with [insert name, and link to, CRM system]" or "Have you checked out the firm's electronic library [insert link]?" or "Check out our Knowledge Management resource page [link] on the firm intranet."[16]

(end of substantive email)

Did you know that the main search box at the top of every ODConnect page can be used to search ODSearch, employees, client and matter information, the firm's blogs and publications, and even Google? Just click the arrow next to the box to select the search scope you want.

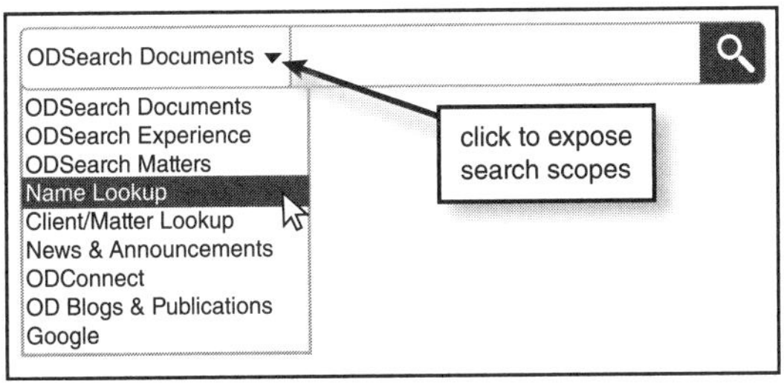

Patrick V. DiDomenico | Director of Knowledge Management | Ogletree, Deakins, Nash, Smoak & Stewart, P.C.
1745 Broadway, 22nd Floor | New York, NY 10019 | Telephone: 212-492-2511
patrick.didomenico@ogletreedeakins.com | www.ogletreedeakins.com

Figure 8.3

An e-mail signature can be used to promote KM concepts or tools. This example promotes the functionality of an intranet search tool.

16. Microsoft's instructions to add email signatures: http://j.mp/Outlook-Email-Sig.

8.8.2 Testimonials and Endorsements

Even though they are not KM professionals, other people in your organization, especially lawyers, may be your biggest KM proponents. The next time lawyers thank you for introducing them to a great new KM resource or tool, ask them to spread the word to their peers ("Thanks for the note, please tell your fellow attorneys about it."). It is often more compelling when your customers (the lawyers in your firm) sing the praises of your KM efforts to other potential customers (the lawyers in your firm who are not yet KM converts). That's why you see customer testimonials on infomercials and advertisements. The infomercial spokesperson is always very convincing, but the actual customers who "can't live without it" really sell the product.

There are several ways you can recruit lawyers and staff members to help promote your KM tools or initiatives. First and foremost, just ask them. Busy lawyers may appreciate your efforts or the tools you've provided, but it is unlikely that they are thinking about your efforts to promote KM to others at the firm. In my experience, happy customers have always been willing to endorse KM initiatives or tools, but don't ask for too much. Lawyers are usually very busy, so they might send you a quick thank-you e-mail, but that doesn't mean they will draft a thoughtful note to be shared with the entire firm. So, make it easy for them to help. One way to do this is to ghost write an endorsement for them. Draft a brief but meaningful note on their behalf that you can post on your firm's intranet or circulate via e-mail if that is a more effective way to reach your target audience.

Another way to ask a lawyer to endorse your KM efforts or tools is to request a small amount of time at a practice group meeting. Take this time to give an overview of a particular KM initiative or tool and then ask one of the lawyers in the practice group to say a few words about their experience and how it helped them in their practice. Selecting the right attorney for your endorsement is important. If possible, select a high-ranking attorney who is well-respected among his or her peers and subordinates. The practice group leader is a good candidate for the job, as he or she usually has these traits and, as the meeting leader, commands the attention of the other attorneys. This technique has been very effective in my promotional efforts. At one firm where I was trying to spread the word about a current awareness and business development tool, a practice group leader who was very enthusiastic about the service was happy to share his experiences with his colleagues. He had already done so with some of the attorneys in passing, but his endorsement of the service during the practice group meeting carried more weight, and all of the attorneys in the group promptly signed up to use the service.

8.9 Key Points

- Once you have established a KM strategy, it's time to start executing on your plans. Taking action is a very important part of your overall KM efforts.
- Deciding which tactics—which actions—will help you achieve your strategy can be challenging.
- The case studies from the U.S. Army JAG Corps and from my firm's experience with implementing an enterprise search system should give you ideas about how to execute your strategy.
- Change management is a systematic approach to dealing with change, both from the perspective of an organization and on the individual level.
- Making changes without taking a structured approach and considering how changes will impact members of your organization can have negative consequences and cause KM initiatives to fail.
- Knowledge sharing is one of the fundamental—and one of the most challenging—activities in KM. It does not happen on its own, and you must take deliberate steps to encourage knowledge sharing in your organization.
- There are many ways to share knowledge in your organization. A few examples are (1) recording interviews of your most knowledgeable lawyers, (2) creating in-house professional development programs, (3) conducting regular gatherings to discuss current work, (4) holding matter-reporting meetings, (5) establishing mentoring programs, and (6) creating an environment that encourages knowledge sharing.
- You should leverage content that your organization already creates in the normal course of business, such as promotional articles, blog posts, and presentations, to enhance knowledge-sharing opportunities.

- You should actively promote a knowledge-sharing culture in your organization. Developing this culture in not an easy task; it takes time, repetition, and a concerted effort.
- When people seek help for KM-related matters, never simply answer the question. Instead "give them the fish and teach them to fish." In other words, provide the assistance requested, but also provide information about how they can find the information themselves. This is one way to promote knowledge sharing in your organization.
- Rely on others to promote KM initiatives. Although members of the KM group should promote knowledge management on a daily basis, promotion by, and testimonials of, others in your organization—especially lawyers—can be even more valuable and persuasive.

Chapter 9

Using Technology Tools to Achieve KM Goals

> You've got to start with the customer experience and work backwards to the technology—not the other way around.
>
> —Steve Jobs

9.1 Chapter Preview and Target Audience

Chapter preview:

1. You'll learn about the role of, and reasons to use, technology in knowledge management and how approaching problems from a business (rather than technology) perspective can produce better results.
2. We'll explore how intranets can be key technology enablers in KM programs and get into some detail about intranet design.
3. We'll spend time on the area of user experience design and why it is important when creating KM applications.
4. You'll learn about common KM technologies, such as enterprise search systems, search enhancement applications, wikis, document automation, expert systems, search filtering, and e-mail filing, and see how they can benefit your KM efforts.

Target audience:
The entire chapter will be of interest to Administrative Leaders, as it broadly describes how to approach technology from a knowledge management perspective. It then delves into some detail about particular technologies and related areas, such as intranets, extranets, user experience design, enterprise search systems, search enhancement applications, wikis, document automation, expert systems, search filtering, and e-mail filing. Sections 9.2 and 9.3, which address the role of and reasons to use technology in knowledge management, will be of particular interest to Lawyer Leaders. I also encourage Lawyer Leaders to read Section 9.6 about user experience, because I believe it to be among the most important aspects of successful adoption of technology tools.

9.2 The Role of Technology in Knowledge Management

Technology is the application of scientific knowledge for practical purposes. Technology is not knowledge management. Knowledge management is not technology. This is a well-known refrain in KM circles. Some KM professionals would say that it has achieved proverb status, while others say it has even become trite. But to those starting out in KM, it's a valuable lesson. The phrase is frequently repeated, because technology is often primarily what people think of when it comes to KM. But to have a true understanding of KM—and to get the most out of it—you must understand that KM is more than just technology. That's not to say that technology is not important for knowledge management or the things we try to accomplish with KM. In fact, technology is crucial to most successful KM initiatives and can help dramatically, because it can help make your work more efficient.

Technology is a knowledge management enabler. This is true, not just of KM efforts in law firms and legal departments, but in KM efforts in all businesses. Just as every other department and function in a law firm or legal department uses technology tools (mainly software applications backed by hardware) to make work more efficient, so do KM departments. But if you view knowledge management as technology, then you will limit its full potential benefits, and all of your KM ideas and initiatives will be technology based. You will see things as technology problems rather than as business problems. On the other hand, if you view technology as an enabler of knowledge management, then you will see more and more ways that you can use the fundamental principles of knowledge management to solve problems and create opportunities.

You should avoid focusing your knowledge management efforts primarily on technology and should instead focus on a problem that may be solved by applying KM principles. People who focus primarily on technology have a tendency to default to technological approaches to problems. If all you have is a hammer, you see every problem as a nail. This can result in unnecessarily complex approaches to relatively simple problems, which can cause low adoption of the technology and overall failure of your KM initiates. Like a Rube Goldberg machine, you may have fun making and operating it, but the complexity will make it little more than a novelty.

Knowledge management is about considering all of your tools, techniques, and approaches, and selecting the appropriate ones that will provide the desired solution. Focusing on what your customer ultimately wants will help you understand the true nature of the problem and develop an appropriate solution, whether that's high-tech, low-tech, or no-tech.

Consider this example: A law firm's practice group leader begins to notice that there is an increase in the rate and amount of writing down (or completely writing off) associate billable time on client bills. This is a problem because it reduces the amount of income generated by the associates, which reduces the amount of profit that can be generated by the associates' work. On deeper examination, it appears that most of the write-downs are for work related to the time associates spend drafting motion papers for relatively routine litigation work. A review of the specific write-downs reveals that the work of five specific associates is written down most frequently, while the remaining associates in the practice group have few write-downs on their work. After speaking with the associates, the practice group leader learns that the five associates have a tendency to draft documents from scratch. That is, when asked to prepare motion papers, they tend to start with a blank page and just start typing.

Although several high-tech approaches could help solve this problem of inefficient document drafting, such as document automation (or document assembly) software, sophisticated search engines to locate model documents, word processor macro plug-ins, etc., some lower-tech approaches may prove to be less expensive and have a greater and more immediate impact. Because the essence of knowledge management is about connecting people so that they can share and transfer their knowledge, a preliminary step might be to assemble the other attorneys who are known to be more efficient document drafters to discuss their approach to drafting similar motion papers. Getting people in a room (or on a conference call) to talk about how they do things is an obvious, but often overlooked, method of learning how to do things more efficiently. In this example, the inefficient associates may learn from such a conversation that they should be using practice-group-approved templates for drafting particular documents rather than starting with a blank page. Not only will this template approach likely decrease the time required to draft the documents, but it will also promote quality and consistency in their work product and cut down on the time it takes senior lawyers to review and approve that work. This preliminary initiative may not solve deeper issues that could arise over time, for example, as the practice group and firm grow in size, or the work of the group grows in complexity. But this right-sized approach may be just enough to do the trick at the moment. Appropriateness of a solution is important. As the proverb goes, "one should not use a hatchet to remove a fly from a friend's forehead."

The foregoing may imply that I am a Luddite or technophobe. I assure you I am not. My point is that it does not take some high-tech effort to implement these approaches. In fact, if you concentrate too much on the technology, you are likely to never do it. You will get hung up on whether you are doing it right or using the right technology, rather than focusing on the point of the effort, which is solving a problem. You'll suffer from analysis paralysis. As with the previous example, it is often better to start simply, with a low- or no-tech approach, and to get going and begin to see some results. This effort may, in fact, lead to a more high-tech approach that will create even greater efficiencies, but that can come later, after you have had a chance to evaluate the benefits of your initial efforts. Like many things, you should approach KM technology at your own pace. If you don't know how to swim, for example, you shouldn't jump into the deep end of the pool. You'll probably have a bad experience, which will likely make you want to stay away from the water altogether. Start in the shallow end, splash around a little and get used to it. Little by little, you'll feel more comfortable, and you will be swimming laps in no time.

9.3 The Reason to Use Technology for KM Efforts

In 1980, Apple co-founder Steve Jobs spoke about the use of technology tools to increase efficiency in competing various tasks. Of course, he was referring to the early days of personal computers, and we have come a long way since then. But he told an interesting story about humans' ability to apply technology—to make and use tools—in order to be more efficient. He recalled the early days at Apple and the original machines that they introduced. In the speech, he mentioned an article in *Scientific American* magazine that reported on the study of various animals and their efficiency of locomotion.[1] The study measured how much energy it took various species of animals to travel a particular distance, "in kilocalories per kilometer or something," as Jobs recalled. The study revealed that the condor was the most efficient animal, because it used the least amount of energy to travel a particular distance. The study noted that human beings came in quite low on the list—about a third of the way down. But, as Jobs reported, someone involved with the study had the insight to test the efficiency of a man riding a bicycle. As it turned out, a man on a bicycle was far more efficient than all other species of animal, even twice as efficient as the condor. This, Jobs said, showed that humans as tool makers have the ability to make tools to amplify their abilities. Amplifying our ability to do work is the reason for employing technology tools in the law (and in any other sort of business). We want to accomplish more with less effort. We want to be more efficient.

In the knowledge management context, some have extended this theme of using tools and refer to this concept as "leveraging our collective knowledge." This is a metaphor for how we can accomplish more with less, but leverage is not really the most apt metaphor. Although levers are simple,

1. http://www.computerhistory.org/atchm/steve-jobs/.

useful tools, the amount of energy put into a lever is, in fact, equal to the power that comes out. But, you may say, "using a lever, I am able to move a heavy object that I am not able to move without a lever, so the power generated by the lever is greater than the energy I put in." Not so. You may be able to move heavy objects using this simple tool by applying an *apparently* small amount of energy, but you must apply it over a relatively large distance. On one end of the lever, energy is applied and the object moves, but it moves only a relatively short distance. Assuming the lever does not dissipate or store energy, the power into the lever must equal the power out of the lever.[2]

A more apt analogy is a more complex tool, such as the bicycle about which Steve Jobs spoke. Even better is a windmill. Chris Boyd,[3] Senior Director of Professional Services at Wilson Sonsini Goodrich & Rosati, has long used the windmill metaphor to communicate the way people should think about using technology to support KM efforts. In their article, "Powering a KM Windmill,"[4] Chris and co-author Ron Friedmann note that a "practical and achievable way to maximize KM results is to capitalize on existing law firm information flows and business processes." Think of a windmill, as opposed to a treadmill. Whereas a treadmill is powered by human effort or an external power source that can be exhausted, a windmill is powered by existing winds, which are not diminished or exhausted because of the windmill. In this way, technology, such as a windmill, can be used to harness power and convert it into useful energy. Think of those information flows and business processes in your firm as the winds that power the KM windmill, generating useful energy to power other efforts. An intranet is a technology tool that epitomizes the value of using the information flows throughout your organization.

2. http://en.wikipedia.org/wiki/Lever.
3. Read Chris Boyd's KM story in Appendix B.
4. Chris Boyd and Ron Friedmann, "Powering a KM Windmill," ILTA's KM Whitepaper, June 2006, http://www.iltanet.org/WhitePaperPDFs/KnowledgeManagement_1.aspx.

9.4 Intranets Are Key Technology Enablers for Knowledge Management

This section is not a deep dive into the technical aspects of designing intranets. Rather, the purpose is to give readers a fundamental understanding of the benefits of using intranets to organize information and provide access to information and applications that legal professionals need to do their work. Although this discussion is not in-depth, I do spend quite a bit of time on intranets, because an intranet can provide the platform for so many other knowledge management efforts. It can be the starting point for your lawyers and staff members to get all they need to do their work. It can also be a virtual community where members of your organization come together to collaborate and work more efficiently.

An intranet is a private computer network built using Internet technologies and designed for the exclusive use of the members of a group, or in this case, employees of a law firm or law department. In short, it is useful to think of an intranet as a private website for your organization. Your organization may have several separate intranets for various groups, or there may be one intranet with various sections, often incorporating access restrictions so that only particular members of a group may access the content available in those sections.

Some people, especially those who don't yet have a firm grasp on knowledge management, will come to see an intranet as the manifestation of knowledge management. Although this belief is erroneous, it is often inevitable, because there will always be a range of understanding of the true nature of knowledge management in any large group. If you've read this far, then you understand this point. In reality, an intranet is merely a technology tool that enables or promotes KM efforts and goals, such as efficiency, knowledge transfer and sharing, and access to information.

Even to those who understand knowledge management, your organization's intranet is likely to be the face of your KM efforts. People will associate—or even equate—the intranet with KM, because it is the most visible and tangible example of "connecting people with each other and connecting people with the knowledge and information they need."[5] You shouldn't worry about this relationship. In fact, at my firm, Ogletree Deakins, we embraced it and call our intranet ODConnect to reinforce the KM theme of connections. Because of this association with KM, it is important to ensure that your intranet is designed properly, is easy to use, and contains valuable information and resources. Like one of the fundamental goals of KM, the intranet should make work more efficient. Thus, the intranet can be like the bicycle or the windmill noted earlier—it enables your workers to be more efficient throughout their workday.

In some ways, the intranet becomes more than a simple work tool. A good intranet will be used every day by everyone in your organization. Thus, as articulated by Jeffrey Rovner in the profile of O'Melveny & Myers (see Chapter 4), the intranet is a representation of the entire firm. You can use this connection to your advantage and take it as an opportunity to use your intranet to promote the development of a knowledge-sharing culture.

9.4.1 The Intranet as the One Place for Everything

Your intranet should be designed as the one place where all employees—practicing attorneys and staff members alike—can go to access all of the information and tools (software applications) they need to do their jobs. Properly designed, your intranet will be the primary technology tool for connecting people to their colleagues and connecting people with the knowledge and information they need. It becomes a true one-stop shop for their information needs. (See Figure 9.1.)

To make the intranet the one-stop shop, the indispensable place where people go for all they need to do their work, you should focus on efficiency and effectiveness. As stated by Peter Drucker, "efficiency is doing things right; effectiveness is doing the right things." In the intranet context, it's important to include the right content (effectiveness) and to make that content readily (i.e., simply and easily) available (efficiency). This point may seem obvious, but it is not trivial. The lack of valuable content and the difficulty of accessing that content are two major causes of low user adoption or outright failure of intranet projects.

5. See Chapter 1 for a discussion of what knowledge management is about and this concept of "connections."

Figure 9.1
Example of a law firm intranet home page.

9.4.2 Typical Information and Resources Displayed in a Law Firm Intranet

The types of information and resources that organizations should make accessible via intranets will vary. Some firms, for example, may favor using an intranet as the sole means of distributing internal firm news and announcements, whereas others favor using other tools, such as e-mail, for this task. Some typical features, types of information, and resources that are commonly offered on intranets may include the following:

- Internal news and announcements (firm-wide or local)
- Calendar of upcoming firm events
- Employee directory
- Practice group list
- Practice group sites with detailed information
- Office location list
- Office sites with detailed information
- Administrative department list

- Administrative department sites with detailed information
- Employee lists (in various groupings, such as by office, by practice area, etc.)
- Employee profiles
- List of software applications available to employees
- Software application informational pages
- List of research resources and applications
- Client information pages
- Matter information pages
- Personalized access to HR or other employee-related information
- Search features that allow easy access to databases or document repositories
- Collaboration sites, such as wikis, blogs, and discussion forums
- Social media features and functions, such as messaging, sharing, and promotion of content throughout the firm

In addition to this typical intranet information, a good intranet should reflect the firm or law department. It can be a vehicle to reinforce the values and culture of the firm. For example, if the firm values open communication and transparency, then keeping everyone in the loop about new developments can be done via a firm leaders' blog, prominently displayed on the homepage of the intranet. This can be a great way for law firm leaders to connect with the entire firm or law department without inundating employees with this type of information via e-mail. An example comes from Foley & Lardner, who formulated a new firm strategy and then created a section on their intranet focused on communicating the strategy to all firm members.[6]

Making an intranet into a center for self-service is another way to not only drive efficiency but also to promote the culture of knowledge sharing. One way to promote self-service is to publish how-to guides and other similar resources. Employees should be able to quickly and easily find information to help them with everyday challenges and questions (e.g., "How do I change my address?" or "Do we have a list of online legal research

6. See Charlotte Lugollo's personal KM story in Appendix B.

tools?"). Making such resources available reduces the frustration of finding information, cuts down on time wasted with administrative tasks, and emphasizes the value of knowledge sharing throughout the organization.

Providing access to administrative forms, templates, and checklists is another way to help employees get work done faster. It has the added benefit of helping to ensure that work is done accurately and consistently. The more resources and valuable content you can provide through your intranet, the more valuable it becomes, and the closer it comes to truly being the one place for all employees to access all they need to do their jobs efficiently and effectively. This does not mean, however, that the intranet should be a dumping ground for all things. You should be selective about what you include, so as not to obscure the important information and create an information-management challenge. See more on this topic in Section 9.6 about user experience.

9.4.3 Managing and Maintaining Intranet Content

The more content that you add to your intranet, the more work is required to maintain it and to ensure that the content is accurate and accessible. Therefore, it is important to have clear processes and procedures to maintain (i.e., adding, editing, and removing) your intranet content.

One way to ensure proper maintenance of intranet content is to automate it whenever possible. For example, if your intranet has attorney profile pages, they may contain an attorney's list of published articles. The attorney may also have a profile on your law firm's public website that contains a similar article listing. If a staff member needs to update these listings separately, then the work is doubled, and the information in the lists might be inconsistent. A better approach is to record and maintain this information in one place and use it for multiple locations. For example, you may decide that the public website, which may have a content management feature, will be the primary repository for this sort of listing. Leveraging this resource, you can set up your intranet to receive a feed of this data to update the attorney's internal profile automatically, whenever it is changed. In the alternative, you may decide to create a separate data repository that can feed both the public website and the internal profile information on the firm's intranet. This is just a minor example, but it points out how structuring information within your firm can reduce the effort involved in maintaining intranet systems and ensuring the accuracy of the information displayed.

Another example of efficiently displaying and maintaining intranet content is the use of client and matter sites. These sites are designed to combine various sources of client and matter information into an easy-to-access and logically organized dashboard-style layout. A matter site, for example, might contain the following information, from various sources:

Information	Source
Client name and number	Matter opening database or financial system
Matter name and number	Matter opening database or financial system
Client contact information	Client relationship management (CRM) application (e.g., InterAction)
Matter status	Matter database
Matter description	Matter database
Open and closed date	Matter database
Attorney origination credit	Financial system (e.g., Elite or Aderant)
Ethical wall restrictions	Access restriction database
File location information	Records management database
Matter documents	Document management system (DMS)
Budget vs actual spend information	Budgeting application
Attorneys assigned to the matter	Time and billing database
Current and historical matter invoices	Billing database

All of this information could, theoretically, be updated manually for all firm matters, but it would probably take dozens of full-time employees to do the work. That is simply not practical. Instead, the intranet can pull this data from various back-end systems and display it in an easily accessible dashboard. One of the principles of knowledge management is to avoid re-creating the wheel. Instead of replicating work, take advantage of data and information throughout your organization to power other systems, in the same way a windmill is designed to take advantage of the prevailing winds to create the energy to power other machines.

The efficiencies are easy to see. When properly designed, a matter information site provides instant access to information that would normally take several minutes (or in some cases, hours) to accumulate manually. An attorney seeking matter information no longer needs to call various administrative departments and ask for this information bit by bit. He or she only needs to visit one well-designed site that aggregates the appropriate information in one place for easy consumption. The benefits to lawyers and others are clear. For example, when a client calls and wants to discuss a bill, instead of hanging up with the client, requesting a copy of the bill from the accounting department, and then calling the client back, the attorney simply navigates to the matter page on the intranet and instantly pulls up a digital copy of the bill. This saves time for the attorney and enables him to deliver instant customer service to the client.

Even adopting the most efficient processes, procedures, and approaches to maintaining content on an intranet can be time consuming. Although everything that can be automated should be automated, not everything can be. People will be needed to create, organize, and maintain intranet content. Even content that is pulled from other systems and fed into the intranet, as described previously, needs to be created *by someone*. As an organization grows, more content is created and needs to be maintained and organized. To ensure that things don't get out of control, organizations need a strategy to manage the intranet content.

There are at least two distinct strategies that you might consider: centralized or decentralized. As the names imply, the approaches differ in that they assign the responsibility of content management to either an individual or a small group (centralized; see Figure 9.2) or distribute the responsibility to multiple people or groups (decentralized; see Figure 9.3) throughout an organization.

The appropriate choice will depend on many factors, including the size, maturity, and complexity of your intranet and the size of the team available to manage content. For example, when an intranet is in its early stages, and relatively few people or groups (e.g., practice areas, administrative departments, offices, etc.) are contributing content, a centralized approach may suffice. Under this scenario, all employees who wish to publish content to the intranet would submit it to a single person or small group (e.g., an

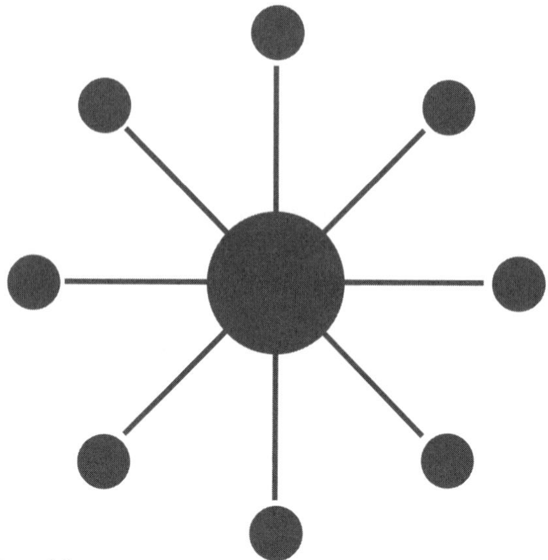

Figure 9.2
Centralized intranet information management model.

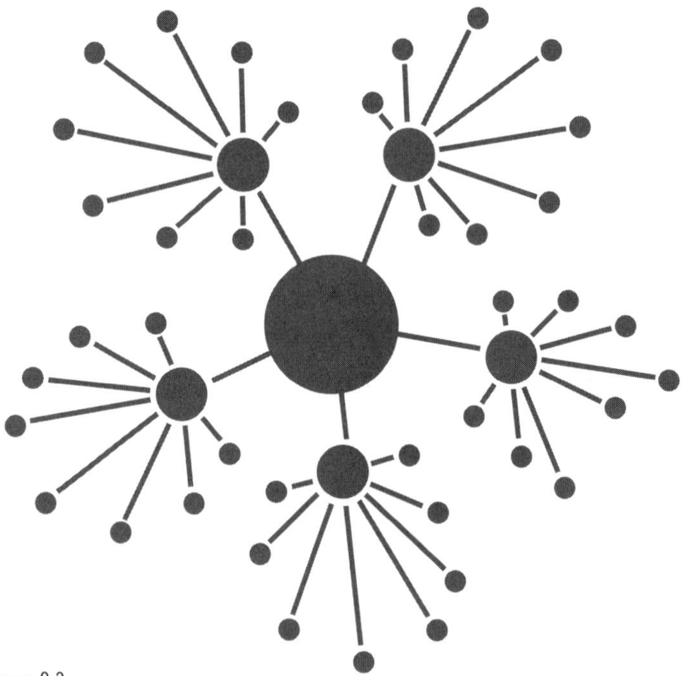

Figure 9.3
Decentralized (or distributed) intranet information management model.

intranet management group), and they would publish the content on behalf of the person who submitted it.

In contrast, a larger organization or one with a more mature intranet may prefer a decentralized model, which empowers multiple contributors to publish content themselves, without the need to submit it to a particular person or group for approval. This is not to say that every member of the organization would necessarily be allowed to publish content. Rather, in this type of decentralized model, certain group members may be designated as the contributors for their groups. They would collect submissions from members of their groups and publish content on behalf of those members. In this model, a core group (often a subgroup of a KM department) provides guidance to the multiple contributors.

There are benefits and detriments to each model. For example, a centralized model puts all of the responsibility and work in the hands of a small group, and therefore can slow down the flow or distribution of information inside an organization compared to a decentralized model. However, because a centralized model has few contributors, the style and format of the content will be consistent and easier to manage. Intranet content management often starts out following the centralized model and changes to a decentralized model as the intranet matures and becomes more widely used and accepted (and as the workload increases). As this happens, it is advisable that all content contributors are trained in the proper processes, procedures, and conventions to ensure that the content distributed throughout the organization has a consistent look, feel, and tone. This also helps ensure the consistency of the organization's brand and core messaging.

9.5 Designing an Intranet

Although I do not intend to offer a detailed guide to creating an intranet, I have been involved in this type of activity at a few law firms, and there is some basic information you should know before embarking on such a project.

Designing an intranet is no easy task. We often make the mistake of thinking that it is simple because we are surrounded (on the Internet) by millions of websites. We also commonly see Internet portals, such as Yahoo!

and MSN.com, which pull together huge amounts of information, such as news, weather, financial information, and the like. We interact with these websites every day, and many of them seem simple and easy to use. If all of these websites are out there, many with enormous amounts of information that is updated frequently, how hard could it be to make a website containing just the information about a single law firm or law department? But beware, things that are simple and easy to use from a consumer's perspective can be difficult to design and maintain. As Steve Jobs said, "Simple can be harder than complex: You have to work hard to get your thinking clean to make it simple. But it's worth it in the end because once you get there, you can move mountains."[7] All of those websites on the Internet don't magically appear. They require a lot of hard work, employees with specialized skills, and appropriate investments of time and money to build and maintain the sites. To design an effective and useful intranet, law firms and law departments must also commit to investing appropriate amounts of time and money, and invest in people with the appropriate skills.

Unfortunately, no turnkey software solution can provide an instant intranet. Successful intranets are unique to the organization for which they are designed. Even though many law firms are similar, no two law firms are identical, and therefore, some degree of customization or configuration of your intranet platform will be required. This is not to say that a website designer or intranet developer needs to start with a blank computer screen and code an intranet from scratch. Although many organizations did this years ago, before the popularization of modern intranet platforms, today this approach would be inadvisable, because the resulting intranet would be slower to develop and more expensive to maintain.

Today, most law firms, and many other organizations, use Microsoft's SharePoint as the intranet platform of choice. In fact, SharePoint is so popular among law firms that the International Legal Technology Association (ILTA) conducts an annual conference, called the SharePoint Symposium, which focuses solely on this platform.[8] The two-day event presents educational sessions in which law firm leaders discuss all aspects of using

7. *BusinessWeek*, "Steve Jobs: 'There's Sanity Returning'," May 25, 1998, http://www.businessweek.com/1998/21/b3579165.htm.
8. http://sharepoint.iltanet.org.

SharePoint within law firms and law departments. The ILTA SharePoint Symposium is an excellent event for KM professionals at all levels of experience to gain valuable insights into the creation and development of SharePoint-based intranets and other applications.

SharePoint is such a popular option among law firm intranets for several reasons:

1. Most law firms use other Microsoft products, such as Outlook, Word, Excel, and other components of the Microsoft Office Suite of applications. This makes for relatively easy integration of various systems into the SharePoint intranet environment.
2. The SharePoint software is often (but not always) included in the Microsoft Enterprise Agreement that many law firms already have, so there often is relatively little or no additional expense to use the software.[9]
3. Because so many law firms and other organizations use SharePoint, there is a large user community from which users can obtain advice about implementation, design, and use.
4. The popularity and large user base has spawned several third-party developers that offer relatively low-cost SharePoint applications (some designed specifically for law firms), which can be added to SharePoint to customize platforms.
5. Many companies that provide back-end software systems, such as accounting and human resources systems, which are popular among law firms, also offer relatively easy integrations with SharePoint.[10]

Whatever application or platform you choose, it is important that you design it to be intuitive and work well. Intuitive, well-designed systems reduce the confusion and frustration that come along with trying to figure out how to get work done. Think of your firm's document management system or intranet. Would you describe these systems as easy to use? If so, then you're lucky. Someone has probably spent a great deal of time

9. Of course, individual agreements vary, so you will need to read your agreement for details.
10. For more information about the use of SharePoint in law firms, see Chapter 17 of *The Lawyer's Guide to Collaboration Tools and Technologies*, by Dennis Kennedy and Tom Mighell (Washington, DC: American Bar Association, 2008).

designing these systems so that they work well. If not, then you're in the majority. I know that doesn't make you feel any better; you're still frustrated and wonder (perhaps sometimes vocally and loudly) why it is so difficult to figure it out. Chances are that nobody thought about or planned how these systems would work and about the human–computer interaction factors that are typically of such importance in the design of consumer-grade software applications.

Law firm applications have historically been accepted as is, and very little, if any, time and effort has gone into figuring out how well they will work when used by the people (lawyers and staff members) they were intended to serve. Such systems were generally developed by techies. And just like lawyers, those techies think and work in a certain way. The problem is that lawyers and techies seldom think and work in the same ways. Therein lies the problem: Systems are built by people who are not expected to use them on a day-to-day basis. What's more, those techies often don't even consult the lawyers who are expected to use the systems, so they don't even get insight into how lawyers work and think. The result is a system that was designed, developed, and completed without appropriate consideration for the customers (or end users) and how they work.

Imagine if other products were designed without consulting customers. You might wonder, how can one even think about building something without considering who would ultimately be using it? It's a good question. Most industries spend significant amounts of time and money doing market research and conducting focus groups before investing even more time and money on the design, development, and manufacture of consumer products. In short, they focus on how the end users will experience their products.

9.6 The Importance of User Experience

User experience (UX) is a term that describes how someone feels about using a particular product, service, or system. More broadly, as Jakob Nielsen and Donald Norman, two UX industry leaders define it, "user experience encompasses all aspects of the end-user's interaction with the company, its services, and its products."[11] So, while UX has more to do than just with people's experience using systems like those designed to support KM efforts, our focus will be on UX in that context.

If you've never heard the term "user experience" before, you're not alone. More likely, however, is that you have heard of it, but only relatively recently. That's because of its growing popularity in common parlance. There are many reasons for the rise of this phenomenon, but I would argue that none are so important as the meteoric rise in the popularity of two things: Apple's iPhone and iPad. These two devices and, lesser so, the devices that compete for their market share have brought UX to the forefront of consumers' attention. The iPhone, which launched in 2007, was many people's first real experience with a common device that was born out of thoughtful design with the entire UX in mind. It was not the first consumer product to give great attention and detail to design and UX. In fact, many products before it did the same thing, but many of them are out of reach of the average consumer (think Mercedes or BMW automobiles or very high-end kitchen appliances). However, I would argue that Apple's devices were the most significant products to do so because of their ubiquity and the very personal relationships that people have with them.

It is important to remember that the experience one has with an iPhone is, as Steve Jobs said about design, not just about how it looks and feels, but also about *how it works*. Some would argue that the way something works is an even more important factor than how it looks. Again using Apple's iconic device as an example, some feel that the iPhone (the physical device) is inferior to many competing devices, such as Android-based smartphones manufactured by companies like Samsung, HTC, and Motorola. Many of the Android-based devices have features such as larger screens, expansion ports, removable batteries, and are lighter in weight than the iPhone. Some would also suggest that the fit and finish of these devices is equal to or better than the iPhone. However, the physical device is only part of the story. The other, perhaps more significant, factor is how these devices work, and that depends on a device's operating system and the application ("app") ecosystem that surrounds it.

11. http://www.nngroup.com/articles/definition-user-experience/.

Apple prides itself on the tight integration of hardware and software in its mobile devices. The company designs both the device (hardware) and the operating system (software), neither of which are changeable by the end consumer (at least not without hacking or "jail breaking" the device's operating system with specialized software, which voids the warranty). This strict control, although frustrating to some who like to tinker with things, generally makes for a stable, predictable, and reliable UX. Contrast Apple's approach to the open Android operating system, which is relatively easy to customize. In fact, major device makers, like Samsung, are known to heavily customize the Android operating system to provide enhancements and purportedly differentiate their Android-based devices from the competition. Some users prefer these deviations from the standard operating system because they offer additional functionality, but others find them to make the UX cumbersome and confusing.

In the end, it doesn't matter which device or operating system you prefer. The point is that starting with the iPhone and the iOS operating system, and continuing with competing devices and their operating systems, we as consumers have been exposed to a vastly different UX than before these devices existed. If you question that statement, then think back to the days of the BlackBerry with its tiny non-touch-sensitive screen (sorry to those who still use one). How would you describe the experience of web browsing on that device? Now compare that to the experience of web browsing on an iPhone, Android device, or even the BlackBerry devices that also ultimately adopted large touch-sensitive screens. It's a whole new and better experience that has raised your expectations about how you can and should interact with electronic devices and software in general.

This phenomenon—the increased expectation of a high-quality experience when we interact with hardware and software—is based on what I call "the consumerization of user experience." This idea is similar to the familiar phrase "consumerization of IT," which refers to people comparing experiences with their personal technology to the experiences they have with technology that they are forced to use at work or in their professional lives. Early on, this comparison was mainly focused on computer system performance. Frustrated employees would lament, "My home PC is 10 times faster than this dinosaur I have to use in the office!" Some people even resorted to bringing their own personal notebook computers to work so that they could avoid the frustration of the standard-issue desktop PC. I recall, several years ago, purchasing (at a then-significant cost) a 20-inch, wide-view, flat-screen computer monitor to attach to my office PC because I found the office monitor (a small 17-inch model) to be completely inadequate. Happily, some things have changed. More office tech has started to catch up to what people tend to have at home.

But now, the consumerization of IT has turned into the consumerization of user experience. It's no longer about computer system performance or the size of the monitor; today it's the entire experience. In the last few years, people have again started wishing things in the office were more like they are at home (or even on their commutes). As noted, the blame (or credit, depending on your perspective) falls squarely with Apple, specifically with the iPhone and iPad (and their competition). After using these devices, going back to the clunky, confusing desktop world of Outlook, Word, and Internet Explorer is tedious and frustrating. The mobile device revolution is a daily reminder of the difference between our personal experience on our mobile devices and our work experience on our PC devices.

The upside (and challenge) for those in KM who are involved with application development is that lawyers have taken note. They are now expressing opinions (some more vocally than others) about how things should work. They want applications, especially those supporting KM initiatives, to be simple, intuitive, and even enjoyable to use. In short, they are demanding a better UX. I spend so much time in this chapter on UX because I believe that a good UX is among the most important aspects that will help ensure good adoption of KM technology tools.

9.6.1 The Five Ds of User Experience Design

Kate Simpson[12] is the National Director of Knowledge Management at Bennett Jones, LLP. Prior to her current role, Simpson was a Knowledge and Information Architecture Consultant for law firms at Tangledom, Inc. In that role, she used her legal education and years of experience to help law firms build systems to support their knowledge management efforts.

12. http://www.linkedin.com/in/katesimpson.

Simpson describes UX as a user-centric view on designing things. It's about asking, "How best should we design it to ensure the solution is the most usable, the most useful, and the most engaging" for the people who will be using it. Simpson told me, "It's only by focusing on the actual end user that we achieve something that's useful, usable, and engaging."

When setting out to create (or redesign) a technology tool, such as an intranet or other application, Simpson recommends a process of UX design that's summarized by what she calls the Five Ds: discuss, discover, design, develop, and deliver. The actual process is much more detailed that what is set forth as follows, but an overview should give you a good idea of some of the key areas to think about.

Discuss. The first phase involves a very high-level discussion to understand what the project stakeholders are looking for. What do they want to accomplish? At this point, a deep dive into the specifics of what will be delivered, what it will look like, and how it will be done is avoided. Is the firm looking for an intranet-type tool that will be the central location for firm-wide information? Perhaps the goal is to make an application that allows clients to ensure that they are in compliance with state laws related to employment applications. The discussion phase seeks to understand the business case of the project, not the details of how it will be built or what it will look like—that comes later.

Discover. During the discovery process, you begin to understand on a deeper level the needs of the users. Beware, however, that focusing on end users does not necessarily mean asking them what they want. Although this is seemingly counterintuitive, asking directly can actually lead to bad design, because people tend not to know what they want when it comes to how software applications (or other things) should be designed. In UX circles, this lesson is summed up in the apocryphal quote, attributed to Henry Ford: "If I had asked people what they wanted, they would have said 'faster horses.'" Part of the point of UX design is to discover, but discovery is not about what people think they want. "You go to users to find out what they *need*," Simpson counsels. "There is no point asking people what they want."

Instead, discovery is about empathy—listening to users and watching how they interact with the tools they already use. Despite the enormous value that is derived from this discovery process, this phase is often ignored. "This is usually the step that's missing at law firms; there's not enough time to do a proper discovery. It's one of my frustrations," Simpson says. "Lawyers like to jump right in and get started on the solution without fully understanding the problem and the problem space." Skipping or skimping on the discovery phase can be penny wise and pound foolish. The relatively small investment in time and money for discovery can prevent headaches—and costly redesigns—in the future. It is always less costly to do things right from the beginning than to have to rebuild something once it's fully formed. Measure twice and cut once, as the wise carpenter says.

Don't make the mistake of thinking that the discovery phase needs to be a significant investment in time or money. You can limit your discovery to a few weeks with a relatively small number of users. You can also get discovery data from other sources. Simpson recommends using the firm's IT help desk and usage statistics. She states: "Some of the best insights can actually come from your help desk, the things people are complaining about, and what they can't use and where the gaps are. I think that's a huge opportunity for any organization, let alone law firms, to discover where people are really struggling." The usage statistics, or metrics, from existing technology tools can also be quite valuable. "I like to back up what people say with what people actually do," Simpson says. "Usage statistics and search logs are among the most useful things that we can get out of an existing system. It also helps with the ROI [return on investment analysis], because you'll be able to then prove how much more usage you get, or not, depending on how successful you've been." Usage statistics can show what parts of a system people are actually using—and what is not used. Measuring how much and how often people use a system is an unbiased way to determine the value of a feature or resource.

Design. After the discovery phase, it's time to design your application. This is a time to think about and incorporate all of the things you learned in discovery. Unfortunately, many organizations give this phase little or no attention, instead moving right on to development. This is a mistake, and frankly, doing so eliminates all the fun. Let's imagine that you're designing an intranet. What will it look like? How will users access the information that it delivers? How will search work? What about navigation? If your firm had a previous intranet, will you gain inspiration from it?

Creating wireframes of your intranet pages is an effective way to begin to visualize how the intranet will look. Wireframes are mockups, or schematics, of the layout and design of the page. Think of them as rough sketches, diagrams, or blueprints of how you want the pages to look and work. Wireframes can be as simple as hand drawings on paper, or they can be created using sophisticated software that makes them look (and act) just like real web pages (the latter are often referred to as prototypes). UX designers differ on whether you should use wireframes, prototypes, or both. Many UX designers recommend keeping wireframes simple, so that they are easy to revise and so that you do not get caught up in the granular details at this stage of design.

That has been my practice. A popular wireframe tool that I have used is called Balsamiq Mockups. You can see from Figure 9.4 that the wireframe page is quite basic and almost looks like it was drawn by hand. This unrefined look is intentional. The purpose is to convey enough information to give the viewer a real sense of what the page will look like without getting into too much detail, such as color and font selection. That level of detail can often distract people and make it difficult for them to focus on the layout and functionality, which is the real goal at this point in the design process.

Wireframes are not just used to help you visualize your application. When combined with requirements, they help guide

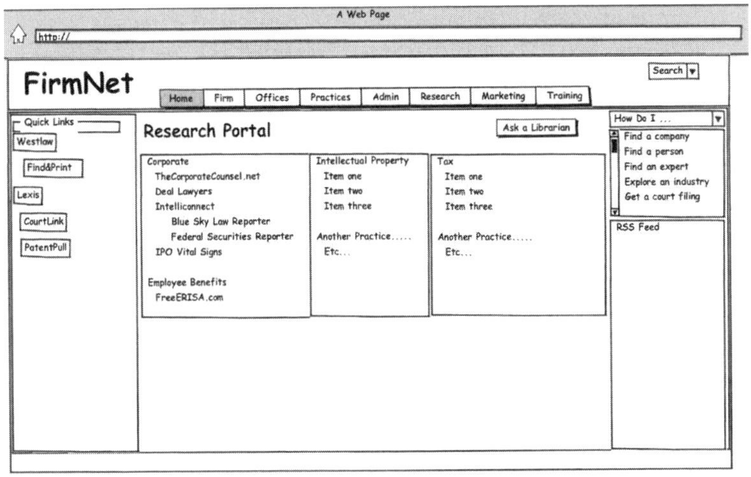

Figure 9.4

Sample intranet wireframe mockup, using Balsamiq Mockups software, courtesy of Nina Platt of the *Strategic Librarian* blog.

software developers on precisely how to build the site. A requirement is a clear, concise statement of what you want your software application to do. As defined by authors Daryl Kulak and Eamonn Guiney, a requirement "is a specific function, feature, quality, or principle that the system must provide in order for it to merit its existence. Requirements also dictate how the system should respond to user interaction."[13]

When creating requirements, it is best to be as specific and precise as possible, because misunderstandings often occur between the designer and the software developer (programmer). Think of the relationship between an architect and a home builder. A blueprint—even if it is very detailed—is not usually sufficient to direct the builder how to act. Detailed, written specifications that accompany the blueprints are needed to effectively communicate precisely what is to be built and how. When designing web-based applications, like intranets, this specificity can be even

13. Daryl Kulak and Eamonn Guiney, *Use Cases: Requirements in Context*, second edition (New York: Addison-Wesley, 2003).

more important, because of the various ways images and icons, for example, can be interpreted. Unlike a wall in a building, an intranet icon is not just a static structure. Clicking an icon on an intranet page causes something to happen, but what? If a wireframe depicts a printer icon, what does that mean? Does it open a printer dialog box, or does it send the print job to the default printer? Does it print the entire web page or just the text of an article on that page? Clearly specifying in your requirements documentation what you want to happen when users take particular actions prevents inaccurate development of what was intended in the design phase. Getting this right the first time will save a lot of time and money.

User testing is another important part of the design phase. As you are creating your application, you will want to know how actual users react to what you are building. This step may seem like it will slow down the design process, but bringing test users into the process early will highlight bad decisions so they can be corrected quickly, before you have spent a lot of time and money going down the wrong path. This doesn't need to be a time-consuming endeavor. Only a small number of users are needed to test the usability of your application. In fact, user experience expert Jakob Nielsen advises that only five test users are needed to surface the great majority of usability problems.[14] "The best results come from testing no more than 5 users and running as many small tests as you can afford," writes Nielsen. Even though his studies have shown that it takes 15 users to reveal all usability problems, he still recommends using only five subjects per test so that you can spend more time and money on additional tests. If 85 percent of the problems can be revealed using small tests with five users, then you can work on redesigning those problem areas and focus additional time and effort on other areas. The most important point when it comes to user testing, according to Nielsen, is that you get no results if you do no testing. He states:

14. http://www.nngroup.com/articles/why-you-only-need-to-test-with-5-users/.

> As soon as you collect data from a single test user, your insights shoot up and you have already learned almost a third of all there is to know about the usability of the design. The difference between zero and even a little bit of data is astounding.[15]

You can use your KM staff for some insights, but don't rely too heavily on their input. It is crucial to have outside testers—people outside of the KM department—because you need to test for *your users* and not *generic* users. Members of the KM department have different perspectives than other users, because they are in the thick of things, especially if they are directly involved in the project. They see the development as it happens and are far too familiar with the way things have been planned and designed to give unbiased feedback. They are also likely to be more tech-savvy than the general population of the employees at your firm. Get real users who represent a cross-section of your organization: partners, associates, secretaries, paralegals, etc. Different users will have different needs, and they can give the diverse feedback you will need to design for your user base.

Develop. The fourth stage of Simpson's Five Ds, development, is when your software developers (also known as coders, programmers, or software engineers) write the software that will eventually become the technology tool (e.g., an intranet) that you have set out to create. There are many types of developers. Some are generalists who can develop software in several programming languages, and some specialize in writing software for particular platforms, such as Microsoft SharePoint.

Finding the right developer is an important factor in your UX design process. The software developer is the builder of the product that you have designed. Just as a home builder cannot simply arrive on the project site and start erecting a house without a plan, a software developer cannot simply start coding without knowing

15. Ibid.

the design plan. This is where communication is critical. All of the work you did in the design phase—creating wireframes, prototypes, and requirements—must be communicated effectively so the developer can build it as it was envisioned.

Good developers are in high demand, and they don't come cheap. Software development is hard, time-consuming work. Thus, development is expensive, and getting the development work done correctly the first time is important, because rework is costly. It is wise to take the time you need to communicate the design to the developers so they accurately build what was articulated in the design phase.

Good communication between designer and developer—like all good communication—is bidirectional and frequent. Don't expect to plop a set of wireframes and requirements on a developer's desk and return in a month to pick up your finished product. My KM guiding principle, "communicate simply and often," is important at this stage. Expect to be in regular contact with your developers so that you can course correct the development as it is happening and ensure that the ship is not veering off in the wrong direction. In my experience, the most successful projects have had regular, structured meetings, conducted by a skilled project manager, involving members of the design team and development team. When you're fully in the development phase, expect to have at least weekly touchpoint meetings, during which the development and design teams can discuss elements of the design that are unclear or unexpected issues that may arise.

And don't be surprised by how many issues arise. It is often difficult to see issues until the developers start creating the software, and complicated elements are revealed. This is especially true if you are creating innovative ways of doing things. No matter how well you plan, you can never account for all possible surprises when you are navigating uncharted territory. To that point, just because you have regularly scheduled meetings to discuss issues, don't wait until those meetings to raise problems that warrant immediate attention. Problems that may have an impact on the project timeline, budget, or essential features of the product should be addressed immediately. These regularly scheduled, and ad hoc, meetings shine light on potential problems and enable the teams to make decisions that will help ensure successful completion of the project on time and on budget.

Getting it right—or correcting it early—is important. Cost restraints on your project will likely be tight. Mistakes and revisions are unavoidable. This is especially true if you are inexperienced or you are doing truly innovative work. You should incorporate time for mistakes and adjustments into your budget. Although you cannot reasonably predict all of the critical problems (i.e., those things that will delay the project and/or increase the cost) that may arise, you can take steps to minimize their impact. Correcting mistakes as soon as possible is one way to do so.

The further along the Five Ds you progress, the more difficult and costly it is to make changes (see Figure 9.5), because of the steps you must retrace to make revisions. For example, if during the design phase you notice something that needs to be fixed, you

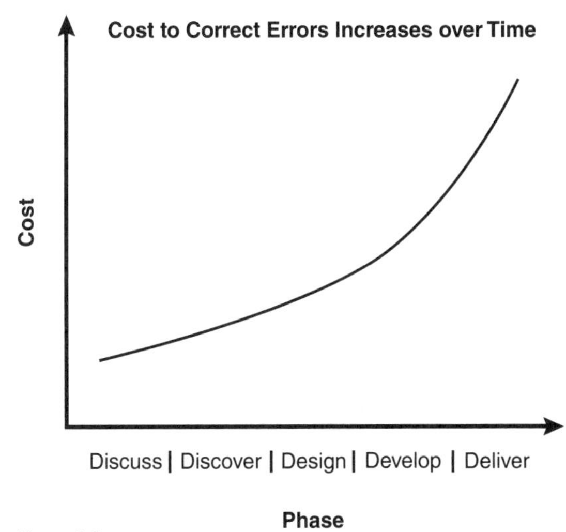

Figure 9.5
The cost to correct errors increases over time.

need only repeat certain steps in the discuss and discover phases. If, however, you do not uncover a mistake until after you deliver the project, correcting it may require a complete rework of all five phases, adding time and expense to correcting the problem. In addition, correcting problems after delivering (or launching) a project causes disruption to the end user and diminished user experience.

Think of this like an automotive recall resulting from a defective part. If the part had been designed, developed, inspected, etc. at the right time during the process, obviating the recall altogether, then the manufacturer would not need to spend enormous sums of money to retrofit cars with replacement parts. Furthermore, the disruption to the car owners, who must now bring their vehicles in for service, has a negative impact on a customer's UX. And remember, UX is not just how someone feels about a product, like a car; it's about how someone feels about a company itself, in addition to its services and products.

Deliver. Delivery is the final stage of the UX design journey, but it really starts up front. You should put a lot of thought into the delivery phase as early as possible, because delivery is really what your project is all about. Launching your product is the first official time that the majority of the users see and can interact with it, but it is not the first time they should hear about it.

As we saw from the examples in Chapter 8 (and as we know from our own experiences), change is difficult for everyone. Your project—no matter how wonderful the user experience you create—will be a change for just about everyone in your organization. Humans are hardwired to dislike change, because it strips us of control. When we have done things in a certain way for so long, they become familiar and comfortable. Even if the established method or approach is inefficient, some people are resistant to change, because they know that it can be a painful experience. They must take time from their busy schedules to learn to do things differently. They must develop new habits.

One effective technique to ease the pain of introducing a new product, such as an intranet, is a soft launch. You may wish to call this a beta launch or a special preview. The idea is to give your users access to the new platform ahead of the official launch date. There are several benefits to a soft launch. First, it allows users to see the way the new platform will look and operate before they are expected to use it. Using a new tool when people are not expected to use it, and therefore not dependent on it to perform their work, relieves the pressure and anxiety of the change. At this point, a new intranet, for example, is not a tool on which they rely; it's just something they can play around with. Seeing and playing with the soft-launch version of the new platform builds familiarity. We like familiarity because it makes us feel safe, secure, and confident.

Second, a soft launch is an opportunity to gain feedback from a greater number of users. Presumably, you engaged in a period of user testing before, and perhaps during, the development phase. Although only a few users are needed to unearth most problems with the system, there is value to gaining feedback from a wider user base. Not only might you become aware of some problems that did not surface during user testing, but more importantly, you have given a wider user base a voice—an opportunity to be heard. Again, change is difficult for many reasons, but loss of control is one of the main factors. How many times have you heard (or even said) "nobody asked my opinion about that!"? People like to know that their opinions count. So, during your soft launch, you should actively solicit feedback and invite everyone to comment. You will invariably receive suggestions that are not part of your design plans, but you can simply thank contributors for their feedback and tell them that it will be added to the list of features for future consideration. This gesture goes a long way toward improving how users feel about your efforts.

A third benefit to a soft launch is that you will get a sense of what kinds of questions your users have without the urgency of having to answer them, as you would if the new product were released officially. If you start to see questions repeated, then you know that you will need to spend additional time on those issues during user training. You may even be surprised by the types of questions you receive. For example, when we soft-launched my firm's new intranet platform, someone asked: "How do I get back to the homepage?" I responded, "You simply click the logo in the upper left-hand corner." Although this action seemed obvious to my staff and me, I understood that it might not be obvious to one or two people out there. But then I got the same question from another user. And another. And another. What was going on here? Doesn't everyone know that clicking a website's logo takes you home? Upon examination, we realized why there was such a disconnect. Although there was a logo in the same place on the old intranet, clicking it did nothing. Furthermore, there was a link called "Home" right under the logo on the old intranet. Users were conditioned to click that link to get to the homepage. So, on the new intranet, which did not have a home link, users were confused. Based on this feedback, we adjusted our planned promotional literature and training materials to emphasize the new feature. Had we not soft-launched the intranet, this problem would have surfaced after the official launch and would have been far more frustrating to our users.

A final thing to remember about UX design is that it is a profession. Just like lawyers, UX designers are highly trained and skilled in their area of expertise. You can attain a good understanding of UX by educating yourself with various resources (find a list of UX resources at www.LawyerKM.com), but most people don't have the time become proficient. Unless you are fortunate enough to have a UX expert in your organization, in most cases, it is a good investment to consult one for help with user experience design.

9.6.2 Helpful Tips to Consider When Designing an Intranet

Plenty of books and other resources provide extensive guidance on designing an intranet. This book does not seek to be one of those resources, but here are a few helpful tips that can make a world of difference in your intranet design:

1. *Simple, minimal design.* It is best to keep the look and feel of your intranet simple and minimal so that your users can focus on the work they are doing or the resources they are looking for. Just as physical clutter can decrease your ability to focus and process information,[16] cluttered, busy web pages tend to overwhelm and confuse users and have the same effect.
2. *Keep things consistent.* Maintaining a consistent structure, look, and feel of your intranet across the site makes it easier for users to become familiar with the intranet. Use consistent color schemes, navigation, and font type and size. Features such as search boxes and navigation menus should be located in the same places across all pages.
3. *Stick with web standards.* Because most people are frequent web users, they have come to expect certain things from web pages: logo in the upper left corner, search box in the upper right or top center, navigation menu across the top or down the left side. Deviating from these standards can confuse and frustrate your users.

9.7 Extranets

As we saw in the last section, an intranet is a private computer network designed for the exclusive use of the members of a group (e.g., law firm or corporate law department). An extranet, on the other hand, is a private computer network operated by a group but designed to allow users from outside the group to have controlled access to various resources.

For purposes of this section, I will use a typical scenario of when a law firm operates an extranet for the benefit of a client. Law firm extranets are typically accessed by clients via the Internet in the same way that you may access your account information on your bank's website. You simply navigate to a website address, enter your login credentials (username and password), which are provided by the law firm, and you are granted secure access to various client and matter-related resources or other applications provided by the firm.

16. Erin Doland, "Scientists Find Physical Clutter Negatively Affects Your Ability to Focus, Process Information," Unclutterer, March 29, 2011, http://unclutterer.com/2011/03/29/scientists-find-physical-clutter-negatively-affects-your-ability-to-focus-process-information/.

Some large clients that employ several different law firms set up their own extranet sites that members of the law firms use instead of the client using the multiple different extranets provided by the several law firms. This gives the client more control over the content on the extranet, and it ensures that the client has a uniform experience when interacting with all of the law firms with which they do business. As beneficial as this sounds, it is not all that common, and there are downsides, such as the client incurring the cost and responsibility of creating and maintaining the sites. Most extranets are provided by law firms for the use of clients.

The purpose of an extranet is to provide a platform that may be used for law firms and their clients to collaborate. In fact, many law firms do not describe these platforms as extranets, opting instead for the less tech-focused, and more meaningful, term "client collaboration site," or something of that nature. Some firms eschew such generic terms altogether and use their own branded name for extranet, or collaboration, platforms.

Like intranets, several extranet platforms are available, so you do not have to build them from scratch. And like intranets, one of the main extranet platforms is Microsoft SharePoint. It is popular as an extranet platform for the same reasons that it is popular for intranets, but, as noted previously, SharePoint requires some configuration (and often, customization) to make it usable. Some other out-of-the-box, web-based extranet platforms are growing in popularity and are much easier to get up and running with little or no configuration or customization. When deciding on which type of extranet platform to use, first start with assessing your needs and your clients' needs. Both types of platforms typically have basic functions and features, such as the following:

- Secure 24/7/365 access
- Electronic file posting, sharing, and transfer
- Discussion forums, wikis, and blogs
- Calendars
- Task lists
- News and publication sharing
- Search

You may need a more customized platform, however, and you should choose a SharePoint (or other similar) platform if you or your clients need features such as the following:

- Custom look and feel
- Dashboards showing matter-level billing and financial information
- Matter budget reporting
- Legal project management or matter management applications
- Portfolio management applications
- Custom tools and databases
- Integration with other Microsoft products, such as Outlook and Excel
- Easier integration with other law firm resources, such as docketing and financial systems
- Easier integration with document management systems
- Easier integration with other law firm systems that are built on SharePoint
- Personalized information
- Workflow processes that involve actions by clients and members of the law firm
- On-premises hosting of files and information because of regulatory or security concerns

From a business-of-law perspective, a good extranet platform can help a law firm obtain and keep an advantage over the competition by providing added value to the attorney–client relationship. This is often referred to as making the client relationship stickier. The benefits of an extranet—providing the features, information, and tools noted earlier—make it easier and more efficient for clients to interact with their lawyers. Like an intranet is to members of a firm or law department, an extranet can be the one place for a client to access all of the information it needs related to its relationship with its law firm. Thus, there is value in the convenience of such platforms, just as there is value in the way online banking makes it easier and more convenient for customers to access their account information and perform certain financial transactions.

9.8 Enterprise Search Systems

An enterprise search system (ESS) is a technology tool that is capable of searching across multiple data sources within an organization (or enterprise) to return relevant search results. Depending on the nature and scope of the ESS that you implement, the search results can be substantive work product, administrative information, or a combination thereof.

Although ESSs are extremely useful tools (many KM professionals report that they are among the most successful and useful initiatives they have undertaken), it would be inaccurate to call them KM systems. Many people with only a cursory understanding of knowledge management make the mistake of equating certain technology tools, like ESSs or intranets, with knowledge management. But, as we have discussed, all such technology tools are merely enablers of knowledge management efforts and not knowledge management itself. That said, many of your day-to-day customers—the lawyers and staff members of your organization—will very closely relate such technology tools with KM or the KM department. This is inevitable, because KM professionals will be the primary champions, principal promoters, and responsible owners of such tools (at least at first, as you are building and developing your KM organization).

Don't get hung up on this connection and be overly concerned that your customers are not fully grasping what KM is really about. It is more important that people are beginning to understand the value of KM and what the KM professionals at your firm have to offer, including tools like enterprise search. A well-executed enterprise search initiative can earn you an incredible amount of credibility and goodwill among the lawyers and staff members of your organization, because you are providing a useful tool that helps them perform their work much more efficiently and easily. Essentially, you are making their work lives easier and more productive. This positive experience goes a long way toward winning people over and convincing them of the value of knowledge management.

9.8.1 How Enterprise Search Systems Work

Although this is not a highly technical description of the way ESSs work, I will discuss some of the basic concepts to make the discussion meaningful to the primary audience of this book: those seeking to initiate or refresh KM programs or efforts in their organizations. It is more important that KM professionals understand the best use of such systems (from the end-user perspective) and allow product vendors and members of your technology department to handle the details of the technical implementation. You will, however, need to have a working understanding of these systems so that you can guide the implementation and identify any red flags or issues during that stage of development.

Most people are familiar with the concept of search systems because of Internet search tools (or search engines) like Google, Bing, and Yahoo!. The basic idea is that a user enters keywords or a search query into a search box, clicks "go," and a list of search results appears. Most people don't think (or care) too much about how the results appear or where they come from. They just click the links that appear and move on. Internet searching is similar, in some ways, to enterprise searching, but there are some differences that make enterprise search challenging.

A significant difference is the accessibility of the data being searched. Internet or Web-based searches typically focus on websites and pages that are designed to be accessed by anyone. Some websites and pages require login credentials for access, but most of the content that a typical Internet user accesses is open and public. In contrast, ESSs, by their nature, search content that is restricted to members of the enterprise or organization for which they were built. Furthermore, some of the data accessible by ESSs are only available to specific groups or individuals within the organization. So, for example, while firm-wide announcements may be accessible by all employees, certain financial information or sensitive client information may only be accessible to small groups or individuals within the organization. Unlike most Internet or Web searches, layers of restriction may be involved with accessing data inESSs. Ethical wall restrictions, for example, are not present when searching the Web, but they are common in law firms.

Another difference between Internet search engines and ESSs is the type of information that is searched. Web search engines can index multiple types of files and data, but websites are primarily written in plain text and formatted in hypertext markup language (HTML) or various revisions thereof (e.g., HTML5). Enterprise search systems, on the other hand, index various databases, e-mail systems, document management systems, and other internal file systems and servers. Thus, the types of data handled by ESSs can be more difficult to access than content of most web pages. Enterprise search systems can be distinguished from some other simpler internal search engines in that they only search single repositories of data, whereas an ESS searches data from multiple, dispersed data repositories within an organization.

When setting up an ESS, you will want to understand the business need for the system and use it to focus on the data that is valuable to your users. Just because ESS technology can be used to search various data repositories does not mean that you should use it to search everything and anything. Don't let the technology drive the project; the business problem you're trying to solve should drive it. Remember that the more complex any technology tool is, the less likely people are to use it. Do your lawyers need to access complex back-office data repositories with a search tool, or are those data sets better left accessible solely by analysts who can easily generate reports from these systems and present them in a more easily digestible format than what could be presented in a search result list? Such search results could make the display of truly valuable information more difficult to comprehend and consume, distracting lawyers from receiving the information they need. Imagine if you did an Internet search and the search result list was filled with unintelligible strings of data. You would likely abandon the search and use a different search engine. Presenting users with clear search results from your ESS is similarly important, and omitting irrelevant or unintelligible data is one way to ensure good results.

One of the primary data sources that ESSs access is a collection of internal documents. Many law firms use document management systems (DMSs) as a single place to store and organize their documents. A DMS is an effective tool for this task, because it allows users to not only save but also categorize documents for easy retrieval. Or at least that's the intention. If you have been involved with law firm KM or technology projects that incorporate a DMS, or even if you have been an end user of a DMS, then you probably have not had a very good experience. Document management systems are often considered a necessary evil, because law firms and law departments need a way to manage their huge collections of documents, but these systems have never seemed to work as well as we would like. Although ESSs typically index more than just internal documents, the shortcomings of search functionality in DMSs have been key reasons why many firms turned to ESSs.

In addition to documents, ESSs can crawl and index other data repositories. Typical law firm data repositories included in ESSs include matter databases and time and billing databases. Crawling the data from these systems allows users to understand who in the organization has experience with various types of matters, industries, and people. Thus, using these search systems allows attorneys to identify and connect with colleagues who have had experience in various types of matters.

9.8.2 Enterprise Search System Case Study

To illustrate the benefits of an ESS, consider the following typical, hypothetical law firm scenario. An attorney with several years of product liability experience recently joined a new law firm as a partner. One of her clients, a pharmaceutical company for which she had done product liability work, asked for help with a new matter involving a claim of age discrimination by an employee. Because she was not familiar with employment law, the partner needed to find a colleague to handle the matter. However, because she was so new to the firm and had only met a small number of the several hundred other lawyers there, she did not know whom she could contact for help to win the new business from her existing client.

There are several ways that the partner could go about finding an appropriate colleague to help, but some are more efficient and effective than others. For example, assuming the firm has a website that contains the profiles of its attorneys, the partner could search and review those profiles, looking for lawyers who list experience with similar cases. This may or may not produce good results, because attorney profiles on law firm websites often do not fully reflect an attorney's actual experience. An attorney may list an area of law as a concentration or specialty, but there is usually no objective way to show the depth of that attorney's experience. The new partner could also send a firm-wide e-mail asking her colleagues to advise her if they can assist with the matter. Again, this method could produce good results, but there are potential issues. What if the appropriate attorney does not respond to the e-mail message because he is on vacation, or too busy, or just because it was buried within hundreds of other e-mail messages?

A well-designed ESS can solve this problem efficiently and effectively. One application of an ESS is an experience search. This allows users to enter search terms (e.g., "age discrimination") and returns a relevance-ranked list of lawyers whose documents, profile information, and other data match the term. More specifically, a single search will look at data in multiple repositories and databases, determine the relevancy of the data, and return results that best match the query.[17] In a typical experience search setup, the ESS may be designed to simultaneously search documents from a DMS, attorney profile information from a firm's website biographies, and billing narratives and time entries from a time and billing system used to generate client invoices. All of these systems contain objective evidence of a lawyer's degree of experience on a particular topic.

So, for example, the search for "age discrimination" might reveal that several lawyers have drafted documents (saved in the DMS) that contain the search term. However, it might also show that a particular lawyer has drafted several hundred more documents containing the term than his colleagues. It might also show that the same lawyer has billed thousands of hours to matters coded as age discrimination matters in the time and billing system, and that his time entry narratives frequently mention the term. Finally, the system might reveal that the same lawyer mentions "age discrimination" as a practice specialty in his website biography. All of these factors combine to indicate that this particular lawyer has the greatest amount of experience with the topic, and his name will therefore rise to the top of the ESS experience search results list. Armed with this information, the new partner can contact her colleague to ask for help.

As you can see from this case study, using an ESS in this way can result in the fast, efficient, and objective discovery of appropriate colleagues to assist with new matters, but this is only one way that ESSs can help. They can also be used to identify previously created work product documents that can be leveraged by other attorneys so that they do not have to create them from scratch. This additional way to boost efficiency is described in more detail in the next section.

17. The ESS can be programmed to give different amounts of "weight" to the data that comes from the various systems when a search is executed, thus helping the system determine the ranking of search results.

9.9 Search Enhancement Applications

In addition to the search tools described previously, there is a class of tools that augments them by enhancing the documents revealed in search results. Although these search enhancement applications are not required to locate previously created documents, they add a layer of data (called "metadata") to a firm's internal documents, making them more useful. The two main providers of such search enhancement applications are LexisNexis, with Lexis Search Advantage (LSA), and Westlaw, with West km. If you are familiar with Lexis's or Westlaw's online legal research tools, then you will better understand how these search enhancement applications work.

Here's how they work from an end-user perspective: A user executes a search of the organization's work product collection and is presented with a list of documents that match the search terms. He then clicks on the title of one of the documents. Instead of opening the document in its native application, such as Microsoft Word, the document is displayed as a web page in HTML. Displaying the document in HTML allows the search enhancement software to instantly scan and recognize certain elements in the document, such as case law and statutory citations, and names of lawyers, judges, law firms, and companies. Those elements, once identified, are converted by the application into hypertext links, like those found on web pages. The hypertext links connect to the provider's (i.e., Lexis or Westlaw) proprietary databases. For example, in the following excerpt, the case citation and the citation to the Federal Rules of Civil Procedure would automatically be hypertext linked, with the familiar blue underlined formatting found on most web pages, which indicates that they can be clicked to activate some function:

> Summary judgment procedure is properly regarded not as a disfavored procedural shortcut, but rather as an integral part of the Federal Rules as a whole, which are designed "to secure the just, speedy and inexpensive determination of every action." *Celotex Corp. v. Catrett*, 477 U.S. 317, 327 (1986) (quoting Fed. R. Civ. P. 1).

Depending on configuration settings, the citations may either be linked to a single Lexis or Westlaw database (e.g., to obtain the case decision or text of the Federal Rule), or they may present a menu of options from which the user can choose, such as an Internet search or other database search. Thus, instead of launching Lexis or Westlaw and typing a citation into the system to retrieve a case or statute, all a user needs to do is click the link for instant access to the resource.

Lexis Search Advantage and West km also offer *real-time* citation checking within documents (see Figures 9.6 and 9.7). The systems indicate to the user—right within the body of the document displayed on the screen—whether the citations contained in it are still valid at the time of the search (not at the time when the document was written). This is possible because, as mentioned earlier, the static document (which may have been written several days, months, or even years ago) is now rendered in HTML, as a web page. This enables the citations to be recognized by the Lexis (Shepard's Signals) or Westlaw (KeyCite) databases that validate the citations.

This citation-checking feature is an enormous timesaver. For readers who are not entirely familiar with the importance of validating citations to legal authorities, let me explain the basics. The U.S. legal system is based heavily on precedent, meaning that judicial decisions and rulings about laws and

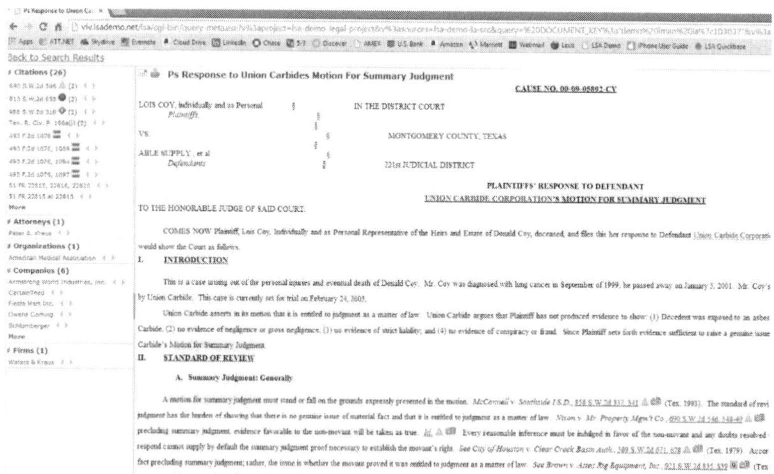

Figure 9.6

Lexis Search Advantage document screen showing highlighted search terms, citation hyperlinks, and Shepard's signals.

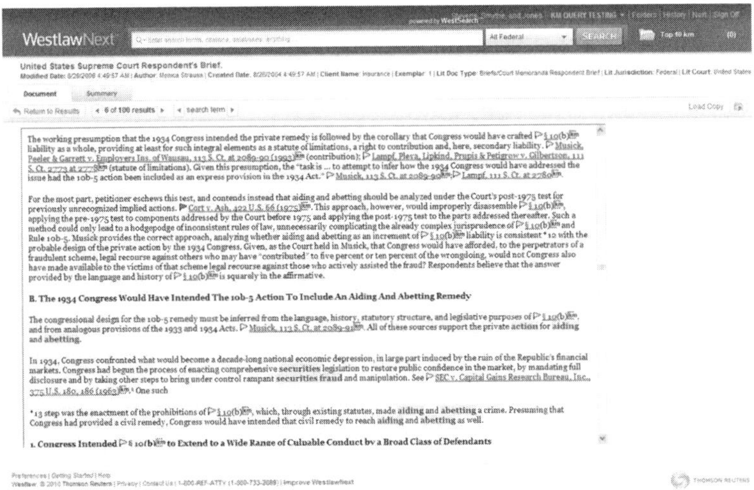

Figure 9.7
West km document screen showing highlighted search terms, citation hyperlinks, and KeyCite flags.

how they are interpreted by the courts are binding or persuasive when the laws are interpreted and applied in cases that come later in time. When lawyers argue points of law, they often point to previous judicial decisions as authority to support their arguments, but because laws can change, and judicial decisions can be overturned or overruled, the precedential value of any given decision can change over time. Thus, it is crucial for attorneys to check the validity of a case citation before using it to bolster his or her argument. Failing to do so is a sure way to lose an argument (or potentially commit malpractice), because the lawyer would be relying on "bad law."

The best way to ensure that a lawyer is relying on "good law" from a previous case is to perform a Shepard's or KeyCite check. Originally, this manual task required a lawyer to look up citations in multiple large volumes and trace citations from case to case, like following a trail of breadcrumbs. I won't go into detail about how agonizing, tedious, and time consuming this process was, but suffice it to say that it was pretty horrible. With the advent of computerized cite checking, this task went from one that could take several hours, via the manual method, to one that could take several minutes by entering citations into a database, which would tell the user whether the citation in question was still good law. Even with the aid of citation databases, however, cite checking is not the most efficient activity. It still requires a lawyer or paralegal to scan a brief, which might contain dozens of citations, type the citations into a database, and then review the results. It is faster than the manual method, but it can still take several minutes, or even hours, depending on the number of citations to be checked.

The automated, real-time cite-checking technology built into the search enhancement tools described previously is much more efficient, because there is no need to manually type citations into a database. When the document is displayed on the screen, the software automatically scans it and identifies the citations in it. It then automatically runs the citations against the Shepard's or KeyCite databases. This all happens passively, in seconds, and as a background operation, meaning that the user doesn't even realize it is happening. The user is presented with the document, which looks normal, except that it has small symbols (colored flags or shapes) next to each citation, which indicate whether there are any problems with the decisions or other authority cited in the document. Because these search enhancement applications do this cite-checking work, which used to take hours, lawyers immediately benefit from this efficiency.

Search enhancement applications add other benefits and features, as well. For example, they can automatically categorize your law firm's documents, regardless of how they have been organized (or even if they have not been categorized). How this works is pretty amazing. Basically, the search enhancement software scans and analyzes all of the documents in your DMS (or shared file folders). Based on the content of the documents (e.g., the words, concepts, citations, and other factors), the software makes determinations about how the documents should be classified. It can then categorize documents by such things as document type, industry, jurisdiction, legal topics, etc., and it creates filters based on the categories. The benefit of this feature is that a user can execute a search against an entire document set, which can contain millions of documents, and then use the automatically generated filters to narrow down the search result set to find exactly what is needed.

As an example, a user can search for documents containing the phrase "motion for summary judgment." In most firms, this search would return a large number of documents—probably too many to review. So, by using filters, the user can narrow that large set of results to a smaller, more meaningful set. Using filters such as document type, dates, jurisdiction, and legal topics can help the user find a summary judgment brief that is right on point.

Online research can be very expensive. Large firms can easily spend millions of dollars per year in online legal research charges. Increasingly, clients are unwilling to pay for this service, because they consider it to be an overhead expense. Thus, recovery rates (the percentage of the amount law firms collect from clients as reimbursement for disbursements) for online legal research expenses continue to decrease. Using an enterprise search engine with a search enhancement application can help reduce the amount lawyers spend for legal research, because the search targets the firm's own documents (no cost per search) and not an actual online search, which incurs a transactional or hourly expense. It is a good practice to train attorneys to first use the firm's ESS to start their legal research. Lawyers may be able to find the documents and legal precedent they need right within the firm's existing collection, obviating the need for an expensive online legal research session.

Another nice feature of search enhancement applications is that they can integrate into the online legal research providers' platforms using federated search technology. So, when lawyers or paralegals do need to use Lexis or Westlaw, the search results displayed in these platforms can include search results from a firm's internal document collection. The internal documents are distinguished with an icon, so they are easy to identify.

In my experience, deploying ESSs, paired with search enhancement applications, has always had a positive impact, as they increase efficiency and make it easier for lawyers to do their work. Many of my KM peers at other law firms have said the same. The increased efficiency and ability to share an organization's collective knowledge that is enabled by these systems is well worth the investment.

9.10 Do Things Once—The Wiki Way[18]

One way to make work more efficient and to avoid reinventing the wheel is to capture and share information in an application called a "wiki." In basic terms, a wiki is an easy-to-edit web page. Invented by Ward Cunningham, wikis are designed to be not only easy to edit but also quick. In fact, Cunningham chose the word "wiki" for his new application because it is the Hawaiian word for "quick."[19]

The best-known example of a wiki is Wikipedia, "a collaboratively edited, multilingual, free Internet encyclopedia"[20] that runs on the free, open-source MediaWiki software platform. Some wikis, like Wikipedia, are accessible to anyone with an Internet connection, but wikis are also available for exclusive groups, such as law firms, where they are often integrated into intranet application platforms.

To understand the nature of a wiki site, think of a digital notebook that is accessible and editable by multiple people. The notebook (a collection of pages) would be the equivalent of a *wiki site*. The individual pages that make up the notebook would be equivalent to *wiki pages*. Users with access to the wiki site can create new pages, edit the content of pages created by others, and link from page to page using hyperlinks. Because wiki sites and pages are shared among group members, and collaboration is encouraged, this often results in shared authorship of wiki content. Once captured in a wiki page, information can be shared easily by simply referring users to wiki sites or pages. (See Figure 9.8.) If the recipient is unwilling to use the wiki, or has other reasons for not doing so (e.g., restricted access to the wiki or limited access to a PC), information from a wiki page can easily be copied and pasted into an e-mail. It is usually advisable to include not only the text of the information from the page but also a link (URL) to the wiki page so that a recipient can access the page for future reference. This step also subtly encourages reluctant users to explore wiki pages without abruptly forcing them to adopt to the change.

18. Based on my 2010 LawyerKM blog post of the same name: http://lawyerkm.com/2010/03/25/do-things-once/.
19. http://en.wikipedia.org/wiki/Wiki.
20. Ibid.

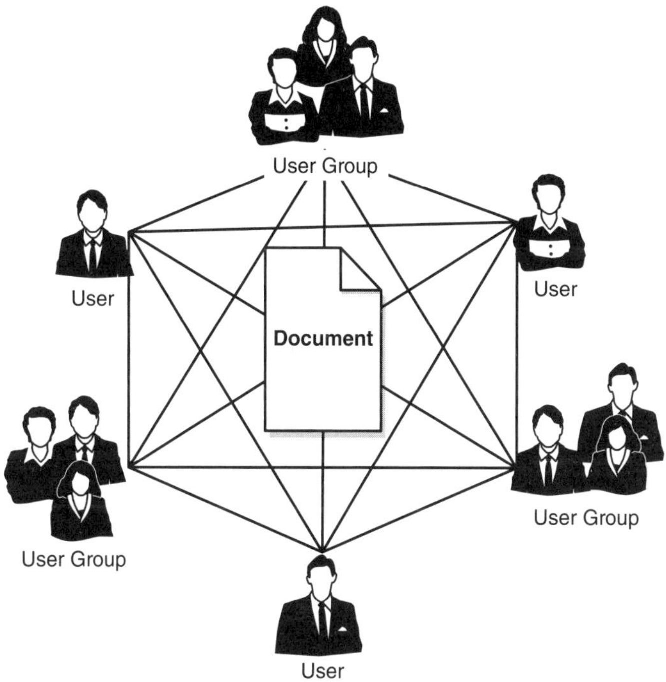

Figure 9.8
Wikis allow users and groups of users to collaborate on the creation and revision of documents in real time.

With the popularity of wikis on the Internet, some law firms have seen potential benefits of bringing this technology behind the firewall, and they have created private, internal wikis for use by groups or even as firm-wide resources. Another factor in this trend is that wiki functionality is built into enterprise intranet platforms, such as SharePoint, and other technology platforms, such as some web-based extranets.

One law firm that has adopted the use of wikis is Goodwin Procter. Fellow KM professional David Hobbie[21] is a Litigation Knowledge Management Attorney at Goodwin. He's a prolific writer on his blog, Caselines,[22] where he has written about the firm's use of wikis. He also published a

21. http://www.linkedin.com/in/davidhobbie.
22. David Hobbie's Caselines Blog, http://caselines.blogspot.com.

paper about his firm's use of Enterprise 2.0,[23] including wikis, in the *KMPro Journal*, a publication of the Knowledge Management Professional Society.[24] Goodwin uses wikis among both administrative departments and practice groups. For example, they use wikis as legal encyclopedias (like a private version of Wikipedia), for administrative project management, as intranet resource pages, and among lawyers for sharing knowledge on topics such as the discovery phase of litigation matters.

Whether wikis are part of your intranet platform or a stand-alone application, lawyers can benefit from their easy collaboration and knowledge-sharing features. Another excellent use for wikis is to capture policies and procedures—at either a department or firm level. I have personally used various web-based and intranet-based wiki platforms to do so.

Like any means of collaboration, probably the most significant key to effective use and value is increased user adoption among the entire group of potential users. The concept here is similar to the "network effect," which is often demonstrated using the examples of telephones or network-connected personal computers. The underlying concept of the network effect is that some tools or networks become more valuable as the number of users of the tools or networks increases. Take as an example, a community of 100 potential PC users. If only two users are connected to each other via a network, and thus able to communicate with the PCs, then the value of the network to the group as a whole is minimal, because only 2 percent of the total group is using the network to communicate.

In fact, such a small user base may detract from existing methods of communication or collaboration and be seen as a distraction from established methods. To ensure that all group members are receiving important messages, it is probably not worth using the PC network to send and receive messages, because some other method is needed to reach the entire community. However, as the number of users adopting the PC network grows, the value of the network increases. It is easy to see that if half of the potential

23. "Enterprise 2.0" is a term coined by Harvard Business School Professor Andrew McAfee to describe the use of web technologies, such as wikis, blogs, and other collaborative social media features, within companies or between companies and their partners or customers. See http://en.wikipedia.org/wiki/Enterprise_2.0.
24. David Hobbie, "Enterprise 2.0 at Goodwin Procter," *KMPro Journal*, 6 (2008): 13–19. http://www.kmpro.org/journal/KMPro_Vol_6_No_1.pdf.

user population were to adopt the networked PC environment, then the network would be considerably more valuable. Significant benefits of a network are realized once a critical mass of users have adopted it. An optimal network is achieved if all potential users have adopted it.

Most of us are too young to have experienced the network effect directly with the advent and subsequent near-complete adoption of certain technologies, like the telephone, but many of us have experienced firsthand the rapid adoption of the Internet. Many of us who have been working in law firms or other business environments long enough have also experienced local network effects with some technologies, like networked PCs and, most notably, e-mail.[25]

9.11 Document Automation

Automating or semi-automating the creation of certain documents is one way to drive efficiency in a law firm or law department environment.[26] Many legal documents contain boilerplate language and need little in the way of customization to make them work from one matter to the next. Often, only the names of the parties and a few variables need to be changed. This is not a foreign concept to most practicing lawyers, who have used fill-in-the-blank forms for some documents for decades. Even before the common use of personal computers in law offices, lawyers (or perhaps more accurately, their secretaries or paralegals) used off-the-shelf legal forms and typewriters to fill in the blanks of such forms. This was an easy way to accelerate the production of such boilerplate documents and ensure that there were fewer errors.

With the advent and subsequent popularization of personal computers and word processing software in the 1980s and 1990s, the use of typewriter-based, fill-in-the-blank forms decreased. Document drafters

---

25. For a detailed description of wikis, and how to set up and use both web-based and internal wiki platforms, see Chapter 20 of *The Lawyer's Guide to Collaboration Tools and Technologies*, by Dennis Kennedy and Tom Mighell (Washington, DC: American Bar Association, 2008).
26. For a more thorough treatment of law firm document assembly, see Chapter 10 of *The Lawyer's Guide to Working Smarter with Knowledge Tools*, by Marc Lauritsen (Washington, DC: American Bar Association, 2011).

could now simply copy the files of previously drafted documents and replace the variables (e.g., party names, courts, basic facts, etc.) with those from their current matters. And just as with the advent of typewriters and carbon paper before it, word processing software reduced a significant portion of the wheel that lawyers typically had to reinvent each time a new matter was begun.

However, for certain document-drafting tasks, especially very high-volume tasks, these copy-and-replace techniques are not efficient enough. That's where document automation (also known as document assembly) tools come in handy. Document automation tools allow you to create templates of commonly used documents and quickly generate finished documents from them by entering variables into an easy-to-use interface. The variables can be entered in a form-based questionnaire, so that the person entering the data need not worry about the accuracy or format of the document. Furthermore, logic-based rules can be used to ensure proper grammar and accelerate drafting. For example, if the subject of a document is identified as male, then the tool can be programmed to use masculine pronouns, such as "he" and "him," without the user needing to change all pronouns manually.

Document automation tools can also be used by clients (or prospective clients) so they can generate their own documents. This involves making the document automation tools available through a website, such as Goodwin Procter's Founders Workbench website.[27] This site contains many useful tools, including Document Driver, a free online document automation tool that allows users to produce documents related to the formation of corporations and limited liability companies. Another example is Wilson Sonsini's Term Sheet Generator, which allows users to create "a venture financing term sheet based on your responses to an online questionnaire."[28] Both of these examples show that document automation can be used not only to offer free services but also to help generate business. Although it is unstated, the hope from a law firm business perspective is that when users of such systems have questions or need help with more complex legal issues, they will consider the firm that offered them these free tools.

27. Goodwin Procter's Founders Workbench, http://www.foundersworkbench.com/.
28. Wilson Sonsini's Term Sheet Generator, https://www.wsgr.com/WSGR/Display.aspx?SectionName=practice/termsheet.htm.

Document automation tools can be used to dramatically cut drafting time and reduce the cost of relatively simple but otherwise time-consuming tasks. As noted previously, they can also be used to offer self-service document generation to clients and prospective clients. For a more detailed case study on document automation, see Chapter 2.

9.12 Expert Systems

A relatively new technology that is starting to gain traction in law firms is called an expert system. An expert system is software that seeks to replicate or emulate human decision making about a task based on a set of rules that are provided by an actual human expert. The goal of an expert system is to provide a user with guidance on a particular topic based on the rules provided by the expert and the variable input provided by the user.

The user of an expert system provides information, typically by answering questions that are designed to elicit facts, which would have a bearing on what guidance the system should provide. The system uses if/then logic, decision trees, and often mathematical calculations to come to a conclusion based on the information provided by the user. A familiar nonlegal example of an expert system is tax preparation software, such as TurboTax, that walks a tax filer through a series of questions that are designed to reach conclusions about how to complete tax forms, claim deductions, etc.

Expert systems are useful for knowledge management, because they can leverage the knowledge of lawyers with particular expertise and apply that specialized knowledge to variable sets of circumstances that are presented by system users. Take, for example, a junior lawyer who knows the facts surrounding a matter and is familiar with the law but does not have a high level of expertise about the laws, rules, and regulations that are implicated by the facts. An expert system that was designed with the input of an experienced lawyer who does have high-level expertise of the applicable laws, rules, and regulations could be used to guide the junior lawyer along as he works on the matter. The guidance could take many forms, such as producing a document, proposing an argument, recommending the collection of additional facts or information, or recommending that he seek the assistance of a human expert.

Some law firms and legal service providers have created expert systems for clients and prospective clients to use as self-service tools. These sorts of client-facing KM applications are becoming increasingly popular. One of the main providers of expert system software for the legal profession, Neota Logic, has several examples of legal expert systems on their website.[29] One example that could be used as an internal or client-facing application is their Family and Medical Leave Act (FMLA) Advisor. This expert system provides a user with guidance, pursuant to federal and state laws, related to an employee's right to take time off from work because of a family or medical-related situation. Using decision trees and if/then logic, the application walks the user through a series of questions, providing clarification and definitions along the way. The questions are designed to elicit facts relevant to how the pertinent laws should be applied to the facts. At the end of the questionnaire, the system provides a report that answers whether the employee is entitled to time off from work to address a family or medical situation. The report outlines the answer and guidance based on the user's input and explains how the system reached its conclusions. The report concludes with recommended next steps and a record of the questions and answers provided by the user.

Not only do expert systems provide specific guidance for users, but they are also a good marketing tool, because prospective clients who use them might realize that they need legal advice that is beyond the scope of the system. These users will likely be inclined to contact the law firm that provides the system. Of course, law firms that use such expert systems need to be careful to add appropriate disclaimers, such as one that advises that use of the system does not create an attorney–client relationship.

9.13 Other Knowledge Management Technologies and Features

In addition to the technology tools discussed previously, there are many others, and new tools are always being developed. The underlying characteristic of all of these technology tools is that they are designed to help lawyers and

29. Neota Logic examples, http://www.neotalogic.com/demos/.

staff members do their work more efficiently and effectively. Some technology tools are more accurately characterized as features rather than tools, platforms, or full-blown applications, because they are merely parts of larger technology tools or platforms. Two examples are search filtering and e-mail filing.

9.13.1 Search Filtering

One example of such technology features is search filtering, which is also known as "faceted navigation" or "faceted browsing." I consider this a feature, because it can be applied to various technology tools and is not really a tool itself. If you have shopped on Amazon.com or used flight search websites like Kayak.com or Expedia.com, then you have experienced search filters.

Kayak.com uses search filters to allow customers to narrow search results and home in on the exact flights that meet their needs. After entering the departure and arrival locations and dates, users can include or exclude flights using checkbox selectors and other tools located along the left side of the screen. This same filtering feature is common in ESSs and in various intranet and extranet applications. When searching for documents, for example, filters can be used to narrow results by selecting or deselecting metadata tags, such as author, document type, matter type, law type, industry, file type, etc.

9.13.2 E-mail Filing

Another technology, which is often overlooked when it comes to knowledge management, concerns filing, storing, and making e-mail messages accessible. As ubiquitous as e-mail is, it is frequently overlooked when it comes to knowledge management and is not often seen as a good source of valuable information. In reality, e-mail can contain some very valuable information that can be useful across an organization. The trick is separating the valuable e-mail messages from those that simply take up space.

One reason for this misconception is that e-mail is often considered personal, rather than part of a matter file. This is based on the traditional use of e-mail in law firms. Before e-mail became popular, law firms conducted almost all written correspondence via letters. These letters were printed and mailed (or sometimes transmitted by facsimile machine) or hand delivered. The same is true of substantive internal memos: They were typed up, printed out, delivered to the partner, and filed in the matter file. Today, a great deal of correspondence and memos have been replaced by e-mail. Partners often prefer an informal e-mail over a formal memorandum of law. The result, over time, has been a reduction of letters and memos, which are typically filed in a DMS, and an increase in e-mail messages containing valuable information.

In addition to the behavioral change, another reason why e-mail messages are not widely shared is because e-mail applications, like Outlook, are not designed for sharing. Many people save e-mail messages to folders, but these folders are generally personal and not shared throughout the organization. To the extent that some people do create shared e-mail folders, the process of accessing the e-mail can be cumbersome. In addition, these shared folders are separated from the main matter folders, which are typically contained in a DMS.

Technology has caught up, and now there are ways to capture e-mail messages so that they can be accessed by people other than just the sender and recipients. One method is to file e-mail messages in a DMS. Although DMSs have been able to store e-mail messages for several years, the practice of filing e-mail messages in DMSs has not caught on widely, mainly because it can be a cumbersome task. To remedy this problem, many DMS providers have added Microsoft Outlook integration, which allows users to save e-mail messages much more easily. Such integrated systems add DMS folders in the Outlook application, which allows users to simply drag and drop e-mail messages into the appropriate DMS folder. Another integrated feature is "send and file," which, as the name implies, files an e-mail message in the DMS immediately after it is sent. A third e-mail–DMS integration feature adds a toolbar to Outlook, which allows a user to file an e-mail message in a DMS folder with a few clicks. Because the DMS is typically a repository that is included in ESSs, the e-mails that are filed to the DMS will appear in searches along with other documents.

Another e-mail filing approach is to use a repository that is separate from the DMS. This approach works well if the organization does not have a DMS or if the DMS does not support e-mail storage. Some e-mail-filing products integrate with Outlook and can be configured to tag and file e-mail messages automatically, based on the content of the message and the sender and recipients. If users do not want the system to file messages automatically, the system can be set up to prompt the user to file (and even suggest an appropriate folder location). Once the e-mail messages are filed, they can be retrieved with built-in search tools. Because e-mail messages can contain such valuable substantive information, e-mail filing and retrieval strategies can add great value to your firm's or law department's KM efforts.

9.14 Key Points

- Although many people equate knowledge management with technology, it is important to understand that they are not the same thing. Rather, technology is an enabler of knowledge management in the same way that technology helps other areas accomplish their goals. Some low- or no-tech solutions to KM challenges might be better than a high-tech approach.
- Using technology to leverage your organization's collective wisdom can be effective—and is in some ways necessary—for KM success. Thinking of technology as a tool, such as a windmill that can harness data flows throughout your organization, can magnify the benefit of applying technology solutions to KM problems.
- Intranets (private computer networks) are key technology enablers for KM efforts. They can be the single place where lawyers go to access everything they need to do their work.
- Well-designed intranets can be enormous efficiency boosters, but do not make the mistake of thinking that creating and maintaining them is an easy endeavor. Intranets take planning, time, dedicated people, and good design in order to be truly useful tools.
- User experience (UX) involves how people feel about a product, service, or system. The increased public focus on good UX design—the consumerization of UX—is the direct result of consumer products companies emphasizing good design in their products and services. This has caused a demand for good design in enterprise applications, such as those created by KM professionals.

- The quality of the UX design is a significant factor in how well your KM technologies will be received and adopted by the people in your organization. Good design can dramatically increase adoption, whereas bad design can significantly compromise your KM application efforts.
- An extranet, or client collaboration platform, can be used to provide clients with secure web-based access to documents, matter information, financial information, news, and other information relevant to clients. Providing this type of resource can add more value to the firm–client relationship and make that relationship stronger.
- An enterprise search system (ESS) is a technology tool that can search across multiple data sources within an organization to return relevant search results. An ESS is valuable because it can dramatically decrease the time it takes for employees to find the relevant information needed to perform their work. Typical data repositories that are searched with ESSs include DMSs or document file shares, time and billing databases, matter information databases, and attorney profile collections.
- Search enhancement applications add a layer of metadata to a firm's internal documents, making them more useful. These applications can add case and statutory law links, citation-checking links, and other valuable metadata, making the research and document drafting process much more efficient.
- A wiki is an easily editable, collaborative web page that can be used to capture various information. Wikis can be useful KM tools, because they make information easily accessible and available to members of a group or an entire organization.
- Document automation tools allow you to create templates of commonly used documents and quickly generate finished documents from them by entering variables into an easy-to-use interface. These tools can dramatically reduce the time it takes to prepare documents, while ensuring consistency and quality of the finished product.
- An expert system seeks to replicate or emulate human decision making based on a set of rules that are provided by an actual human subject matter expert. Expert systems can guide users (either internal lawyers or clients) on a particular topic based on the rules provided by the expert

and the variable input provided by the user. These systems leverage the knowledge of subject matter experts so that it can be applied to various situations without the actual input of the expert.

- Search filtering is a feature of search engine applications that can help a user narrow a set of search results—or filter out irrelevant information—making it easier to find the exact information someone is looking for.
- E-mail filing technologies can be very useful in KM efforts, because e-mail messages, which are often considered personal, are increasingly taking the place of more formal communication methods, like letters or faxes. The ability to easily add e-mail messages to digital case files and make them accessible to others—even if they were not recipients of the e-mail message—is an effective way to make important matter information available to those who need access to it.

Chapter 10

The Role of Legal Project Management in Knowledge Management

Let our advance worrying become advance thinking and planning.

—Winston Churchill

10.1 Chapter Preview and Target Audience

Chapter preview:

1. You'll learn the basic principles of legal project management.
2. We'll explore how knowledge management and legal project management support each other.
3. You'll learn what clients want and how legal project management can help you deliver it.
4. We'll outline the basic steps involved in legal project management.
5. You'll learn what KM professionals can do in light of the increasing popularity of legal project management.

Target audience:
This entire chapter should be of great interest to Lawyer Leaders and Administrative Leaders. Because legal project management is such an important and currently popular topic, I recommend that everyone read this chapter thoroughly.

Legal project management (LPM) is currently the hottest topic in law firms, legal departments, and on the conference circuits, but it is a relatively recent phenomenon and nascent discipline. It gained increased popularity shortly after the global economic crisis of 2008, an event that also rekindled interest in knowledge management, as mentioned earlier. This is not a book about legal project management, and there are several good books on the topic that I highly recommend.[1] However, a brief note about LPM is appropriate because (1) there is a great deal of overlap between LPM and KM, and (2) many knowledge management professionals are leading LPM efforts at their organizations.

10.2 What Is Legal Project Management?

Like knowledge management, there is no established definition of legal project management, but there is a reasonable amount of agreement about the nature of it. In essence, LPM is about defining, planning, budgeting, and performing legal work efficiently and effectively.

In their recent book, *Legal Project Management in One Hour for Lawyers*, authors Pamela Woldow and Douglas Richardson, whose work I highly respect, define LPM as "a systematic approach for scoping, planning, managing, and controlling legal work within clearly understood—by both law firm and client—time, budget, and performance requirements that also captures lessons learned after a project is complete in order to enhance

1. Pamela H. Woldow and Douglas B. Richardson, *Legal Project Management in One Hour for Lawyers* (Washington, DC: American Bar Association, 2014); Jim Hassett, *Legal Project Management, Pricing, and Alternative Fee Arrangements: What Firms Are Doing* (Amazon Digital, 2013); and Susan Raridon Lambreth and David A. Rueff Jr., *The Power of Legal Project Management* (Washington, DC: American Bar Association, 2014).

future performance."[2] I like this definition because it is pragmatic, and it helps lawyers understand LPM in the context of *action*—what to do and how to do it.

In his book, *Legal Project Management, Pricing, and Alternative Fee Arrangements: What Firms Are Doing*, Jim Hassett, whose work I also highly respect, takes a different approach and defines LPM more broadly, but perhaps less pragmatically: "Legal project management adapts proven management techniques to the legal profession to help lawyers achieve their business goals, including increasing client value and protecting profitability."[3] Hassett's reference to "proven management techniques" is surely a reference to (non-legal) project management, which is an established field and discipline that has been practiced in many industries, varying from construction to software development, for several decades. The world's premier organization that promotes and provides education on project management, the Project Management Institute, was established in 1969.[4]

There are other good and useful definitions of LPM; Hassett lists some in his book. I point out these definitions not to debate them, but rather to point out the similarities between LPM and KM. In many ways, the two disciplines have very similar—often identical—goals and benefits to lawyers and clients. This will become clearer upon a little deeper investigation into the field of LPM.

Before we go much further, however, I must point out that knowledge management is *not* a "component of the larger discipline of legal project management," as Hassett has articulated.[5] Knowledge management and legal project management are separate disciplines with often overlapping objectives and goals, so it is understandable that some people may equate the two or subordinate one to the other (some believe that LPM is a component of KM, which is also erroneous). To support his statement, Hassett points to examples of firms that have shared and improved preexisting checklists or have developed templates to increase efficiency. Another firm

2. Woldow & Richardson, *Legal Project Management in One Hour*, vii.
3. Hassett, *Legal Project Management, Pricing, and Alternative Fee Arrangements*, 22.
4. http://www.pmi.org/About-Us.aspx.
5. See "Research update on knowledge management: Opinions are split" on Hassett's website, Legal Business Development: http://adverselling.typepad.com/how_law_firms_sell/2013/12/research-update-on-knowledge-management-opinions-are-split.html.

with which Hassett has worked has established an LPM committee "whose mission includes identifying existing firm documents that can be used as templates for future legal projects so that professionals at the firm don't constantly have to reinvent the wheel."[6]

Yes, creating templates and checklists and identifying documents that can be reused are KM activities, but they are just a few examples of KM activities (among many), as we have seen throughout this book. Furthermore, these are basic KM activities, which, although important and fundamental, don't represent the complete value of knowledge management. As I stated in a comment[7] to Hassett's blog post, I would caution that while KM is a key component of LPM, it is not *merely* a component of LPM. Applying one KM activity (e.g., sharing checklists) to the discipline of LPM does not mean that the discipline of KM is solely part of LPM. Rather, the examples point out that KM principles, activities, etc. can be applied to (and greatly benefit) various other initiatives and efforts, including LPM.

10.3 Why Is Legal Project Management Important?

Legal project management helps provide clients with the cost certainty and financial transparency they desire. Two of the fundamental components of LPM, matter budgets and project plans, provide the degree of certainty about legal spend and scope of work that clients want. They also help clients understand the proposed course of action that a lawyer plans to take in a matter. When clients are better informed, they can make better decisions, and they will be more pleased with your legal service.

Many lawyers have historically been reluctant to create budgets and project plans for their matters. There are various reasons, including the popular excuse that "my matters are unique, so it would be impossible to provide an accurate budget or project plan." The reality is that even unique, personalized, or "bespoke" legal work can be budgeted and planned. Probably the

6. Ibid.
7. http://adverselling.typepad.com/how_law_firms_sell/2013/12/research-update-on-knowledge-management-opinions-are-split.html?cid=6a00d8341c72a653ef019b03b66218970c#comment-6a00d8341c72a653ef019b03b66218970c.

main reason that lawyers have not made budgeting and planning matters a standard procedure is that they have never had to. For years, clients have, for the most part, simply accepted the amount charged by their lawyers. If lawyers may simply bill as many hours as they see fit, without considering the cost to clients, assuming that they will be paid for all the time that they spend, then why would any lawyer spend any time preparing something as restrictive as a budget or project plan? These devices could only potentially limit an otherwise virtually unlimited scope and budget for a matter. As we know, however, the days of clients blindly paying lawyers "whatever they charge" are long gone. Clients now want some degree of certainty regarding their legal spend, and they are no longer shy about challenging the amount or propriety of legal fees, thus they are increasingly requiring attorneys to provide budgets and project plans.

Although most firms have been slow to adopt LPM efforts because of the perceived complexity (e.g., they assume that LPM requires sophisticated software), some simpler, low-tech approaches can have profound effects. A simple, effective approach to providing budgets and project plans is to use a template. Because the structure of many legal matters is quite similar in many respects, usually at least the outline of a matter can be formed into a project plan template. In a typical litigation, for example, certain steps will almost always be taken. Experienced lawyers know this, and even in highly specialized matters, some degree of procedure is followed. This procedure makes it possible to create a project plan for most matters. In fact, the American Bar Association (ABA), along with the Association of Corporate Counsel (ACC) and a group of law firms, produced the Uniform Task-Based Management System,[8] a set of standardized codes and task descriptions that are designed to help facilitate the analysis of legal work and fees. These code sets can be downloaded from the ABA website and used as a guide to create a collection of templates for your project plans and budgets. Creating templates from these sets and reusing them for each of your matters is a good, low-tech starting point.

8. http://www.americanbar.org/groups/litigation/resources/uniform_task_based_management_system.html.

10.4 Knowledge Management and Legal Project Management Support Each Other

Lawyers don't typically use the word "project" to describe what they do. Lawyers work on matters or transactions, litigate cases, or do deals, etc. They don't think of these things as projects, but they are. A project is simply an activity or undertaking that is finite—one that has a beginning and an end. Contrast this with a process, which is an ongoing, continuous activity (e.g., a billing department's activity of preparing and sending out bills to clients). As mentioned, the term "legal project management" grew out of the similar, but not identical, field of project management, hence the use of the word "project" to describe what lawyers would typically call something else. If it helps, you can swap out the word "project" with "matter" or "transaction" or whatever you like. In fact, some people in LPM circles have proposed changing the name from legal *project* management to legal *matter* management. This appears to have been a short-lived effort, though, and the use of "project" in LPM has stuck. The point is that LPM is about managing a finite piece of legal work that you perform for a client. As the aforementioned steps indicate, you will start the work, execute it, complete it, and move on to the next project.

If lawyers do, in fact, work on projects, then don't they also manage those projects? The answer is yes—and no. Many lawyers, when introduced to the idea of LPM, declare that "I already do that" or "I already know how to manage a case." This may be true, and some lawyers do manage their legal work well, but most don't do it in a way that fulfills their clients' desires (especially as the desires of clients have changed in recent years). Clients are no longer satisfied with excellent legal work and favorable outcomes. Today, those things are expected and even assumed—they are "table stakes," as the popular expression goes. Increasingly, especially in the current competitive environment, clients want more.

What do clients want? As Woldow and Richardson succinctly put it, they want value, efficiency, predictability, improved communication, understanding of their business, and alignment of their interests with the lawyer's actions.[9] Looking at what clients want, it is clear to see that LPM and KM

9. Woldow & Richardson, *Legal Project Management in One Hour*, ix.

have overlapping purposes and goals. How can KM and LPM contribute to providing clients with what they want in the environment of the new normal? Let's review what clients want and how LPM and KM can help provide it:

- *Value.* Value doesn't mean cheap or inexpensive. Value is about what something is worth. Most clients don't want to take advantage of their lawyers or get something for nothing. Most are willing to pay a fair price for excellent service and results. KM and LPM seek to help lawyers deliver that excellent service and results in the most efficient way possible. From the KM and LPM perspectives, delivering value is about delivering more than what's expected—more than just table stakes.
- *Efficiency.* We've discussed efficiency throughout this book, as it is a fundamental aspect of knowledge management. It is about achieving maximum productivity with minimum wasted effort or expense. Avoiding the reinvention of the wheel by reusing work product is among the most basic ways that KM can help with efficiency. Implementing KM technology tools is another approach that helps lawyers be more efficient. LPM can help lawyers be more efficient not only by incorporating KM approaches in the execution phase, but also by proper planning, scoping, and monitoring. On a broader scale, the post-project reviews (or after-action reviews, in KM parlance) can be a time for lawyers to review what they did and come up with new and more efficient ways to approach future work.
- *Improved communication.* Improving communication is another fundamental part of KM that overlaps with LPM efforts. Recall the theme of connections when describing what KM is about. Connecting people with people—both internally and externally—is one of the main goals of KM. Connecting attorneys with each other, but also connecting attorneys with their clients, is the focus. KM addresses this in many ways, from low tech to high tech. Simply creating and reusing matter reporting templates is an example of an easy way to apply KM principles. At the higher-tech end of the spectrum, KM teams are often responsible for creating collaborative environments, such as extranets

or client collaboration platforms, to link attorneys with their clients for more efficient and effective communication. From an LPM perspective, you will see as follows, where we address the basic steps of LPM, how communication is a central theme that pervades almost every step of the LPM cycle.

- *Understanding a client's business.* KM assists attorneys in understanding a client's business in many ways. The KM themes of providing "the right information to the right people at the right time," helping attorneys and teams develop "what we know" about clients, and connecting attorneys with information about clients and their businesses are, again, fundamental components of KM. This can be accomplished via the on-demand services of a KM researcher or practice support lawyer, or through establishing client information centers or news and information feeds on intranet client sites. LPM reinforces this theme by seeking to promote the attitude of partnering with clients, rather than merely doing work for clients. An attorney who partners with a client looks out for that client in all aspects of the client's business, rather than merely seeking to complete the work for which he or she was retained.
- *Alignment of interests.* Alignment of a client's interests and a firm's behaviors can manifest itself in many ways. As the old adage goes, clients don't have legal problems, they have business problems. Your business clients are concerned with conducting their business. No businessperson ever wants to hire a lawyer, but it is often a necessary evil. Laws and regulations (and sometimes disputes) can get in the way of conducting business. Law firms are businesses, too, and lawyers make money when clients hire them to help them with legal issues that arise from conducting their business. A lawyer might seek short-term gains by overlawyering a matter (e.g., spending excessive time on a matter to "win" the case when a quick, cheap settlement would be the better strategy for the client from a *business* perspective). This approach may put more money in the lawyer's pocket now, but if a lawyer does not operate with the goal of aligning his or her interests with the client's interests, then the relationship with surely be short-lived. LPM and KM

can help align interests by, among other things, employing the principles discussed earlier.

Let's take a deeper look at legal project management, what it's all about from a more practical perspective, and why KM professionals should learn more about it.

10.5 The Basic Steps of Legal Project Management

Many legal project management authors and proponents have mapped out the recommended steps to take when applying the principles of LPM. Although there are different approaches,[10] it is helpful to outline the fundamental steps. Keep in mind that, as with knowledge management, you must select the steps and approaches that are appropriate for you and your firm. There is no all-purpose option when it comes to how to do legal project management. Woldow and Richardson succinctly outline the five general steps of LPM: (1) defining, (2) planning, (3) executing, (4) monitoring/measuring, and (5) reviewing. The following excerpt is reprinted with permission from their book, *Legal Project Management in One Hour for Lawyers*, available from the ABA Law Practice Division:[11]

The Five Steps of Legal Project Management

1. Defining Project Objectives and Scope
    - Information gathering to understand the client's business, needs, and expectations
    - Discussions with the client to agree upon project phases, deliverables, and desired outcomes
    - Discussing project scope, time, and cost
    - Agreeing on billing arrangements
    - Discussing possible events or risks that may impact the engagement

10. See, e.g., Chapter 4 of Hassett's book, *Legal Project Management, Pricing, and Alternative Fee Arrangements: What Firms Are Doing*, in which he outlines the approaches of nine law firms.
11. Woldow & Richardson, *Legal Project Management in One Hour*, 2–3.

2. Project Planning
   - Defining the project phases, tasks, and performance standards
   - Developing timelines and milestones
   - Selecting the project team (firm side and client side)
   - Budgeting
   - Getting appropriate tools in place
   - Planning communications
   - Planning approaches for handling unexpected events and risks
3. Executing the Plan: Doing the Legal Work
   - Deploying the right lawyers to the right tasks
   - Making task assignments and delegating authority effectively
   - Giving timely, objective, and specific feedback
   - Managing team performance, dynamics, and morale
   - Ensuring collaborative team and client communication
4. Monitoring and Measuring Progress
   - Tracking progress of phases and tasks
   - Avoiding scope creep, bottlenecks, redundancies, or other inefficiencies
   - Tracking budget-to-actual
   - Making project adjustments when unexpected events occur
5. Post-Project Review
   - Evaluating outcomes in terms of agreed project scope
   - Identifying what went well and what needs improvement next time
   - Discussions with client to give and get real-time feedback
   - Identifying lessons learned, resources needed, and surprises that can be avoided
   - Aligning post-project review with the firm's knowledge management function to aggregate cumulative learning and put it in a form accessible to all in the future

Reviewing the steps involved in legal project management, you'll immediately notice obvious overlap between LPM and KM. Central KM themes are clear: information gathering and distribution, improving communication by discussing and clearly defining the work and plans to accomplish it, increasing efficiency in executing legal work, capturing data about the progress of the work and budget, and reviewing the overall engagement with the goal of improving future matters.

10.6 What Should Knowledge Management Professionals Do in Light of the Rise of LPM?

Knowledge management professionals have a unique opportunity to lead LPM efforts, or at the very least, to collaborate to help them succeed. The overlap between the goals and objectives of KM and LPM make KM professionals a perfect fit. At many firms, including mine, Ogletree Deakins, KM professionals are leading the LPM charge. At others, including several profiled in this book, LPM is a part of the KM department or it falls under the direction of the head of knowledge management.[12]

In many firms, LPM is at a similar maturity level as KM was several years ago—finding its footing and figuring out how to make it work. For those firms that have been through the growing pains of KM, those experiences and lessons learned can help in your LPM efforts. For those firms that have not yet started KM or LPM initiatives, this is a great opportunity to approach both fields simultaneously, to unify the efforts and make an even more profound difference than with KM efforts alone.

10.7 Key Points

- There is a great deal of overlap between legal project management and knowledge management.
- LPM is about defining, planning, budgeting, and performing legal work efficiently and effectively.
- LPM can help lawyers provide the value-added services and deliverables that clients are increasingly demanding, such as cost certainty/predictability, transparency, improved communication, and understanding of the client's business.
- Many KM professionals are leading LPM efforts at their organizations.
- The increasing popularity of LPM initiatives creates opportunities for KM professionals.

12. See examples in Appendix B: Milena Higgins of Fish & Richardson; Mara Nickerson of Osler, Hoskin & Harcourt; Charlotte Logullo of Foley & Lardner; Felicity Badcock of King & Wood Mallesons; Steven Lastres of Debevoise & Plimpton; Lisa Gianakos of Pillsbury Winthrop.

Chapter 11

The Future of Knowledge Management in the Legal Profession

Prediction is very difficult, especially if it's about the future.

—Niels Bohr

11.1 Chapter Preview and Target Audience

Chapter preview:

1. You'll learn why I believe that knowledge management will continue to flourish in the legal industry.
2. We'll explore how a spirit of innovation and entrepreneurship, combined with a new social-sharing mindset, will keep KM a relevant and important discipline well into the future.
3. You'll see how advances in technology will support KM, and how client demands will be the fuel that drives KM innovation into the future.

Target audience:
This chapter will be of great interest to Lawyer Leaders and Administrative Leaders. After all, who wouldn't want to know about the future?

I'm reluctant to make any predictions about the future of knowledge management, because in the worst-case scenario, I'll be completely wrong, and in the best, we'll all shrug and say, "Well, that was obvious." One prediction that I feel comfortable making, however, is that by the time this book goes to print, or at least by the time you read it, some of my predictions will have seen the light of day. To paraphrase William Gibson, in some ways, the future of knowledge management is already here—it's just not very evenly distributed.[1]

The field of knowledge management has come a long way in a relatively short period. From a legal industry perspective, there have been fits and starts, times of great interest, and times when some have declared KM dead (I hope that after 10 chapters, we can agree that KM is alive and kicking!). As one KM colleague noted, perhaps nothing has been better for the health of KM than the global economic crisis of 2008 (and beyond) and the ushering in of the current (and perhaps permanent) state that we call the new normal.

I believe that one reason for the longevity and resiliency of KM over the years is the nature of the people who are drawn to the field. Knowledge management professionals are an innovative and entrepreneurial bunch. They seek out new and better ways to do things. They are not satisfied with the status quo. They seek constant improvement. As entrepreneurs, they search for change, respond to it, and exploit it as an opportunity.[2] This is a fundamental reason that the future of KM is so bright.

11.2 Collaboration and Interaction

It is difficult to talk about the future without talking about technology. But the future of KM is not *just* dependent on advances in technology, although such advances will certainly play a significant role. There is an underlying factor that I believe is equally—and perhaps more—important. That is the nature of how people interact and work. With the popularity and proliferation of social media and social networking, we are seeing a change in the way people interact and behave. People are becoming more collaborative and willing to share. People are more forthcoming with information that, in

1. William Gibson (paraphrased), http://en.wikiquote.org/wiki/William_Gibson.
2. Peter F. Drucker, *Innovation and Entrepreneurship* (New York: HarperBusiness, 2006).

a bygone era, was once considered better kept confidential. Helping others and sharing information is becoming the new default behavior. This new mindset, characterized by collaborating, cooperating, and sharing information and ideas, is the breeding ground on which knowledge management thrives and grows. This cultural shift, on a societal scale, is a factor that will predispose younger generations (some of whom are already law students and in the workforce) to embrace knowledge management.

There is also an indication of the mindset change in the way we are training our future lawyers. Several law schools have programs that stress the importance of innovation and try to prepare our future lawyers for a different kind of legal industry:

- Suffolk University Law School offers a concentration in Legal Technology and Innovation. The university's website describes the program as follows: "The concentration—which is similar to a major—will prepare students for 21st century legal employment with specialized courses on important legal innovations and technologies, such as automated document assembly, legal project management (LPM), knowledge management and virtual lawyering."[3]
- The Georgetown University Law Center has a Technology Innovation and Law Practice Practicum that culminates with a competition called Iron Tech Lawyer, in which students create and demonstrate applications and vie for prizes for Excellence in Design, Excellence in Presentation, and the all-around best app.[4]
- Fordham University Law School offers a course called Law Firm as a Business, which includes lectures on knowledge management and legal project management.[5]
- Vermont Law School has a Center for Legal Innovation whose curriculum includes topics such as legal document automation and legal project management.[6]

3. http://www.suffolk.edu/news/26454.php#.VT-p7YH3aK0.
4. http://www.law.georgetown.edu/academics/centers-institutes/legal-profession/legal-technologies/iron-tech/index.cfm.
5. http://law.fordham.edu/registrar/17003.htm.
6. http://www.vermontlaw.edu/Academics/Focused_Studies/Center_for_Legal_Innovation.htm.

These are just a few examples of law schools focusing on the future of the practice of law. You can read about others in the ABA Law Practice Magazine article, "Teaching the Technology of Practice: The 10 Top Schools," by Richard Granat and Marc Lauritsen.[7]

11.3 Social Media versus Knowledge Management

Given the cultural shift described earlier, it is ironic that some people believe that knowledge management is dead because social media has effectively replaced it. In reality the opposite is true: KM has been enhanced and will become even more well-developed *because* of social media. The desire to pit social media against knowledge management is based on the misunderstanding that the two are contradictory. Specifically, some people mistakenly believe that knowledge management is about managing and controlling information while social media is about letting information flow freely.[8] Despite the misleading word "management" in the name, those who have read this far know that KM does not attempt to manage or control information or knowledge in the way that a casual observer, or one with a cursory understanding of KM, might think. Knowledge management has always been about connecting people and their knowledge to advance business objectives. There is no prescription in knowledge management that some knowledge overlord or gatekeeper decides who can share what with whom. To the contrary, KM promotes the same free flow of knowledge and information as social media.

The key difference between knowledge management and social media is the domain in which each originated. Knowledge management is an institutional endeavor. It is concerned (among other things, as we have seen) with connecting people with others to drive efficiency within a particular organization or enterprise. Social media, on the other hand, evolved on the

7. Richard Granat and Marc Lauritsen, "Teaching the Technology of Practice: The Top 10 Schools," http://www.americanbar.org/publications/law_practice_magazine/2014/july-august/teaching-the-technology-of-practice-the-10-top-schools.html.
8. Anthony J. Bradley and Mark P. McDonald, "Social Media versus Knowledge Management," *Harvard Business Review*, October 26, 2011, https://hbr.org/2011/10/social-media-versus-knowledge.

Internet and is about connecting and sharing with anyone and everyone, mainly without limitations.[9]

One way in which social media will help the development of knowledge management is through the adoption of social media and social networking application features into the internal applications that are used in law firms and law departments. These applications are core components of social networking websites like LinkedIn, Facebook, and Twitter. They include the ability to easily share digital content, reshare that content, endorse—or "like"—that content, and comment on and discuss the content with others. Another key feature of social networking applications is the ability to build and share information about yourself in a profile. Lawyers are most familiar with this in the context of LinkedIn, but other social networking applications, such as Facebook, Twitter, and others, allow profiles as well. Sharing information about yourself through a profile encourages interaction and facilitates collaboration and information sharing.

Although some progressive law firms and law departments are already adopting social media features in their organizations, this practice is still in its infancy. As enterprise-class software continues to develop and emulate consumer-grade web-based applications, we will see increased adoption of social media features in applications used by law firms and law departments. This will not diminish the importance of knowledge management in the future, but rather, like other technological advances, it will be an enabler—and even a catalyst—of knowledge management.

11.4 Technological Advances

Advances in technology will also certainly have a profound effect on the future of knowledge management. I won't go so far as to predict the near-term massive proliferation of robot lawyers or tacit knowledge-extraction devices that attach to our temples (sounds painful), but even current

9. Some social media applications limit their scope or reach to particular groups, but for most social media applications, such limitations are subfeatures of the main applications. For example, the default nature of Twitter is for users to post messages that can be read by any other Twitter member, but users may also send private messages to other Twitter users.

technology is giving us clues about where we may find ourselves in the relatively near future. The most notable example is IBM's Watson supercomputer.

IBM piqued the interest of many KM professionals when it announced the Watson supercomputer, which uses artificial intelligence and natural language-processing technology to (among other things) answer questions posed in natural language rather than terms connected with Boolean operators (e.g., and, or, not). Watson became famous after beating two champion players on the television quiz show *Jeopardy!* in 2011. Soon, Watson was adapted to commercial uses in the healthcare industry for cancer treatment, the financial industry, in retail, and even in the art of creating unique food recipes.

The IBM Watson Group is a new business unit, based in New York City's Silicon Alley and funded with more than $1 billion, dedicated to the development of innovative ways to commercialize uses of the company's supercomputer.[10] What does this mean for knowledge management at law firms? Probably the most basic (if it could be considered basic) or at least straightforward application of Watson is to replace—and far surpass—the enterprise search function that many law firms use today. Today's enterprise search technologies are impressive, but they pale in comparison to what could be accomplished with Watson's artificial intelligence technology. If Watson could process 200 million pages of structured and unstructured data for its *Jeopardy!* challenge to answer questions related to general knowledge, then certainly it could ingest every legal textbook, treatise, statute, regulation, court opinion, and other piece of legal research ever published to answer questions that frequently come up in the practice of law. Watson could also process every piece of legal work product prepared by a law firm, analyze it, and spit out answers to legal issues both simple and complex. By the time you read this, I predict that at least one law firm will have announced just that, if not something more ambitious.

In fact, we may be closer than we think. In early 2015, a team of students from the University of Toronto showed the potential of Watson in

10. "IBM Forms New Watson Group to Meet Growing Demand for Cognitive Innovations," January 9, 2014, https://www-03.ibm.com/press/us/en/pressrelease/42867.wss.

the legal profession when they won second place in IBM's Watson University Competition.[11] The students built a Watson-powered application, called ROSS, which analyzes massive amounts of unstructured data from legal documents, statutes, court opinions, and so on, and answers legal research questions posed to it in natural language. The system—sort of like a super-charged Lexis or Westlaw—provides a rating to tell the user how confident it is with the answer. The user gives the system feedback on the answer with a simple thumbs-up or thumbs-down, which ROSS uses to get smarter. ROSS's creators, who have already turned their competition entry into a startup business, refer to it as "an artificially intelligent attorney," which learns and becomes more accurate the more it is used.[12] It won't be long before ROSS is in the hands of lawyers and perhaps even nonlawyers. That is, unless the nascent company and its robot lawyer gets acquired by one of the big legal research providers or some other opportunistic player seeking to disrupt the industry.

Another application of Watson that will likely surface in law firms sooner rather than later is what IBM calls The Debater, which was announced in May 2014. This iteration of Watson is designed to construct arguments, both pro and con, based on a given set of data that is made available to the system. If Watson consumes every federal statute, regulation, court opinion, treatise, etc., could it be used to help attorneys construct arguments in preparation for appearances before the Supreme Court? Could this technology be used in a courtroom during a trial to test potential objections before making them, and indicate the likelihood that the objection will be overruled or sustained? Will this technology be banned from courtrooms, as Internet-connected devices once were, because it could give one side an unfair advantage?

Although it is unlikely that Watson, or similar artificial intelligence technology, will soon replace attorneys entirely, it is not unreasonable to think that they may replace some functions of associate attorneys. This would not be the first time for this to happen. When I first started practicing law as a litigation associate, I frequently found myself in large conference rooms

11. "IBM Awards University of Texas at Austin Top Spot in Watson Competition," https://www-03.ibm.com/press/us/en/pressrelease/45861.wss.
12. http://www.rossintelligence.com.

surrounded by bankers boxes full of paper documents to review, separating the relevant from the irrelevant. In those early years, no computers or sophisticated software were involved. But slowly, over the years, as the volume of digital documents increased, and it became far too expensive to have attorneys doing manual document review, computer-assisted document review became popular. This was followed soon by filtering and "predictive coding," or the ability of software to learn how to classify documents, so that attorney reviewers can focus on documents that are likely relevant.

Some people may fear (rationally or not) robot lawyers stealing the jobs of law school graduates, but it is just as likely that the "legal robot revolution" will create jobs. These may not be traditional law firm associate attorney jobs as we know them today, but they may involve other functions that will be just as important (and perhaps as lucrative). Just as advances in technology have a way of creatively destroying some things, they also destructively create other things, including opportunities for savvy law firms to differentiate themselves from their competition.

The rise of electronic discovery again provides a good example. Although electronic review and predictive coding of litigation documents arguably took work away from young associates who once flipped through piles of paper for days and weeks on end, these technologies also gave rise to "e-discovery attorneys," litigation support analysts, and even entire law firm practice groups that focus on this litigation subspecialty. Just search the Web for "e-discovery practice group," and you'll see dozens of examples. In fact, in 2010, one consultancy's research found that "87 of the AmLaw 200 firms have an area or practice group dedicated to handling e-discovery matters."[13]

But what do these advances in technology mean for the professional development of attorneys? How will recent law school graduates learn how to hone their research skills when they can simply answer most legal questions as easily as I can know the square root of pi by using a calculator (or the calculator app on my iPhone)? How will young associates learn how to be effective law firm partners? How can we save the legal profession as we know it from complete disruption and even death? All of these questions

13. Bob Ambrogi, "Of the AmLaw 200 Firms, 87 Have an E-Discovery Practice Group," October 18, 2010, Catalyst, http://www.catalystsecure.com/blog/2010/10/of-the-amlaw-200-firms-87-have-an-e-discovery-practice-group/.

assume that the practice of law today will be substantially similar to the practice of law in the future. They assume that it will be important for law school graduates to have good research skills. They assume that partnership (or its equivalent) will be a desired—or viable—business construct for future generations of legal professionals. They assume that it is desirable to save the legal profession as we know it.

Most practicing lawyers would likely argue that most of these assumptions are sound, but many consumers of legal services would welcome a legal services paradigm shift. Most consumers don't care how a service provider arrives at positive results. If a provider can do it faster and cheaper, then consumers won't likely care if the service was provided by an Ivy League graduate or a piece of silicon. And just as nobody ever shed a tear for the declining ranks of bowling alley pinsetters, switchboard operators, bookbinders, and travel agents, the changing (and likely declining) role of legal professionals—including lawyers—will likely be met with dry eyes.

11.5 Client Demands

It's probably safe to assume that the legal industry will survive (and thrive) for quite some time in ways that are at least vaguely similar to its current form. That does not mean, however, that there will not be changes in what clients expect from their lawyers. We don't need a crystal ball to know that clients will likely continue to demand more for less when it comes to legal services. For years, lawyers have heard the cries from clients demanding greater value for their legal spend. These cries are not likely to stop and will probably grow more intense.

Clients also continue to demand pricing options, such as fixed or guaranteed pricing. If a matter is based on a fixed price, then the only way for a lawyer to make a profit is to spend less money executing the work than the lawyer received to complete it. Knowledge management's role in ensuring efficient handling of matters can help ensure profitability on such matters. In fact, there is no greater direct relationship between increased efficiency and increased profits than when a matter is guaranteed to be completed at a fixed cost. If KM efforts can help a lawyer complete a matter in 10 hours that would otherwise have taken 20, then the profit margin more than doubles (assuming a profit margin was built into the 20-hour budget). Each minute saved as a result of the efficiencies gained from knowledge management is pure profit.

This is another key reason that the future of knowledge management is bright. As we have seen throughout this book, the primary purpose of knowledge management is to improve the efficiency with which lawyers do their work and deliver legal services to their clients while maintaining or increasing quality. Greater efficiency means more for less, which means happier clients. But some might say that efficiency has its limits; you can only squeeze so much wastefulness out of a process or activity before it has reached its peak of efficiency. That's true, and that's when the shift in focus must go from efficiency (i.e., doing things right) to effectiveness (i.e., doing the right things). As Peter Drucker noted, "there is nothing quite so useless, as doing with great efficiency, something that should not be done at all." So, in some ways, the future is not as much about finding a better solution to a problem as it is about eliminating the need to solve the problem in the first place. However, with new ways of doing things comes the opportunity to make the new ways we do them more efficient. There is always room for improvement, and knowledge management can help.

11.6 Key Points

- One of the fundamental reasons that KM has become so popular and that it will continue to be important in the legal profession is because of the innovative and entrepreneurial nature of the people who are drawn to the field.
- Changes in the way people live and work—how they increasingly interact and collaborate—are significant factors in the future of knowledge management. Law schools have even begun to offer courses that emphasize the importance of knowledge management, legal project management, technology, and innovation.

- Contrary to some theories, social media will not destroy knowledge management. In fact, social media and KM share similar characteristics, and the increasing popularity of social media will boost the importance of KM.
- Advances in technology, such as artificial intelligence, will have a great impact on the way we practice law and on the importance of knowledge management. As they have in the past, technological improvements will further enable knowledge management and help make us all more efficient and effective legal professionals.
- Client demands for improved efficiency, better outcomes, and greater value will be the primary factors that drive lawyers to accept change and embrace knowledge management.

Appendix A

Additional Law Firm Knowledge Management Organizational Structures

In Chapter 4, we looked at the organizational structures of several law firm knowledge management departments. Following are some additional descriptions of law firm KM department organizational structures.

Addleshaw Goddard, LLP

Addleshaw Goddard, LLP[1] is a U.K.-based international law firm with approximately 700 lawyers and other fee earners. The firm began its formal KM efforts when Mark Gould became Head of Knowledge Management in September 2006. Previously, the firm had engaged in KM efforts in various ways but in a less formal manner. In fact, Gould started with the firm as a Professional Support Lawyer (PSL) in the firm's competition/commercial law practice in April 2001, fresh from a long career as a legal academic. Read Gould's personal KM story in Appendix B.

Gould left the firm in May 2014, and his role has not been replaced. Although he was Head of KM there, he reported to the firm's Chief Operating Officer, then to a Director of Knowledge & Learning, and most

1. http://www.addleshawgoddard.com/.

recently, to the Quality Partner (see Figure A.1). When he left, the firm reverted to its previous KM arrangements for the time being. What follows is a description of the situation before May 2014. In addition to leading the firm's 20 PSLs and KM-aligned paralegals, Gould was also a key member of the firm's Quality Team and played a key role on several major project and program boards.

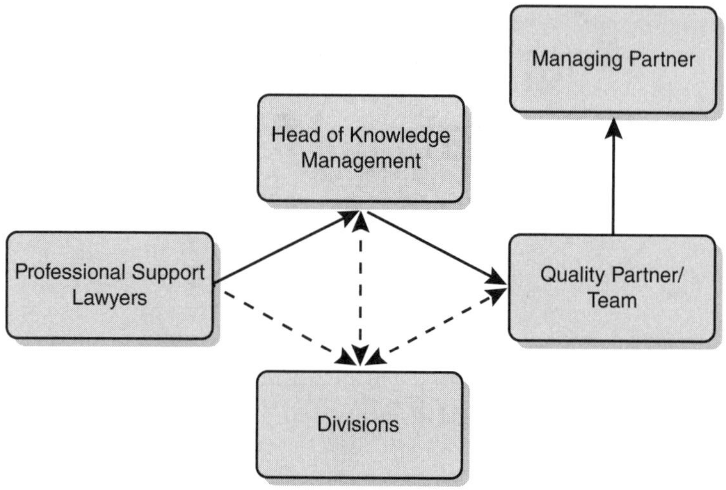

Figure A.1
Addleshaw Goddard knowledge management structure.

In comparison to most U.S.-based law firms, 20 PSLs sounds like a very large group of non-revenue-generating lawyers. However, the PSL role is much more common in the United Kingdom, where firms typically have larger KM lawyer teams than they do in the United States. Although they are expensive, such PSL teams add great value that simply cannot be replaced by technology tools.

From a substantive law perspective, Addleshaw Goddard's KM team works hand in hand with the firm's practice groups. All of the PSLs are budgeted and managed as a central resource, but each of them works almost exclusively within a practice group. In effect, this results in joint management: The practice groups dictate *what* each PSL should prioritize (what would generate most value for the practice group), and Gould defines *how* those things should be done. Gould also manages some of the "what" when the PSLs are engaged in joint projects outside practice group control. Because a key driver for the firm's knowledge work is to reduce the firm's risk profile, the KM group works closely with the Risk team. That group is very similar to the KM group in that it comprises lawyers with practice experience who now focus on supporting the business of the firm.

From a business services perspective, Gould's KM group collaborates with the Information Technology department, which is responsible for supporting all of the firm's technology systems. Each of those systems has a business owner, and Gould owns some of those, including internal and client-focused collaboration systems, the intranet, and the extranet. The other key collaboration in terms of delivery of legal services is with Business Development. In this respect, the PSLs often draw on their expertise when working on client initiatives, and they may be called on by Business Development to support pitches and tenders.

The firm also has a growing Business Transformation group, which is focused on developing process maps and legal project management. The KM group works closely with that group, as the knowledge team is often the destination for those activities when they transition from active to completed projects. The PSLs work closely with the firm's Research Services team, which covers core legal and business research and manages information resources, and the Learning & Development team, which is responsible for all skills-based training across the firm, for lawyers and others. The Head of KM coordinates activities with those groups and ensures that they are aligned with each other.

Gould also shared his thoughts on the principles that guide KM efforts at his firm. He noted that a regular review of guiding principles is important to keep in line with the needs of the firm. As noted earlier, this is good advice and crucial to success in knowledge management. He offered the following statement:

> The overall purpose of our knowledge and PSL activities is to contribute directly to improvements in (1) divisional and firm-wide profit margins, (2) quality of work and service delivery, and (3) the firm's risk profile. In a way, that is consistent with the firm's purpose: Enabling our clients and people to succeed and flourish.

Faegre Baker Daniels, LLP

Shawn Swearingen[2] is the Director of Client Technology Solutions and Knowledge Management at Faegre Baker Daniels, LLP, a large law firm with 750 attorneys in 13 offices in the United States, the United Kingdom, and Asia.[3] FaegreBD's KM department officially launched in January 2011, but before that the firm was engaged in KM activities under the department name of Practice Support and Advocacy. This name change to include "knowledge management" either in the department name or in the titles of some department members is a growing phenomenon and indicates the growing popularity of KM in law firms.

Swearingen has been the head of KM since the establishment of the department. Before that she was the predecessor-department's Practice Support and Advocacy Manager since September 2008. Her background in libraries, primarily law libraries, has served her well in her KM leadership role. "I started as a research librarian and then was a director of a law firm library," said Swearingen. "I made the switch into more of a technology/knowledge management role in the fall of 2008." A background as a research librarian can be quite beneficial in law firm KM departments, because it provides an understanding of substantive legal issues and concepts, which helps KM professionals communicate more effectively with the lawyers they seek to help. Swearingen's educational background also serves her well in her role. She has an undergraduate degree in English and a Master's of Library & Information Science, and she is a Certified Knowledge Manager through the Knowledge Management Institute. KM certifications are rare in the legal industry but more common in other industries.

KM Department Organizational Structure

Swearingen reports to the firm's Chief Information Officer, and her KM team comprises 10 members. She is also a member of the firm's Technology Advisory Group, Professional Development Advisory Group, and the

2. http://www.linkedin.com/pub/shawn-swearingen/36/8a6/490.
3. http://www.faegrebd.com.

Legal Process Improvement Working Group. The teams within the KM department are as follows:

The Practice Support Team is led by a Practice Support Manager and consists of five people who are responsible for the firm intranet and extranets.

The Contact Relationship Management Team has three members who all report to Swearingen. The CRM team is responsible for client/prospect data and supports the Business Development and Marketing department.

The Knowledge Management Team is the smallest group, with one person responsible for knowledge-sharing tools and processes (other than intranet/extranet/CRM). The main focus is on the firm's document management system, document drafting, collaboration, and the like.

The KM department also has two dedicated SharePoint developers and a host of other software developers who work with the KM teams, but they are not a part of the KM department. (See Figure A.2.)

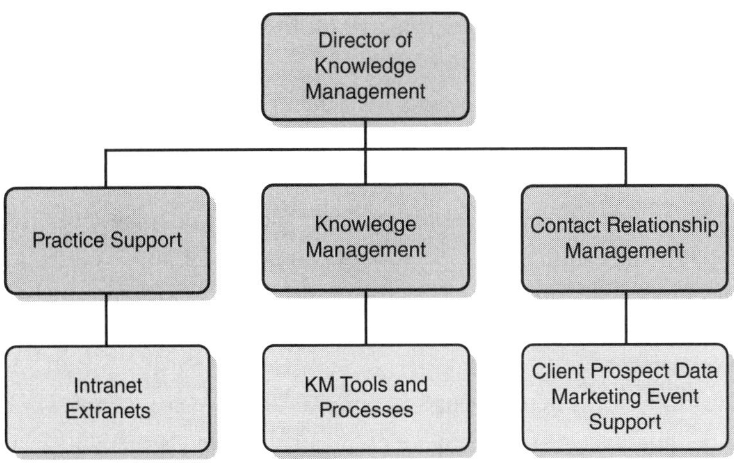

Figure A.2
Faegre Baker Daniels knowledge management structure.

The FaegreBD KM department collaborates regularly with many of the other firm departments. The level and degree of collaboration depends on the projects that are underway at any given time. "Across the board though, we most often collaborate with the rest of our technology organization," Swearingen said. "Outside of technology, business development and marketing department would be a close second. The KM department works with all operational/legal/consulting teams to find solutions to meet needs." As KM can be amorphous and have projects and responsibilities that overlap with many other law firm departments, this is not surprising.

KM Principles at FaegreBD

Swearingen articulated a familiar theme about approaching KM from a law firm perspective. She stated: "At the core of what we do is connecting people to the knowledge they need to do their jobs more efficiently and effectively so we can deliver cost-effective and high-quality services to our clients." The following three components are critical to FaegreBD's KM work and philosophy:

- *People.* The firm's value lies within the deep and varied knowledge possessed by our people. Our people are our main source and consumers of knowledge. The KM team focuses on promoting an environment where the members of the firm are able to share and reuse both explicit and tacit knowledge.
- *Process.* The KM team works with members of the firm to offer best practices and guidance on the processes for capturing, storing, applying, and reusing knowledge, and also for innovating.
- *Technology.* Often, the people and the process need to be supported by technology, which allows knowledge to be found and accessed wherever it resides. The technological tools are the most visible aspect of our work, but without people and process, it would not exist.

FaegreBD's KM department and approaches are nice examples of how, with the guidance of some fundamental concepts and principles, KM can be deployed and sustained. It also shows that KM is not a one-size-fits-all proposition. What works at FaegreBD may not work at your law firm or in your legal department.

Foley & Lardner, LLP

Foley & Lardner is a large international law firm with more than 850 attorneys and 20 offices. The firm's KM efforts are led by Charlotte Logullo, the Director of Practice & Client Solutions. The firm had been engaging in KM activities for several years, but the official efforts began in August 2011, when the firm implemented a new strategic plan.

Although the department is called Practice & Client Solutions (P&CS), its work is rooted in knowledge management, and as Logullo reports, "the group name was created not without some careful thought and much discussion." The decision to avoid the KM label for the department was based on the varying levels of understanding of the nature of KM at the time. This practice of avoiding the term "knowledge management" is not too common, but it has been adopted by some firms, especially those who have had failed attempts at KM efforts in the past (which was not the case at Foley). Nevertheless, as evidenced by the department's vision and mission statements, they are clearly focused on knowledge management:

- *Vision.* Improving efficiency by reducing the need to rediscover knowledge. Leveraging Foley & Lardner's collective knowledge through systems and processes to support and facilitate the identification, capture, dissemination, and use of the firm's knowledge to meet our business objectives.
- *Mission.* Focus on knowledge management as a core competence in order to succeed in the next decade by providing our clients and lawyers with the content and process that maximize our ability to:
  a. Provide greater efficiency and process improvements for monitoring and effectively managing legal matters
  b. Access, utilize, and integrate the knowledge bases existing within and outside of the Firm
  c. Develop and utilize best practices
  d. Foster collaboration with clients

Logullo reports to the firm's Chief Information Officer and has five employees in her department. The department's organization chart is depicted in Figure A.3. A P&CS Consultant (supported by a Web Content Specialist) reports directly to Logullo and focuses on technology tools. Knowledge management, process improvement, analysis, and legal project management (LPM) efforts are led by a KM analyst, who also reports to Logullo. This group collaborates with and supports the firm's Pricing Director and Department Operating Officer, leading LPM objectives for Alternative Fee Arrangement (AFA) clients. In addition, they work with assigned KM Liaison Attorneys assigned by each practice group. Finally, the group includes a Technology Communications Consultant, who is responsible for marketing the use of business technology systems, building awareness programs, and special projects.

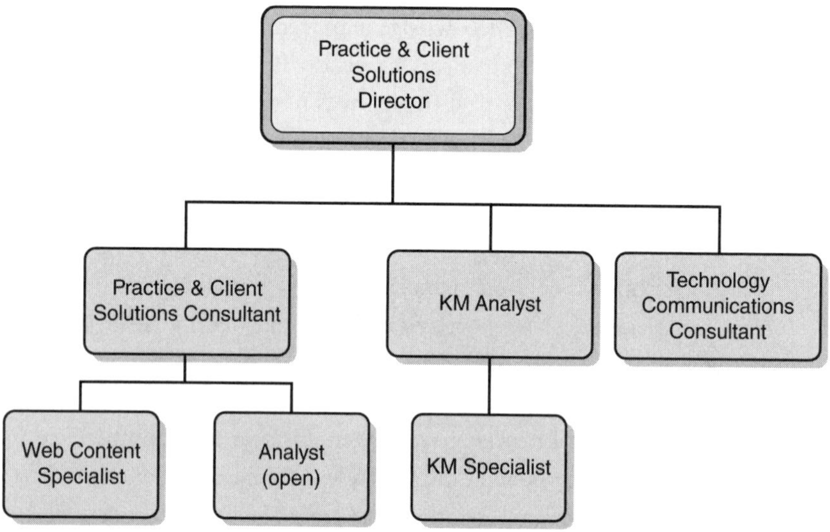

Figure A.3
Foley & Lardner knowledge management structure.

Because of the nature of their work, the P&CS department collaborates extensively with the Technology department. In addition to the main P&CS team, there are three software developers and a web system manager who report to the Technology department, but whose work is mostly dedicated to the work of the P&CS department.

Although the Research & Information Services department (Library) is not under P&CS, they liaise with this group on numerous projects. That department is led by the Director of Research & Information Services, who reports to the Chief Operating Officer. The group consists of eight research librarians, two competitive intelligence analysts, and nine technical services librarians.

In addition to running the P&CS department, Logullo is also a member of the firm's Technology Leadership, Firm Research & Development Committee (R&D), and Legal Project Management Steering Committee.

Foley clearly values interdepartmental collaboration. This is evident because the P&CS department frequently collaborates with Department Operating Officers, Marketing and Business Development, Professional Development (Training), Information Governance (Professional Responsibility & Compliance), Finance & Accounting, and the firm's Chief Strategy Officer on several firm-wide initiatives.

Fox Rothschild, LLP

Fox Rothschild, LLP is a national law firm with more than 630 attorneys practicing in 20 U.S. offices.[4] The Chief Knowledge Officer, Catherine Monte, leads the firm's KM department. Monte's background is as a paralegal and librarian, and she holds a BA in English and a Master's degree in Library Science (see her personal KM story in Appendix B). Monte started with Fox Rothschild in 2000 after previous roles as Head of Information Services at Clifford Chance, Head of Reference Services at Dewey Ballantine, Reference Librarian at Pepper Hamilton & Scheetz, and paralegal at Drinker, Biddle & Reath. These varied roles prepared her well to lead the KM efforts at Fox Rothschild.

Although she has been with Fox since 2000, she acquired the CKO title in 2006, a few years after the department name changed to Knowledge Management Services. Fox's Firmwide Managing Partner recognized Monte's

4. http://www.foxrothschild.com.

previous KM experience and made the forward-thinking decision to change the name of the department to better reflect the services that it offered.

Knowledge Management Organizational Structure

There is a dual-reporting structure at Fox, with Monte reporting to the Chief Operating Officer and the Firmwide Managing Partner (see Figure A.4).

The Knowledge Management department comprises 23 people and encompasses three service teams: Library Services, Knowledge Solutions, and Business/Competitive Intelligence. KM is also responsible for SharePoint development in the firm. SharePoint is used for the intranet, client extranets, and team sites. Each group reports to Monte.

Library Services is responsible for legal research projects and supports firm-wide monitoring and news aggregation initiatives. The group is led by the Director of Library Services (a former practicing attorney) and is assisted by a Research Services Manager (also a former practicing attorney), five research analysts, and a three-member Serials/Acquisitions team.

The Knowledge Management Solutions team is technology-based and is responsible for the firm's intranet, team sites, and client extranets. They also support the practice groups with custom solutions such as a Bankruptcy Referral network, Gaming Opinions library, Entertainment Deal database, and others. The team is led by the Director of Knowledge Services and is assisted by a KM Applications developer, a KM systems administrator, two web developers, and a data steward.

The Competitive Intelligence and Risk Mitigation groups focus on business research and support needs on the nonlegal side, primarily business background and financial risk assessment research, as well as market and industry research. In addition, the Risk team works in close conjunction with the firm's General Counsel, and the Competitive Intelligence team is involved in numerous business development programs and initiatives. The group is led by the Director of Business & Competitive Intelligence and is assisted by a Business Research Manager, two risk analysts, and two competitive intelligence analysts.

The KM department is in the beginning stages of an enterprise search system deployment as well as a project to provide mobile access to news and KM data repositories. In addition, they are finalizing their SharePoint 2013

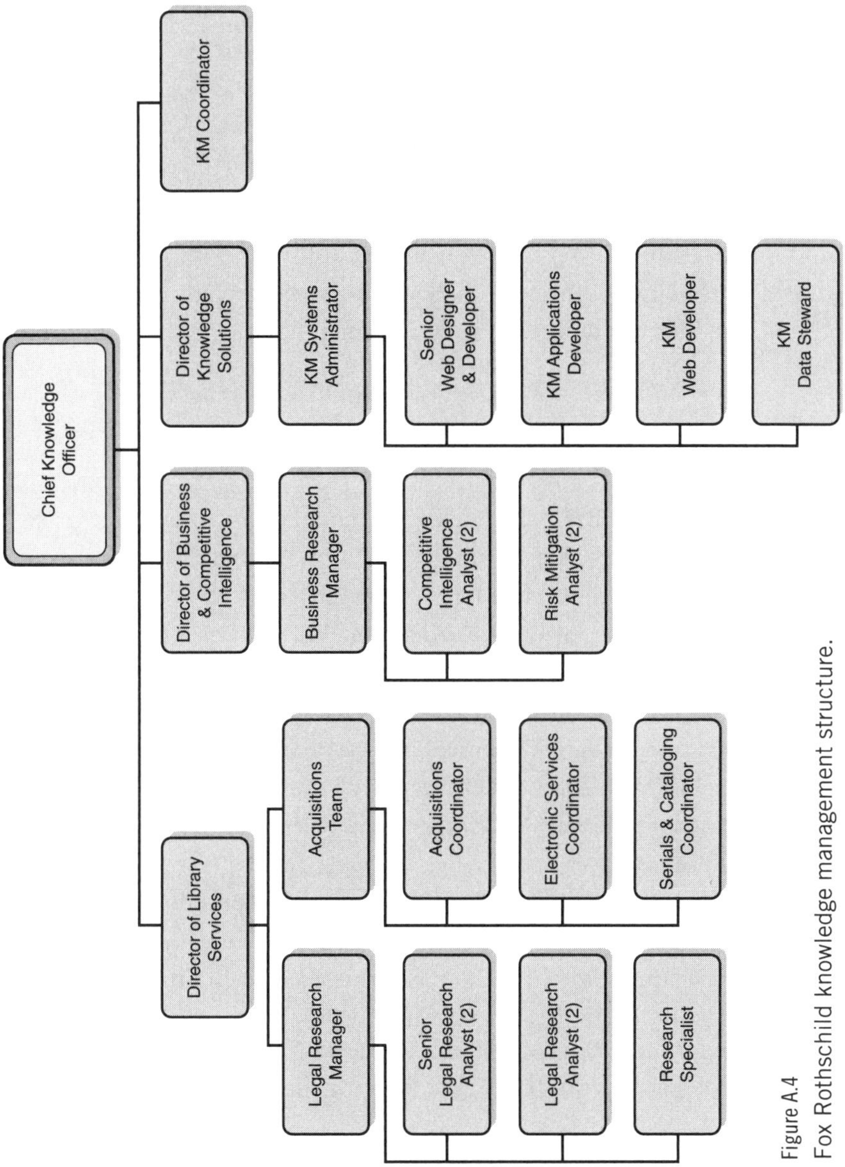

Figure A.4
Fox Rothschild knowledge management structure.

design for the intranet, extranets, and team sites. Other initiatives include exploring information standards/big data and legal project management.

The KM team frequently collaborates with Professional Recruitment/ Development (i.e., CLE programs, partner retreat), Marketing (business development initiatives and training), and Information Technology (data integration projects).

Vision and Mission

At Fox, KM is a broad umbrella that can cover a variety of information projects. "Simply defined," said Monte, "it is all about providing external and internal information to attorneys in a holistic service package. Our mission is to support attorney collaboration, strengthen relationships with clients, and improve business process streamlining."

Goodwin Procter, LLP

Goodwin Procter, LLP is a full-service, international law firm with approximately 850 attorneys in eight offices.[5] The firm's formal KM department started in 1999, which is relatively early on the legal KM history timeline. The department is currently led by Anne Stemlar, who has served as Director, Research and Knowledge Management Services since 2011.

Like many law firm KM leaders, Stemlar is a lawyer. She graduated from The University of Iowa with degrees in history and psychology, and then earned her J.D. from Marquette University Law School. In addition, she earned a Master of Library and Information Science degree from the University of Wisconsin—Milwaukee.

David Hobbie, whose personal story is included in Appendix B, is another member of the KM team at Goodwin. He has been a Litigation KM Attorney since 2005 and practiced as an associate doing civil litigation at two large law firms for eight years before moving into knowledge management. Hobbie earned an undergraduate degree in history from Oberlin College and a degree in violin performance from Oberlin Conservatory of Music. His J.D. is from the University of Michigan Law School.

The KM department structure has Stemlar reporting to the Chief Information Officer. In addition to Stemlar and Hobbie, the department also

5. http://www.goodwinprocter.com/.

includes a Business Law department Knowledge Management Attorney (Hobbie's counterpart), two KM coordinators, and one KM specialist. KM cooperates extensively with the IT department, Business Unit Managers, chiefs of the administrative departments, Marketing, Professional Development & Training, Finance, and Research and Library Services. (See Figure A.5.)

Importantly, the Goodwin KM department has support from practicing partners, as well. There are two KM partners, one for the Business Law department and one for the Litigation department, and the two KM attorneys have a dotted-line reporting arrangement to them.

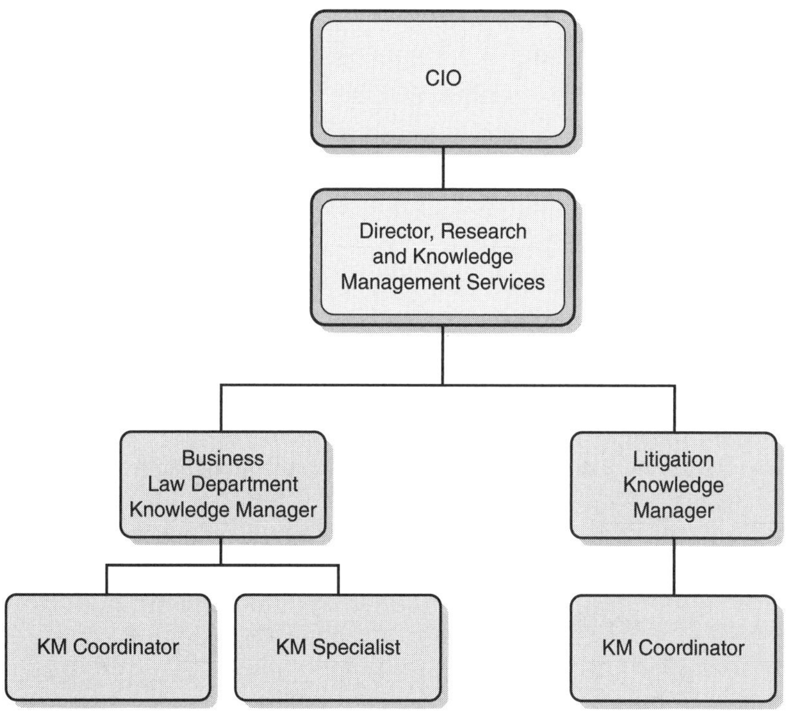

Figure A.5
Goodwin Procter knowledge management structure.

King & Wood Mallesons (Australian Partnership)

Felicity Badcock[6] has been the Head of Knowledge Management at the Australian partnership of King & Wood Mallesons (KWM) since November 2009.[7] She is a former practicing lawyer who subsequently established a career in information technology and knowledge management. The KM department at KWM was established in 1998 (when the firm was Mallesons Stephen Jaques). Badcock reports directly to the Chief Operating Officer and has a team of 22 full-time equivalent employees, broken into three subteams: Research and Information, Precedents Administration, and Search and Registration (see Figure A.6).

The Research and Information team responsibilities include:

- Legal and business research
- Legal and business research training
- Library and online resource management
- Monitoring legal and industry/sector developments
- Curating and publishing current awareness newsletters
- Practice team and sector team knowledge support

The KM department's Precedents Administration team is responsible for:

- Administering the firm's precedents and other knowledge resources, including PrecHelp (an online guide to precedents), clauses, forms, dealbooks and example advices, opinions, and papers
- Delivering legal excellence training (e.g., plain English writing, contract drafting, and statutory interpretation)
- Creating and maintaining Word templates and macros (in cooperation with the Client Technologies team) to help users process documents faster and with fewer errors

Finally, the Search and Registration team's responsibilities include:

6. http://www.linkedin.com/in/felicitybadcock.
7. King & Wood Mallesons formed on March 1, 2012, as a combination of Chinese firm King & Wood PRC Lawyers and Australian firm Mallesons Stephen Jaques.

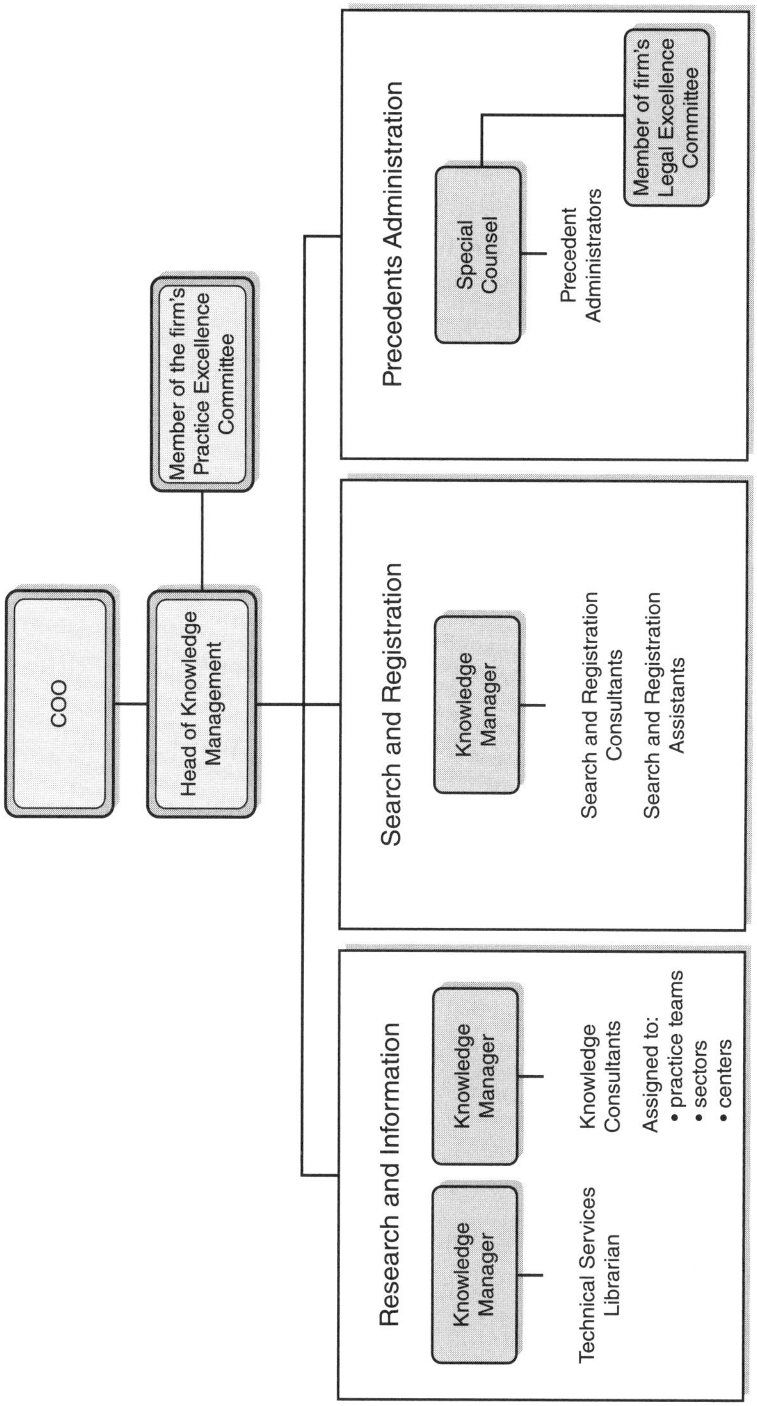

Figure A.6
King & Wood Mallesons (Australian Partnership) knowledge management structure.

- Company and business name searching
- Company lodgings
- Court filing and litigation searching
- Property searching and lodging
- Search and registration training

In addition to all of this, The KM team's other responsibilities include managing and promoting use of the firm's knowledge systems and resources; facilitating and promoting the sharing of knowledge and information; identifying opportunities to apply knowledge systems and processes to improve the efficiency and quality of legal service delivery; and supporting the firm's social media initiatives.

Like other firms, the KM department at KWM cannot do it all alone. Badcock and her team collaborate with several other departments, committees, and practicing partners and lawyers. They most frequently collaborate with the Practice Excellence and Legal Excellence Committees, support functions including Technology, Legal Logistics (which incorporates Applied Legal Technology and Legal Project Management), Business Development, People & Development (including Learning & Development), and Finance.

King & Wood Mallesons' KM efforts are an example of a mature, well-developed program. This is not surprising, because many non-U.S.-based law firms (especially those based in Australia and the United Kingdom) are usually more mature, from a KM perspective, than their U.S. counterparts. Many of these firms embraced KM as a discipline earlier than U.S. firms, and there has been a propensity among them to realize the value of people, specifically professional (or practice) support lawyers (PSLs), over technology. This is one reason that many U.K. and Australian firms are further ahead of the KM curve than U.S.-based firms in many aspects.

Littler Mendelson, P.C.

Littler Mendelson, P.C. is a large international labor and employment law firm with more than 1,000 lawyers in more than 60 locations.[8] The

8. http://www.littler.com.

firm's KM department, established in 2001, is led by Scott Rechtschaffen.[9] Rechtschaffen graduated with an A.B. from the University of California, Berkeley, majoring in history and psychology, and then went on to obtain his J.D. from Cornell University Law School. He started with Littler in 1984 as an associate practicing labor and employment law and became a shareholder at the firm in 1990. He became involved with KM at the firm and eventually was made Managing Shareholder, Knowledge Management. In 2009, he was given the title Chief Knowledge Officer, reporting to the Chief Operating Officer. As CKO, Rechtschaffen maintains his shareholder title and is also co-chair of the firm's Innovation Council.

KM Organizational Structure at Littler

Littler has one of the larger KM teams among U.S.-based law firms, with more than 30 people (see Figure A.7). Among the KM department members are:

- Chief Knowledge Officer
- Senior Director of Knowledge Management
- Firm Principals (equivalent of a nonparticipating shareholder for those in management positions) (2)
- Director of KM Innovation
- Managing Editor, Publications (also serves as KM department administrative manager)
- Knowledge Management Attorneys (12)
- Manager of Client Service Applications
- Technologists and Content Administrators (3)
- Research Attorneys (2)
- Director of Library and Research Services
- Research Librarians (6)
- Library Assistants (4)
- Client Services Coordinator
- Applications and SharePoint developers (within the IT department)

9. Scott Rechtschaffen is Chief Knowledge Officer of Littler Mendelson, P.C., and he was awarded the 2011 International Legal Technology Association (ILTA) Knowledge Management Champion—Distinguished Peer Award. Read his personal KM story in Appendix B.

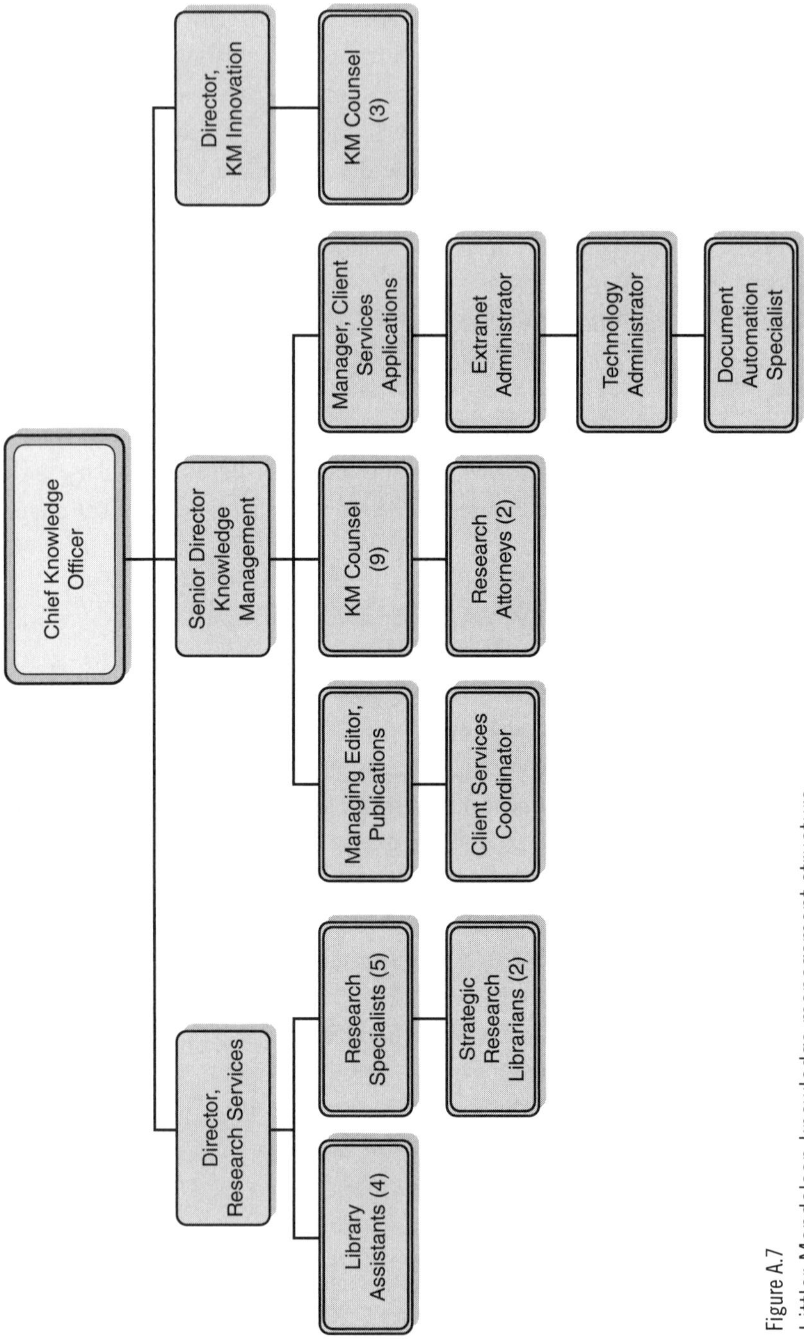

Figure A.7
Littler Mendelson knowledge management structure.

Littler's KM department is considered to be one of the major corporate departments supporting the firm's attorneys. They collaborate extensively with the IT department on major attorney- and client-focused development projects. Rechtschaffen said:

> KM often stands as the interface between IT and the attorneys and clients; enabling IT to gather and understand the requirements and specifications necessary for successful product development. The IT department routinely asks KM to assist in refining development projects to ensure that their application development work will meet the needs of the firm's attorneys and clients.

Knowledge Management works closely with the Client Relations department on innovative client development projects. They support and manage all of Littler's publication efforts, including the firm's blogs, client alerts, print publications, and numerous subject-specific books. In all, KM generates about 15,000 page-equivalents of content each year. The KM department also supports the firm's major client events, including conferences, regional breakfast briefings, and webinars. Finally, the KM department collaborates with the Product Development department, which is responsible for various client-facing technologies, the Learning Group, which is the firm's in-house client training division, and other service departments, such as the Client Planning team, the Litigation Support department, and the Professional Development department.

Littler's KM Vision

"Littler firmly believes that the traditional law firm model is imperiled." Rechtschaffen said "It's threatened by dramatic changes in the market, including the rise of alternative legal service providers, changing demands and expectations of clients, and significant advances in technology." Although he acknowledges that KM is not the panacea for fixing the legal business model, he believes it is clearly one of the major components for successfully reinventing how legal services should be delivered more efficiently.

KM is very important at Littler, especially because it has so many attorneys spread over so many offices. "KM is the glue that binds our attorneys together, giving them a common base—a town square, if you will—for sharing knowledge, collaborating, and ensuring that we are serving our clients' best interests in the most expedient way possible," Rechtschaffen said. With effective KM, attorneys do not reinvent the wheel, become their own isolated fonts of information, or hoard their knowledge. They are encouraged to share their expertise, their experience, and their lessons learned to benefit their colleagues and, most importantly, their clients, and they understand the value of doing so. As Rechtschaffen puts it: "Knowledge management at Littler stands at the forefront of our efforts to reimagine and build the new model of how law firms should be delivering legal services to their clients."

Pillsbury Winthrop Shaw Pittman, LLP

Lisa Gianakos is Director of Knowledge Management at Pillsbury Winthrop Shaw Pittman, LLP, a large international law firm with more than 600 lawyers in 14 offices around the world.[10] Gianakos has been with Pillsbury since January 2011, when she left Reed Smith as that firm's KM Director. She has an interesting background and is one of the leaders in the legal KM field. Unlike many large firm KM leaders, Gianakos is not a former practicing lawyer, but rather, she has a background in information technology. Her first real specialty was as a network engineer (Certified Novell Engineer) but she also became a jack-of-all-trades as a result of her experience doing five years of legal technology consulting for small to medium-sized law firms in Washington, D.C.

Gianakos's start in the legal industry was as a web master, although she was really doing intranet/web development, at Hogan & Hartson (now Hogan Lovells). While at Hogan, she went back to graduate school, which is where she first heard the term "knowledge management." She realized that much of what she was doing at work fell into this discipline, but the term just wasn't used much at the time (1999). In fact, Gianakos's final paper in graduate school was titled "Applying Knowledge Management to the Legal Profession." "I remember doing a web search for KM and 'law

10. http://www.pillsburylaw.com/offices.

firm' or 'legal' and getting only four real hits," Gianakos said. "One was an article by Nina Platt. Another, I don't recall the details other than it talked about Skadden Arps, and there was a quote by Charmaine Polvara, who I later worked with." After she finished her degree in 2000, Gianakos went to work for a consulting company heading up their new legal program. After that, in 2001, she joined LeBoeuf, Lamb, Greene & MacRae, LLP as their Director of KM, and she has been in similar roles since then with firms such as Hunton & Williams, Reed Smith, and now Pillsbury.

KM Department Organization

At Pillsbury, Gianakos reports to the firm's Chief Information Officer, and there are a total of 14 others in the KM department (excluding an offshore team). One unique aspect of Pillsbury's KM program is that the Marketing Technology efforts fall under KM. The group is headed by a Marketing Technology Manager, who reports to Gianakos and has five marketing technology coordinators as direct reports.

The firm's Intranet/Extranet Web Development Group (previously called the Client Services Group) is led by a Web Development Manager, who reports to Gianakos. He has five web developers and a SharePoint architect reporting to him. In addition, the Web Development Manager has a three-person offshore team that provides web development support (primarily for Lotus Notes—a legacy system that is being phased out).

The firm's Knowledge Development Manager reports to Gianakos and provides business analysis services, monthly metrics/reports, content manager training and support for the intranet, and manages document automation projects and other projects, as assigned. Like many firms, Pillsbury is looking closely at legal project management, and although there is no official LPM group, the function falls under the KM department, and Gianakos has proposed a new LPM Manager position for 2014. (See Figure A.8.)

The KM department's high-level goals are consistent with good KM practices and themes: connecting and efficiency. The KM team seeks to enable better client service by (1) putting people in touch with people ("know who") and (2) providing better and faster location of work product, samples, precedents, and tools related to preparing documents ("know how").

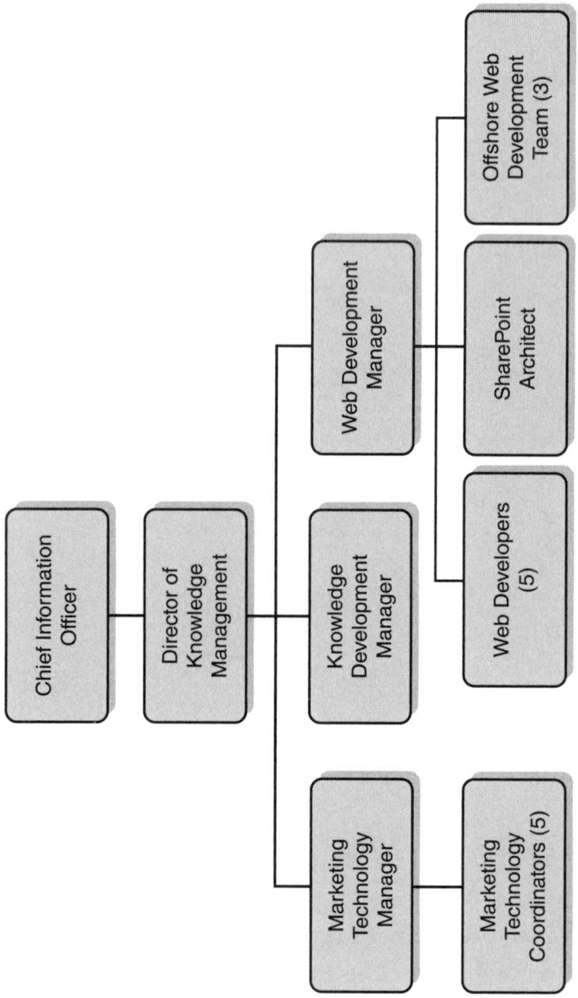

Figure A.8
Pillsbury Winthrop Shaw Pittman knowledge management structure.

KM Collaboration at Pillsbury

Gianakos's team works closely with several other groups throughout the firm—Marketing, Business Development, Client Team Services, and Library & Information Services, to name a few. She stated:

> We work with Marketing primarily for communications and branding. They are a key stakeholder for our intranet and provided excellent creativity and design when it was initially launched. They assist,

in particular, with our home page design (and upcoming redesign), as that is our most valuable real estate and where our chairman's messages are promoted, as well as other marketing news about the firm.

Because Marketing Technology is part of KM, Gianakos's team also works with Business Development, either directly supporting the systems they use (such as CRM, ERM, and business intelligence tools) or in integrating business development data into the firm's intranet and extranet to expose to other groups, as needed. With direction primarily from Business Development, KM also promotes the firm through many social media channels and provides social media monitoring and reporting. They work with Client Team Services to implement changes they would like in order to improve client service, whether through the extranet or other public-facing solutions.

Library & Information Services is another collaboration partner for KM. Primarily through the firm's intranet, KM works extensively with the library in incorporating and applying taxonomies to various library resources so they are easily accessible to the attorneys and practice groups. A current project involves working with the library on improving the delivery of news via the intranet, as well as methods for (partially) automating and/or improving how practice and industry newsletters are pulled together and distributed.

Promotion and Training

Promoting KM resources and ensuring that attorneys are well informed about KM tools is an important component of the services provided by the KM department. The team provides KM orientation to all new attorneys, and they offer practice-area-specific training and awareness opportunities when new tools and resources are introduced. Often, the goal is not to teach lawyers all they need to know about a particular resource, but rather to make them aware of the resources so that they know what's possible in the hope that they will ask for more detailed training when it is needed.

The team is also a proponent of the "give them a fish and teach them to fish" approach. "We monitor 'all-attorney' emails as well as posts to our bulletin board," Gianakos said. "When KM can help answer questions or at least point attorneys in the right direction, we provide the answer we have found, as well as a reminder of what tool we used or how we derived the answer." It's kind of a hand-holding way of leading attorneys to these tools for future self-service. This approach to ongoing education is a great way to continue to develop the knowledge-sharing culture of a firm and seek out ways to turn everyday interactions into teachable moments.

Anonymous Law Firm A

Anonymous Law Firm A is a global law firm with more than 1,000 lawyers in more than 15 offices. Although the formal KM department began in March 2008, the firm had long engaged in KM activities and initiatives. Before 2008, the KM efforts were a part of the Attorney Development Group.

The department is led by a Senior Manager, whose background is common among KM leaders: A former practicing lawyer, she practiced corporate law for six years and moved into KM as a practice support lawyer in 2006. Now, as the head of KM, the Senior Manager reports to the firm's Chief Information Officer. The department is lean but effective. The Senior Manager has two direct reports: a Senior KM Content Coordinator and a KM Specialist. (See Figure A.9.)

Among other things, the Senior Manager and her team are the business owners of several technology tools designed to help the firm's lawyers practice more efficiently and effectively. These include the firm's SharePoint-based intranet and enterprise search system. Because of the firm's and KM department's reliance on these technology tools, KM collaborates frequently with the IT department, specifically the SharePoint administrator, developers, and document management analyst. As KM at the firm is not all about technology, the KM department also collaborates with other departments, such as the Library and Attorney Training.

The firm's overall KM objective reflects a common theme in mature KM organizations—one we have explored earlier. It is to "leverage the firm's collective knowledge, processes, and technology to support both the practice of law and the business of law by: (1) connecting people to information, (2) connecting people to people, and (3) increasing attorney productivity."

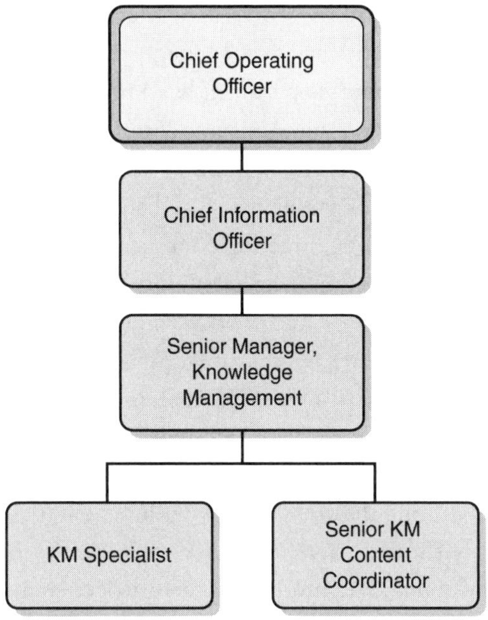

Figure A.9
Anonymous Law Firm A knowledge management structure.

Anonymous Law Firm B

Our final profile is of an anonymous, midsized Canadian law firm that provides its clients with a wide range of legal services, including corporate transactional work and litigation. The firm has had a formal KM program since 2007, but it has opted to label the group Practice Support rather than knowledge management.

The group is led by the Director of Practice Support, who is a former practicing lawyer with a diverse background. He practiced law with firms in Europe and Canada and was also in-house counsel with one of Canada's Big Five banks. He also served for several years as Knowledge Director at another Canadian law firm. The Director of Practice Support reports directly to the firm's Managing Partner, which is a beneficial arrangement to have such direct reporting lines. The Director of Practice Support has additional duties, including serving on the firm's Risk Management Committee and overseeing the Library and Litigation Management departments.

The firm's Practice Support department has a total of eight members. Two of the members, the Director and Assistant Director, are lawyers who focus on substantive legal KM issues. The Library Services group has a manager with three librarians reporting to her. Finally, there is a manager of Litigation and eDiscovery, who has one litigation support specialist reporting to her.

The Director of Practice Support shared with me the firm's Practice Support Team Mandate:

> The Practice Support team is dedicated to supporting the firm's members and advancing the firm's strategic goals. It aims to make it easier for firm members to work more effectively (doing things right) and efficiently (doing the right things) with a view to improving the quality and consistency of legal services provided to our clients by capturing, packaging, and mobilizing the intellectual and social capital of the firm; supporting and engendering a culture of knowledge sharing, collaboration, and firm-first attitude; alleviating inefficiencies and introducing process improvement; bridging the gap between emerging knowledge management technologies and the traditional practice of law. The Practice Support team collaborates with the Library team to provide top-quality resources and knowledge services to all firm members.

In addition to the Practice Support Team, the firm has a Practice Support Committee, which provides direction for the Practice Support Team. The Committee is made up of five partners (one from each practice group, other than the tax group), the Director, and the Assistant Director of Practice Support. The Director of Practice Support also shared with me the Practice Support Committee Mandate:

> The Practice Support Committee provides direction on, and acts as an advocate of, the initiatives of the Practice Support team. Their participation in the assessment of proposed initiatives and implementation of approved initiatives of the Practice Support team assists the

Director of Practice Support and the Managing Partner in ensuring that all activities of the Practice Support team align with the firm's strategic plan and the aim of the Practice Support team.

As we have seen, the involvement and support of high-level firm or department leadership demonstrated here can be a crucial element in effective KM efforts.

Appendix B

How Some Knowledge Management Professionals Got Started

> Share your knowledge. It is a way to achieve immortality.
>
> —Dalai Lama XIV

The knowledge management community is full of smart, interesting, and generous people. While researching and writing this book, I had the pleasure of speaking with many knowledge management professionals, some of whom I knew and some I had met for the first time. Whenever I spoke with someone, the conversation inevitably turned to how we got involved in KM in the first place. I found the stories fascinating, and when discussing the topic with one KM colleague, John Gillies, he suggested that I devote part of the book to those stories. I loved the idea. The only thing better than that would be to let my KM friends and colleagues tell their own stories, in their own words. I floated the idea around to my KM cohorts, and several took me up on the offer. These are their stories, written by them and edited for consistency. I sincerely appreciate all of their contributions.

John Gillies

John is Director of Practice Support at Cassels Brock & Blackwell, LLP. He started this role in October 2007.

How Did You Get Started in KM?

I didn't enter the KM field; I backed into it. I started out thinking I was doing one thing, but it morphed into something else, which turned out to be KM! My background was as a banking lawyer. I had done some banking and lending-related work when I worked in a French law firm in Paris from 1979 to 1981, then as an associate at McCarthy & McCarthy (as it then was) in Toronto for four years, and finally for 15 years in-house with one of the big Canadian banks. In 2000, however, the bank had an internal reorganization, and the young partner hired from outside to head the legal group terminated most of the lawyers older than she was, including me.

Among the people I spoke to during my subsequent job hunt was the head of the tech law group at McCarthy Tetrault (as it had since become known), whom I had known from my previous time there. He was looking to have the firm establish an online legal information service for subscribers (modeled on Linklaters' Blue Flag offering, among others). For that, he needed someone who was bilingual, with big firm experience, and experience in the then-new field of Internet law (which I'd had at the bank). It was serendipity. So, I was engaged to write the business plan for this initiative, which was eventually approved, with the authorization to hire six lawyers to get it up and running. I was hired, followed immediately by Joshua Fireman, to co-lead the project.

After an RFP process to select the right web design company, we set to work with ii3 to plan the browser-based application we envisaged. A few months into the project, however, the powers-that-be decided that it would be more prudent to first build an internal repository, which would then serve as the springboard for the proposed external service (which, sadly, never got built).

In the course of all the reading that I had done during that time in exploring the different aspects of this project, I saw frequent references to "knowledge management," which was then still a relatively new field. Finally, one day, the light bulb went on, and I realized that what we were doing was, in fact, KM. Eureka!

In any event, we continued on, and within 15 months of our start we launched, in December 2001, a browser-based KM repository, designed to capture key matter documents, annotated by lawyers from the matter, which were tagged, categorized, and available to be searched. Particularly for its time, it was a very progressive system and ended up winning a tech design award.

The design and build process was exciting, particularly since I'd never been involved with a project anything like this. Joshua and I essentially divided the role so that he was more involved in the outward-facing aspects of the project, like liaising with partners, library, admin staff, and vendors, while I dealt more with the technical aspects, like taxonomy and synonym rings. (I learned more about taxonomy, which was another discipline I'd never heard of, than I would ever have anticipated!)

At the time, I think I most resembled the character Ray Kinsella in [Canadian author] W.P. Kinsella's novel, *Shoeless Joe*, who hears a voice that says, "If you build it, he will come." I was so enamored of this wonderful tool we'd created that I just assumed that if we explained to people what it could do if they fed it the proper "diet," then they would be inspired to immediately contribute mounds of useful content, full of insightful context. "Naive" would be an understatement!

There comes a time in the life of every KM professional when he or she realizes that, in law firms, unless you have something that either directly improves lawyers' billings or clearly answers the question "What's in it for me?," adoption is going to be a huge challenge. It took me awhile to realize that I wasn't really in the business of KM but of change management as a means to KM: "I'm here to help you, and if you just change pretty well every aspect of how you currently practice, you're going to be much happier!"

The happiest surprise in getting into KM was first discovering the community of KM professionals in law firms around North America and second developing good friendships with so many of them. I have gotten to know many very intelligent, highly creative, and innovative people who are a real pleasure to know. I particularly enjoy the opportunity at conferences to engage in discussions with my counterparts, because I leave those discussions enriched and energized by what my friends have shared with me. The people in this field are driven by a desire to share knowledge, starting with their own, and we are all the collective beneficiaries of that drive. I find that if I am asked to speak on some KM topic on a panel with others, I come away with far more useful information than whatever I have been able to impart.

The most innovative project I have been involved in was the KM repository at McCarthy Tetrault. It was exciting to be part of something designed to help significantly transform lawyers' practices. But the most fun was the launch of our first enterprise search tool. I had come up with the name that we branded it with, "SearchWell," by riffing on the firm's name of Cassels Brock & Blackwell, and I thought the name worked well on a couple of levels. SearchWell was very well received, but that's not surprising when users go from not being able to find what they need to finding all that and more. We were also somewhat ahead of the curve in the introduction of search, so it was also fun to try and figure out what we needed to do.

The key difference, for me, between the practice of law and working as a KM professional is in the type of goals of the projects you work on. In practice, everyone on the team is working to achieve the desired goal. The goal tends to be fairly well defined: closing a transaction, defending a lawsuit, etc. Because the fundamental goal of KM is to change behaviors, on the other hand, we're inevitably on very small teams constantly swimming upstream (or so it feels), trying to get people to do things differently. As a result, the goals we aim for tend to be more amorphous, where success is much harder to measure. And there's rarely a time when we can say, "Done!" I'm still struggling with the same sort of things as when I got into this gig at the turn of the century. So you have to learn to be more self-sufficient and satisfied with what you know you've accomplished, because the external markers are usually not there. Sometimes I miss those defined goals and easily measured markers of accomplishments, but mostly, not!

This has been a great gig for me—way more fun than I had ever anticipated. When I changed jobs four years ago, I proposed to my new firm that I put in four good years and then join my wife in retirement. But I'm enjoying this so much that I intend to keep doing it as long as it stays fun. (My grandfather continued practicing medicine until age 87, and I think I would probably chuck this in before that, but who knows?) So, it seems to me the most important thing that we KM professionals need to do is not to let the practicing lawyers know how much fun we have doing this, because if they find out, they'll all want to do it!

Carolyn Austin

Carolyn is Precedents Manager at K&L Gates, LLP (Australian offices). She started in this role in May 2006.

What Do You Do?

My team is responsible for:

- The development, maintenance, and delivery of consistent, relevant, and current precedents across all practice areas in Australia
- Promoting knowledge sharing and utilization via creation, storage, and reuse of knowledge assets, and supporting our designated knowledge champions

How Did You Get Started in KM?

To begin at the beginning, I started out as a graduate lawyer in a top-tier Australian law firm and, after a couple of years, gravitated toward commercial litigation. It was a diverse commercial practice but included some pretty large cases, involving massive amounts of documentary discovery and general management of evidence. What I loved most about my job was coordinating all the logistics of the matter, usually toward a court deadline. Working with the partner, I would manage teams of paralegals through the electronic discovery process; pull together voluminous briefs; coordinate the communication with senior and junior counsel; and just about roll everything down to court for the first day of the hearing. I suppose it wasn't too far from what might be called legal project management today. Having to be across the latest in legal technology was great fun, too.

After my daughter was born, I came back to full-time work thinking everything would be fine. Well! I had a few months in which to realize that if I continued to work as I had been, I would not see my daughter from Monday morning until Friday night, most weeks. For me, this just wasn't a choice I could make. At that time, doing my job on a part-time, job-share, or other flexible basis would have been totally unthinkable. It just didn't happen back then, particularly in litigation. This was the moment when I happened to see an advert in the paper—my firm was advertising for a part-time precedents lawyer to work with document analysis and coding for a document automation system. I jumped at the chance, and that's when I joined my firm's precedents team. It was such a happy and enlightened team to work with. I got a great grounding in the importance of process and protocols when building a solid precedents function. Here was not only legal technology to learn and apply, but interesting projects to coordinate. I loved the work, and tried my hand at designing litigation automation, even learning a little programming along the way.

Another child later, I moved across to another firm, this time in a precedents lawyer role. It was back to legal drafting, in an environment that valued plain language principles and using a consistent style. Over time, I became manager of the precedents department nationally, and part of the senior administration team. Now I had the chance to participate in leadership and management training, which I really enjoyed. So, in many ways, I was lucky to have the right background at the right time, when this thing called knowledge management burst on the scene and changed everything.

Clients began to ask questions about how their law firms were managing knowledge. Our firm decided to appoint a Director of Know-How. My precedents team integrated with the library and formed a Know-How group. Initially, I admit to a healthy dose of lawyers' skepticism, but as I started to learn what KM was about, gradually I became fascinated by the concepts and potential of this new discipline. Fascination became conviction, which became enthusiasm. I got the chance to move into a new team within Know-How, called Innovations, as a know-how projects manager. Now, instead of precedents, I was working on things like developing intranet sites, facilitating after action reviews, assisting with strategy, and participating in a diverse portfolio of projects for both internal and external clients, designed to create value and build a better firm. I was encountering a wide range of ideas and practices (play theory, anyone?). It was an incredible time of exploration and learning, and I will always feel a particularly close bond with my colleagues who went through that journey with me. In many ways, I am still on it.

To get to grips with my new passion for KM, I went back to university and studied for a postgraduate qualification in Knowledge Management. This was a great experience, and I found it a really great way to solidify and deepen the insights gained from being a practitioner. You meet some great people in those classes, who are working across a wide range of industries. It really helps to broaden your horizons beyond law firms: the cross-pollination of ideas can be a fertile source of innovation.

Then back in 2006 I moved to a middle-sized firm in Australia, as national precedents manager. It was back to an emphasis on precedents development—only now, I saw precedents as key knowledge assets, part of a wider, holistic approach to managing knowledge flows, with a focus on organizational value. We started conversations about how to extend and connect what we were doing with other aspects of the business, and again, I found myself and my team involved in a diverse array of knowledge-based projects, working collaboratively with colleagues in information technology, finance, learning and development, library, and marketing. In 2013, the firm combined with K&L Gates, a global firm with 48 offices and over 2,000 fee earners around the world, and since then, the horizons have been almost unlimited. Our challenge has been all about taking what we do and exploring with our international colleagues whether we may have the capability to meet business needs across a broader, deeper, globalized client base. It's an exciting time and place to be.

The most surprising thing I have found about KM is KM itself. It is a discipline that has the ability to be constantly changing, growing, flowing into all sorts of unexpected places and directions. My biggest challenge, and also my biggest joy, has been learning to deal with ambiguity and continual reinvention. As a knowledge manager, often you find yourself without a clearly defined roadmap, or even a clearly defined set of expectations. You sometimes need to feel your own way forward, making your role work for your organization as you go. You are creating models for the future, then continually shaping and refining them. No two weeks are the same. It's exciting stuff and can sometimes be a little scary for lawyers who transition to KM, because we tend to come from a background of relative structure and certainty. I'm sometimes asked if I would ever go back to practice. My answer is a firm no, and I think most knowledge managers I know would say the same.

I've also been fortunate throughout my career that my role has involved teaching young lawyers about precedents, knowledge, and plain language drafting. Coming into contact every year with a new group of seasonal clerks or graduates, who are just starting out on their career in the law, and having the privilege of being part of their learning experience, is a very valuable thing indeed. These days, my teaching career has come full circle, and I lecture a couple of times each semester in the postgraduate knowledge management program at the university from which I graduated. Teaching knowledge managers about KM in the legal profession is a nice balance to teaching lawyers about KM.

Looking back, I feel incredibly lucky that I found my way into this career. It started as a work/life balance choice but has ended up to be more encompassing and engrossing than my first career choice could ever have been, for me. Now that the kids are grown up, the hours I work would sometimes make the most dedicated commercial litigator sigh with recognition. But I can honestly say I love every minute and look forward to every day at work and the new challenges it brings. How many people get to say that?

Chris Boyd

Chris Boyd has been the Senior Director of Professional Services at Wilson Sonsini Goodrich & Rosati since August 2006. He is also the International Legal Technology Association (ILTA) Knowledge Management Peer Group Steering Committee Vice President.

What Do You Do?

I lead several of our firm's talent management programs, including attorney recruiting, associate relations, diversity, knowledge management, and professional development. Every day, my teams and I seek to hire the best attorneys for our firm and our clients and provide them with the training and tools to provide superlative value to both. Within KM specifically, we focus on connecting attorneys and legal support staff with the firm's three

Ps: work product (model forms and sample documents), projects (matter profiles and documents), and people (internal and external experts).

How Did You Get Started in KM?

Short version: I'm a former practicing lawyer who started my legal career in 1992, switched to full-time KM in the consulting industry in 1997, and then moved into legal KM in 2001. I decided to do KM for a living for two reasons. First, I really like making things work better, and leading KM enables me to do just that for the legal profession. Second, I like getting paid for results rather than for billable hours.

Longer version: I grew up in Washington, D.C. and went to Princeton University, where I majored in public and international affairs and graduated in 1987. I then spent two years in Boston working for a wonderful management consulting firm named Corporate Decisions, Inc. (CDI). CDI's goal was to help its clients grow their share of current markets, successfully enter new markets, and make more money. The four partners, all alumni of Bain, taught us all how to do ground-level market research and, once we had the necessary data, apply our analytical skills and judgment to present and implement pragmatic steps. I learned more about how to think, analyze, recommend, and execute at CDI than at any other time or place in my life. It was also a fantastic place to begin to learn techniques for making things work better.

I moved to Palo Alto, California, in 1989 to go to Stanford Law School. I dutifully spent two years taking classes and leading a law and business society, but I grew restless with a classroom-only education. So for the fall of my third year, I set up an externship in Paris at the International Chamber of Commerce Court of Arbitration, which supervises arbitration proceedings between companies in contract disputes. I helped the court's attorneys manage cases and steadily improve the overall arbitration process. The court competes for arbitration business with the American Arbitration Association and other international arbitration organizations, so it needs to provide efficient, fair, predictable, and final adjudications to keep and grow its share of the international arbitration market. I wrote my externship paper on ways that the court could continue to improve its processes—yet again, focusing on ways to make things work better.

I graduated from Stanford Law School in 1992 and spent the next year in Reno, Nevada, clerking for Ninth Circuit Court of Appeals Judge Melvin Brunetti. The following year, I started work as a corporate and securities associate at my current firm, Wilson Sonsini Goodrich & Rosati (WSGR), based in Palo Alto, California. We represent growth companies of all sizes, mostly in the technology and life sciences industries. I worked for a variety of client companies, ranging from brand-new startups to mid-cap public companies. In addition to helping clients day-to-day with a variety of legal matters, I represented them on venture financings, public offerings, buy- and sell-side acquisitions, and public company reporting. The Internet boom began in the mid-1990s, which were consequently a period of tremendous growth in Silicon Valley. WSGR and its peer firms were fortunate to benefit from an explosion in demand for corporate legal services, and we worked hard and grew fast.

While I spent most of my days working for clients, I also started to do some legal KM, though we didn't call it "KM" back then. One of the junior partners I worked for shared my passion for process improvement, so he and I embarked on a series of projects that will sound very familiar to today's legal KM practitioners: We set up physical forms files in abandoned library filing cabinets, drafted lists of firm experts on various topics and circulated them, and even developed a prototype document assembly wizard for IPO prospectuses. We really liked our informal investments in practice efficiency, but we couldn't devote enough time to them given that they were off-the-books, "after-hours" projects, and neither of us had that many "after hours" to give.

After four years as an associate, I got married in 1997 and soon decided that I liked the work and loved the clients, but not enough to spend 60- to 80-hour weeks practicing law for the rest of my life. So I left the firm and went to work for one of my clients, USWeb, as Director of Corporate Methodology (and yes, I kept the business card). USWeb, a rapidly growing web consulting firm, tasked me with consolidating website development best practices into a standard, documented process, and then deploying it firm-wide. Those legal knowledge managers tasked with doing this for the M&A or patent litigation practices will empathize with just how challenging this was. But I really liked the work, so for the next four years, I worked for web services companies doing a wide variety of KM, ranging from intranet development to expertise location to standardized processes and work product. Overall, the work of designing, developing, and deploying resources to help people tap into their colleagues' expertise to do better work faster—and thus making professional services work better—really appealed to me.

Working for three technology companies in four years was a roller-coaster ride. My first company went public, the next one was sold, and the last one went bankrupt. Par for the course in Silicon Valley in the boom-bust period of the late 1990s, I suppose. While working for the last company, which managed and marketed a highly secure multiparty extranet to law firms and law departments, I had the good fortune to meet Jeff Rovner, one of the pioneers and leading lights of legal KM. Jeff at the time had set up an impressive legal KM operation at the now-defunct firm of Brobeck, Phleger & Harrison, and I was fascinated to learn about the resources they had developed.

After my last company went under, I thought of Jeff's operation and decided to see if WSGR would be interested in setting up a legal KM program. It turned out that not only was WSGR interested, but it had also just started a program. WSGR hired me to lead the program in 2001, and I've been doing it ever since. I now also lead our professional development and attorney programs. Every day, my teams and I seek to hire the best attorneys for our firm and our clients and provide them with the training and tools to provide superlative value to both. I really love what I do, and I'm very grateful to WSGR for having given me the opportunity to do it.

Mark Gould

Mark Gould is now an independent KM consultant and was Head of Knowledge Management at Addleshaw Goddard, LLP between September 2006 and May 2014. This is how he described his work before moving on.

What Do You Do?

I am responsible for creating and sustaining the environment within which people across the firm can develop and share knowledge to underpin the work we do for clients. At the moment, my focus is on leading and directing the firm's PSLs, but it is likely to shift toward improvements in collaboration and social business over the next couple of years (as our IT platform matures).

How Did You Get Started in KM?

My original calling was as a legal academic. Law is taught as an undergraduate subject in the United Kingdom and is much less closely linked with practice than it is in the United States. After my first law degree, I did a research Masters at the European University Institute in Florence, Italy. From there, I joined the teaching staff at the University of Hull (just for a year) and then the University of Bristol.

My focus as a legal academic was, again, quite far from practice. I taught subjects like Public Law (which is probably much closer to political science in the United Kingdom than constitutional law in the United States might be—one consequence of not having a written constitution), Administrative Law, European Union Law, and Jurisprudence. My research interests tended toward the arcane as well, covering topics ranging from the role of the Law Commission in English law reform to governance and rule-making in the nascent public law of the Internet.

For various reasons, I decided to change careers after 12 years in academia. This coincided with a family relocation to the north of England, and I was offered a job as a PSL in the Trade & Regulatory group at Addleshaw Booth & Co. (then based primarily in Leeds and Manchester). This was a new role for me and for the firm, although there were a few other PSLs in other practice groups, so I was able to define it to fit my capabilities as well as the needs of the group. In fact, I found that there were many aspects of the PSL role that match the skills required of academics. This is probably especially true in a practice area like competition law, where few issues are settled, so research and training can be characterized as academic with a dash of practice and commercial reality.

Addleshaw Booth & Co. merged with the London firm Theodore Goddard in May 2003, creating Addleshaw Goddard. The merger almost doubled the number of PSLs across the firm. During the post-merger integration, I worked closely with the integration team on reviewing library holdings.

This was probably the point at which I started to think about moving on from a PSL role, because I enjoyed the coordination and liaison challenges arising in the review work. I was also increasingly aware that the enlarged PSL group was in need of some form of coordination. Neither firm had had any form of central knowledge function, and so I proposed that we start by coordinating the PSLs better.

Having sown the seed, it took a couple of years before the firm decided that a properly constituted knowledge function would be a good idea. Finally, in September 2006, I was appointed as the firm's first Head of Knowledge Management. My initial contact with KM came when I was scouting for suitable roles in late 2000. At that stage, I joined a KM group on the U.K. conferencing system CIX (equivalent to the Well), but found that much of the discussion was over my head. On reflection, this was probably because it required an understanding of business life that I didn't then have. (I have a similar issue now in trying to describe to my school- and university-age children what I do. They have no comprehension of how an organization works, and so they struggle with the notion of knowledge work.)

I kept that initial contact with the KM field alive over the next few years by reading articles and books on the topic, but my first exposure to the wider legal KM community came when the firm appointed an external consultant to review the PSL function, with a view to developing our knowledge capability. She had been one of the first PSLs in the United Kingdom, and had moved into a management role before settling up as an independent consultant. She was very helpful in guiding me toward the new role and in supporting me in my first years in it. I found that her openness about her experiences in other firms was typical of others in the field. This is one of the things that I think marks out legal KM folk; we tend to be very happy to share with each other the ups and downs of our roles, in the confidence that we will keep each other's secrets where necessary.

When I started as Head of KM, I spent some time talking to people who had joined the firm in the previous 18 months or so. This helped me get a feel for the things that worked well (and not so well) in other firms, as well as the things that people were looking for from our KM function. This was immensely helpful for several reasons. I had only a limited perspective on legal KM, having only worked at one firm and in one practice area. Talking to lawyers at all levels (from junior associates to experienced partners) in a wide variety of practice areas and from a wide range of different types of firms, I got a real sense of the importance of different approaches to legal KM. I also had discussions with senior people within the firm, but those meetings tended to have a different focus. People who had been at the firm for longer tended to have a very similar outlook to each other, so it was useful to be able to provide evidence of other ways of approaching KM.

During my time in this role, I have concluded that the most important facet of knowledge management (certainly in law, if not elsewhere) is the creation and maintenance of connections among people. When I first joined the firm, I was lucky to share an office with one of the most well-connected associates in the firm. As a result, I got to know many more people across the firm than I might have otherwise, as people dropped in to speak to her. Many of those people are now quite senior, and my strong connection with them has proved valuable. My own personal knowledge management strategy depends on nurturing and learning from personal connections, as well as more traditional forms of learning through reading and attending conferences.

This emphasis on personal connectivity is also a critical aspect of the KM work that I do together with the firm's PSLs. When I first proposed that the PSL group should be better coordinated, my impression was that coordination was self-evidently a good thing. In fact, my experience in actually drawing the PSLs together as a group has been that the benefit of coordination comes from better connections among them, and in the awareness of the work that they each do. The result is that their knowledge of, for instance, changes in the law in areas other than their own is improved. Our PSLs also work closely with some of our key clients, to such an extent that they are considered by those clients to be their PSLs as much as ours. The depth of those relationships arises from a focus on quality connections.

One of the things that flows from strong personal networks is trust, and trust is a key component of a successful knowledge environment. I am fairly sure that firms with low levels of trust between lawyers cannot do anything meaningful with knowledge management. They may be able to implement various technology solutions (e.g., know-how databases, enterprise search, and so on), but the real value of those systems will not be realized. I think (and I have had feedback to support this) that I am trusted by many people across the firm, which I have found helpful in promoting various initiatives over the years. In part, this is a result of having been part of the firm for some time. I wonder whether someone new to the firm would find it much harder to gain the support of key partners and other stakeholders.

Most of my time in the role has coincided with the difficult market conditions of the last five years. This has meant that the firm has been able to make very little capital investment in knowledge systems. As a result, I (and the PSLs) have had to be quite resourceful in using the firm's other systems to support knowledge sharing. There is a limit to how much we can achieve though, and my biggest challenge has been to keep people interested in the future of knowledge management.

On a more positive note, I think that the way the legal sector is changing is positive for knowledge management generally. Every firm is facing the need to change, and most are doing so in ways that match sound business practice in other sectors. This might include better pricing, process mapping, project management, increased use of paralegals, or improved collaboration. For any one of those initiatives to succeed, knowledge management is necessary. My firm is doing them all, which means significant amounts of change and brings really positive challenges in the short and medium term.

Since leaving law firm life, I have been building a business aimed at helping firms use their knowledge more productively. My experiences at Addleshaw Goddard made me realize that my real interest was in moving the firm toward different and better ways of working. In fact, I think this has to be a core purpose for anyone involved in knowledge management. Even on a small scale, changes in knowledge processes must bring improvements in efficiency, effectiveness, or quality. Those improvements can only stick if people change the way they approach their work. However, a knowledge leader within a firm also has to deal with operational management and administration, which can make it hard to focus on important strategic projects. My move into consulting is an attempt to redress that balance, as well as immersing myself more deeply in the changes that are happening across the whole legal sector.

Milena Higgins

Milena Higgins is Director, Litigation Knowledge Management at Fish & Richardson, P.C. She started this role in August 2012.

What Do You Do?

I provide strategic oversight and support in driving business process improvements for our litigation group. My involvement spans everything from traditional KM projects, such as our best practices efforts to legal project management, litigation budget-monitoring software, and change management. I combine my passions for people and technology to architect the next generation of knowledge management solutions that will enable Fish & Richardson to provide better value to our clients.

How Did You Get Started in KM?

I vividly remember the moment I learned about knowledge management. It was like someone had opened the door to a world I didn't know existed. It's as if someone took all of the favorite things about my previous jobs and put them together to create the role of legal KM. Because I am not a lawyer, I always felt a little bit like an outsider in this industry. Learning about knowledge management made me eager to leverage my experience in litigation, my training as a scientist, and my growing interest in business to find new ways to contribute to the legal industry.

The year was 2010. Up to that point, I had spent the bulk of my professional life in patent litigation. I was at a point in my career where I felt restless and was looking for a new challenge. I didn't yet know what I wanted to do next, but I knew I needed a change. I set out to explore my options. I started talking to people I knew and learning about the various possibilities. This was about a year and a half after the economic downturn of 2008, so there were already some indications that the legal industry was changing. The more I read about the industry, the more intrigued I became. Unlike most people I know, I really like change. So I found the news about our industry changing really exciting.

Let me take a step back to add some context. I am a physicist by training. I literally stumbled into patent law when looking for jobs right out of graduate school. I took a job as a Science Advisor in a growing Intellectual

Property department at Robins, Kaplan, Miller & Ciresi in Minneapolis, Minnesota, not really knowing what I was getting into. It turned out to be a wonderful career. I loved my job. I enjoyed working with really smart people, learning about different technologies, and helping the litigators solve really complex puzzles.

After eight years at Robins, I got recruited out to join the in-house legal department at 3M. There I learned the client's perspective. Now the business units were my clients, and I quickly learned how important it was to know their business in order to do my job well. After two years of patent prosecution at 3M, I returned to Robins to manage a growing group of Science Advisors. As the Chief Scientist, I learned to manage people. I also learned a lot more about the business of running a law firm. But like many such roles in a law firm, I could only focus on that a small fraction of the time, because the rest of my time was devoted to billable client work.

By 2010 I started feeling that I was outgrowing my job. I was still really enjoying growing as a manager. My hope was to make a transition to a nonbillable management role, so I started having those conversations with my boss. I also started talking to others in the firm to learn of other opportunities that might lie within the firm. It was during one of those conversations with Dave Rigali, the firm's CIO, that I discovered knowledge management. When I learned that there were people who help firms be more efficient by providing technology solutions, I was hooked! I didn't expect that there were people in law firms doing that as a full-time job. I immediately started learning more about knowledge management, joined several LinkedIn groups, and was reading a lot of industry news articles. I was so intrigued, that a year later, I started a KM committee at Robins.

My interest in business was also growing. In 2011 I decided to apply to business school. That fall I enrolled in the University of Minnesota's Management of Technology program. This opened my eyes to a whole lot more exciting tools and methods of running and improving a business. I learned not only the business basics, like accounting, marketing, and communications, but also things very particular to technology-driven businesses, like new product development, technology foresight and forecasting, and managing innovation.

During the summer between my first and second year of school, I learned about the KM job opportunity at Fish & Richardson. Even though I was hoping to find something at Robins, this was simply too perfect to pass up, so I jumped in with both feet. I got the job and felt like the luckiest person alive! A year and a half into it, I still smile every day as I drive to work. I have my dream job. In some ways things haven't changed all that much—I still work with super-smart people, learn about cool new technologies, and help litigators solve complex problems—but the problems I help solve today are different. I work with our Litigation Practice Group Leader, Ann Cathcart Chaplin, to implement her vision for the new and improved litigation group at Fish. I help her manage change. I focus on helping the litigation group become more efficient, adapt to the changing legal industry, and hopefully stay a step or two ahead of the competition. And that is great fun!

I was in the midst of trying to figure out what to do next in my career. Learning about knowledge management was the Aha! moment that gave me clarity. From that point forward, the pieces started falling into place. In a way it feels like I have been preparing for KM work my entire career. Today I combine the problem-solving skills I learned as a physicist with the people skills I learned as a manager and the business skills I learned at 3M and in my MOT training, stir in all those years of being in the trenches of patent litigation, sprinkle my experience developing custom legal tools, and bring it all together to help the litigation group at Fish embrace and thrive in the new normal. I continue to enjoy the journey and look forward to the challenges ahead. I am especially looking forward to watching (and perhaps even influencing) the evolution of the legal KM profession as our industry embraces the opportunities that lie ahead.

David Hobbie

David Hobbie is a Litigation Knowledge Management Attorney at Goodwin Procter, LLP. He has held this position since 2005.

What Do You Do?

I support my firm's Litigation department through search, matter experience, collaborative technology, litigation analytics, and substantive knowledge management resources.

How Did You Get Started in KM?

My first real job, after college, was at the Climate Institute, a small international nonprofit focused on climate change (global warming and ozone depletion). I drafted proposals, wrote, and did some basic project management. My boss John Topping was a lawyer; in fact, he had been a trial lawyer before moving into politics and then environmental policy. Rumor has it he had taken IBM to trial for a small business client—and won!—but the client went under anyways. I was intrigued that he had been able to do so many different things with his career after coming out of law school, and I was also impressed by my labor lawyer uncle Charles Hobbie, who had argued several cases before the U.S. Supreme Court on behalf of unions. So, off to law school I went.

I was certainly correct that a law degree is (was?) a good preparation for a variety of types of work. After law school, I joined what came to be known as Bingham McCutchen, a large law firm that had grown significantly. After five years there, I joined the Boston office of another large firm, Eckert Seamans Cherin & Mellott. At these places I did all kinds of civil litigation; at Bingham, nominally I was in the securities litigation group, but I spent most of my first few years litigating a single construction arbitration and also did environmental litigation/negotiation. At Eckert Seamans, again I worked on a broad variety of cases, including product liability, education, trade secret, and small business litigation. At a large firm, you're provided with tremendous training and support, but you also tend to be limited in your hands-on experience. The Boston office of Eckert Seamans functioned like a smaller firm—within three weeks of starting there, I was second chair on a trial in Massachusetts Superior Court, and I later handled motions and small cases entirely on my own.

I was able to work as a litigation associate for eight years, because I enjoy and am good at legal research, and perhaps because I am easy to get along with. In my private life, after all, I am an accomplished classical musician, focusing on chamber music, string quartets, and the like, which call for intense collaboration with a small group of other musicians. But the adversarial side of litigation work repelled me. I remember one partner saying, after a tough negotiation, "You know, the clients expect you to get angry sometimes." I dwelt on my capabilities and realized that I liked learning about legal issues and thinking about the law, and also didn't mind being in an office a lot of the time. I preferred being in a helper role, though, rather than an adversarial one.

Fortuitously I saw an ad in the *Massachusetts Lawyer's Weekly* for a litigation knowledge manager position at Goodwin Procter. It described work that focused on developing sets of precedents, samples, and models for a large litigation department and representing the litigation department's perspective in firm-wide technology initiatives. Like the good researcher I am, I looked up some background information on knowledge management (I think I read Peter Drucker and other *Harvard Business Review* articles on KM) and on the limited public information about the firm's KM program. I interviewed with two partners and the director of KM and started at Goodwin Procter in October 2005.

I was happy to get the job, but I really had no idea just how fortunate I was. First of all, legal knowledge management jobs do not exactly grow on trees. To illustrate this point, I occasionally organize a meeting of those attorneys and other professionals who do legal knowledge management at law firms in Boston, and we comfortably fit in a medium-sized conference room. Second, I joined a program that was one of the real innovators and pioneers in the field, getting underway as early as 1999 and with a highly capable staff (including Trudy Ernst and Doug Cornelius, among other colleagues) that connected with the legal KM leaders of North America. Third, legal knowledge management turned out to be a really good fit for me. I'm passionate about helping other people practice law more effectively and efficiently; I love learning about new technologies and sharing what I know; and the legal knowledge management community consists of people who also highly value sharing and collaboration.

Rick Krzyminski

Rick Krzyminski has been the Knowledge Management Director at Baker, Donelson, Bearman, Caldwell & Berkowitz since December 2012. Before this role, he spent several years at Mayer Brown & Platt, where his interest in the then-nascent Internet lead to his breakthrough moment when he began working on the firm's intranet.

What Do You Do?

My role is leading a team that is responsible for delivering KM solutions to its lawyers, administrative staff, and clients, and working closely with IT and other groups to lead large projects. I am a member of the firm's Technology Committee, Marketing Data Committee, Task-Based Billing Committee, and Online Client Services Committee.

How Did You Get Started in KM?

"Sometimes it's better to beg for forgiveness than ask for permission," said Gail Munden, Director of Legal Information, in response to my question of whether I should start an intranet at Mayer Brown & Platt (MBP) in the mid-1990s. We were looking for a way to organize the helpful web links we were using for research at the time and make them available to all Library staff and lawyers. At the time, no one had desktop web access, and we were discussing adding two to four shared terminals in the Library. The Internet was just starting to take off, and home users were in the early stages of signing up for Earthlink and AOL—accessing with 14.4-baud modems. (I still remember those beeps and screeches of dial-up connections like it was just yesterday.) I gathered the links I had collected and organized them by practice group and by topic. I then picked up an *HTML for Dummies* book, learned how to code web pages, and the MBP intranet (and my involvement in KM) was born.

A few short years earlier, in 1993, I had graduated from The University of Illinois–Chicago with my BA in English Literature and was looking to find work while I figured out what I wanted to do with the rest of my life. At the time, I was thinking about possibly going to law school, so when I heard about an opening in the MBP Library, I jumped at the chance. Those first few professional years were spent working in various traditional legal library roles, as well as getting exposure to newer technologies (e.g., online catalogs, research materials in CD towers, etc.). I mention these early years for several reasons. First, I learned much in these years and received valuable mentoring from my supervisor at the time, Bobby Towns, who taught me the value of hard work and professionalism. Second, I firmly believe that technology and usability are essential components of delivering successful KM, and these early years prepared me well for what was still to come. Finally, these early years in the Library helped me develop a great base for building relationships with lawyers and understanding their practice. I had the opportunity to get to know them as incoming Summer and Fall Associates. Years later, when they were becoming partners, those great relationships had already been established, and it made it much easier for me to approach them and for them to feel comfortable working with me. Little did I know that 20-plus years later, I would still be working to make lawyers' jobs easier.

I enjoyed the work I was doing, and I was learning constantly, but it wasn't until that breakthrough moment when I started the firm intranet in the mid-1990s that the notion of using new technology to organize information and make it accessible to lawyers, thereby increasing their efficiency, began to firmly take hold in my mind. Before long, other administrative information began to creep onto the intranet, as well as the beginnings of data and application integration. What started as a small site that was stored on a file share grew to require its own server, which was dubbed RickuServe by Eric Anderson, MBP's Operations Manager at the time. My name had become synonymous with the intranet, due to my passion for my work, Gail's willingness to take a risk, and the unforeseen emergence of the World Wide Web.

Things became so busy that we needed help. We initially hired two people to work with me to keep up with demand for new intranet sites. Eventually, every practice group, administrative department, committee, and office had its own intranet site to collaborate with each other and to share the necessary information with other groups within the firm. I worked very closely with a few lawyers who were very adept at compiling their relevant practice group information and were looking for a mechanism to be able to share their knowledge. We didn't call it knowledge management at the time, but that's exactly what it was. A few years later, in approximately 2002, after MBP merged with London's Rowe & Maw, I was introduced to a more formal approach to knowledge management common to the U.K. legal industry. We began meeting regularly with KM leadership and practice support lawyers from across the pond to combine our intranets and develop new ways to provide access to relevant information. The blending of cultures and continued learning proved to be the next step in my development.

Of course, knowledge management is about more than lawyer efficiency and internal collaboration. It also plays a huge part in delivering client service that goes well beyond what an intranet is able to deliver. The way that I became involved directly in client services is also a unique story. In the early years of the commercial World Wide Web, firms were still developing their organizational structures to support what the new platform offered and were struggling with what many were calling the Wild West. At Mayer Brown, for instance, Marketing was working on all aspects of the public website using a homegrown content management system, IT was responsible for setting up extranets using a third-party solution, and I, from the Library, was managing our HTML-based intranet. Our web offerings had evolved separately over the course of these early years, with varying degrees of knowledge in each group, different tools, and, in some cases, duplicate effort.

By 2004, we realized we could streamline the delivery of web services by utilizing the strengths of each of these three groups. The individuals from each group that were responsible for the technology and content for each of the web channels (i.e., intranet, extranet, and Internet) were merged to form a new group called Knowledge & Web Solutions (KWS). The next four years would be economically prosperous for law firms, which allowed this new team to grow and prosper. The number of projects we delivered over the course of a given year were far more than the separate groups could have accomplished. At the same time, we worked very closely on several more mergers, adding seven Asia offices and two Brazil offices to the mix.

During this time, I went from managing the intranet alone to running all three web channels as the Assistant Director of KWS. My team, at its peak, consisted of 13 individuals supporting our clients, 1,800 lawyers, and 23 offices worldwide. The KWS team was responsible for implementing SharePoint and developing the intranet's search capabilities, delivering thousands of client extranets, hosting hundreds of knowledge bases, and maintaining the content of the firm's public website. During this time, I worked very closely with Howard Niden, the firm's CIO, who brought years of experience from his Price Waterhouse Coopers days. Howard was a great mentor and taught me about what KM means from a corporation's perspective, which has been very valuable in my professional development. The three things I'm most proud of during these years are as follows:

- Developing a distributed SharePoint publishing platform where owners of all sites would identify site publishers who would be responsible for directly maintaining their own content. This was developed along with a very extensive governance plan that was passed through our technology committee and strictly enforced.
- Developing a plan for KWS to document and share our collective knowledge internally (KM's not just for lawyers!), as well as processes by which we worked collectively with other groups (lawyers, staff, IT, Marketing, etc.) to efficiently deliver projects.
- Getting on board with IT's formal project management initiative and helping to enhance the formal, repeatable processes and communications that are part of each project.

By 2012, after 19 years at Mayer Brown, it was time for a new challenge, and an opportunity presented itself. Meredith Williams, Chief Knowledge Management Officer at Baker Donelson, was looking for a KM Director to lead a team responsible for delivering KM solutions to its lawyers, administrative staff, and clients. I had been familiar with Meredith's work for years through ILTA and respected her accomplishments. Additionally, during the interview process, I was quickly impressed by the firm management's commitment, support, and passion for knowledge management. The firm culture to which I was being introduced was quite impressive and the type of environment that is conducive to the success of a firm in this day and age. This culture, combined with the types of projects that were targeted for 2013, made my decision a no-brainer.

In a little over a year, I have enjoyed working with Meredith, helping to develop what we call a KM dream team, and delivering some very successful projects, including Enterprise Search. We have interesting projects coming up, along with the development of our next strategic plan. I look forward to the upcoming challenges and growth opportunities. Looking back, it's interesting to me how fortunate I am that various developments over which I had little or no control (e.g., the emergence of the Internet, great people that I've been fortunate enough to work with, law firm mergers, and continued learning opportunities) have had such a profound impact on my career. If I were to give one piece of advice to others entering the KM field, it would be to embrace change. To me, using one's knowledge and experience to address change and maximize the opportunities it provides is one of the fundamental values of KM.

Charlotte Logullo

Charlotte Logullo is Director of Practice & Client Solutions at Foley & Lardner, LLP. She has held this position since August 2011.

What Do You Do?

The Practice & Client Solutions Group is focused on improving and supporting the delivery of legal services through innovation, knowledge sharing, and enhancing the value received by the firm's clients in support of the firm's strategic initiatives. I am responsible for defining, coordinating, and facilitating these objectives. I am a member of the firm's Research & Development Committee, Legal Project Management Steering Committee, Technology Leadership Team, and have participated in various other firm strategic initiative groups.

How Did You Get Started in KM?

My background is likely very different from most of my colleagues in this field. I grew up in the United Kingdom. My family owned several hotels and restaurants, and I was raised in an environment of caring for and catering to customers, so my focus on client service was established at an early age. This focus continued throughout my early career; when working for a legal document retrieval company, I was intrigued with the level of service that large law firms provided to their clients. As an account representative, many large firms were part of my client list, and I really enjoyed providing the level of service these firms expected and provided. I got to see this first-hand when joining Foley in 1996 as a Legal Assistant in the Business Law Department.

In January 1997, I joined the Professional Development department as part of a team of trainers that were tasked with training for their conversion from MS-DOS to Windows and WordPerfect to MS Word. For two years in this role, I traveled to every office across the firm and was able to gain the knowledge and understanding of the different cultures in the different Foley offices. In 1999, a new CIO joined Foley, and with this came many new opportunities. For me it was a new role as the Southeast Region Technology Manager, overseeing at that time six offices and 12 staff members consisting of technology specialists and learning coaches (trainers). The firm was in a transition with the consolidation of all technology under one central management. This position was a key Technology Department liaison for all attorneys and staff in the southeast region. This included responsibility over communications, technology training, problem escalations, project management, and support of the firm's southeast region offices, comprising more than 300 end users including more than 150 attorneys. In this role, I was exposed to work with people at all levels within the firm, including clients.

In the quest to provide excellent client service and in response to several client requests, and being that the CIO was very progressive, we were at the time working with a newly hired internal technology consultant to develop a client-facing extranet. This led to further work and development of client-focused technologies that were provided to the firm's clients at no cost as a value-add. In my role managing training and several of the firm's Learning Coaches, I worked with the consultant to create a program to educate the firm on different technology services we could provide not only internally, but also to clients. We hosted a number of internal tradeshow-style Technology Open House sessions that were hugely successful and popular. About this same time, the CIO and internal consultant worked with an external consulting company to gauge the temperature of the firm attorneys for their understanding of knowledge management and the implementation of a formal program. The interest for a formal program and varying levels of understanding of KM at that time was fairly low, as was management support, so as a firm we did nothing.

In 2004, right before taking leave for the birth of my second child, I accepted a newly created position as Senior Technology Consulting Manager. The previous consultant had left the firm, and with this new role, I now managed all facets of the firm's technology service products for clients, including our proprietary client collaboration system—FOLEY ClientSuite. I was also responsible for coordinating the strategic use of technology within law departments and practice groups and worked with them to evaluate and improve the use of technology within the firm. As a member of the firm's Client Service Initiative, I identified essential applications required for business use and led the development of the client-facing Budget Management Tool, which was designed to monitor legal spend in real-time. I led several other technology initiatives and assisted in strategic technology planning. I added a staff member to my team to focus on internal marketing and communications.

In early 2011, the firm implemented a new strategic plan. I worked with the Chief Strategy Officer and led a team to create a new internal website focused on communicating the strategy to all firm members. Among the core strategic objectives was not only being an innovator in service offerings, but also in the manner in which these services are delivered. This included key action steps focused around KM and process improvements. Other strategic objectives included action steps that aligned within all the areas in which I had been working. I was asked to lead a KM task force comprising attorneys from across the firm to complete several action steps associated with the strategic plan. At that time I also had some new initiatives in the FY12 budget, including the replacement of the firm's intranet portal, so I requisitioned to have another new staff member. The prior CIO recognized the need to formalize the creation of a KM department and move some firm strategic initiatives away from management by the Technology department, so the Practice & Client Solutions Group was formed in August 2011. The group name was created with careful thought and much discussion. We knew that management was in support of KM, but lawyers at that time had very different levels of understanding. It was felt that it would be limiting to name us the KM department, as it would be restrictive and not inclusive of the many other areas that we were working that were not, at that time, widely considered in the legal industry to be under the KM umbrella.

It appears that my move into KM occurred as a natural progression of a series of opportunities and events, similar to how Foley itself has evolved. This firm has always focused on excellent client service, and the initiatives my group manages help lead to Foley being known as a firm that always delivers excellent quality work, value, and client service.

Catherine Monte

Catherine Monte is Chief Knowledge Officer at Fox Rothschild, LLP. She has held this position since 2006.

What Do You Do?

I lead the firm's KM department, which consists of three main service areas: Library Services, Knowledge Services/Solutions, and Business and Competitive Intelligence.

How Did You Get Started in KM?

My entrée into KM—and the legal sector in general—was somewhat accidental. I applied for an editing job at a law firm after I graduated college. I had an English major and had absolutely no idea what I really wanted to do with my life. I figured, I can read and write fairly well, so why not editing? But when I went in for the interview, the HR representative said she didn't think I was a good fit. My heart sank, but in the next sentence she said there was another job available—a paralegal position in the Litigation department, and she thought it would suit me better. I ended up taking this position and spending a lot of time researching in the library, which led to my interest in obtaining a Master's degree in Library Science.

I immersed myself in several research-related jobs, and after a few years secured a management position in the New York City office of a U.K.-based firm. Because the office was relatively small (about 50 attorneys), I was responsible for some administrative functions: records, library, and eventually KM, which is an integral part of all major U.K. firms. I worked in close conjunction with the professional recruitment/marketing attorney, who was instrumental in introducing me to KM concepts and culture while also connecting me to PSLs and other counterparts internationally.

One of my official KM assignments here was to create a system to index and capture U.S. securities documents. Many U.S. transactional attorneys in London and Hong Kong needed to connect with their counterparts in New York and share best practices. There was nothing in place to do this, and we had to start from scratch. Luckily, there were colleagues in London who had a tried-and-true system. so we used their system as a baseline and architected a U.S. model. It was exciting to be in on the ground level of that process and see it through a few phases of execution. It was one of my most rewarding achievements.

When I left the U.K.-based firm and moved into my current position, I wasn't sure how my former experiences would segue into my new role. I had left a very large international firm with 30-plus offices in many countries. The new firm had only eight offices and all were in the United States. What sorts of needs would they have for sharing precedents, best practices, and collaboration? As it turned out, they had very similar KM needs, especially as the firm grew in attorney size and in offices. Though still only in the United States, attorneys practice in multiple jurisdictions and have a need to share across 19 offices and more than 40 practices. The KM team is actively involved in practice group meetings and strategy sessions with practice groups and partners to improve productivity, streamline business operations, and increase client development/retention. The varied backgrounds of the staff—lawyers, librarians, business analysts, and technologists—come together in what I consider to be the perfect amalgamation of talent.

I suppose if I had to provide advice to someone starting out in the library/information/KM profession, it would be the following:

- Be open to opportunities and new ideas.
- Take chances and be willing to volunteer for new projects, even if you don't have specific past experience.
- Create collaborative rapport with colleagues.
- Learn from more-experienced mentors and be a mentor for others.
- Be more proactive than reactive.

Mara Nickerson

Mara Nickerson is Chief Knowledge Officer at Osler, Hoskin & Harcourt, LLP. She has held this position since September 1998, though at the time the title was Director of Professional Development and the scope of the role was simply professional development and precedents.

What Do You Do?

I am responsible for the oversight, strategic direction, and management of Knowledge Management, Professional Development, the Library, and Conflicts and Records. I am also on the firm's Practice Management and Innovation Committee and the Conflicts & Ethics Committee.

How Did You Get Started in KM?

I am a lifer at my firm. Professionally born and raised at Osler. I feel this has had a huge impact on my ability to move into and grow the KM role here. I joined the firm right out of law school after completing my LLB and MBA degrees. I practiced in the corporate area. Eventually, as much as I enjoyed doing deals, with a busy family life I started to consider alternative career options. At the same time, the Corporate department started feeling it needed to invest in the creation of precedents. So I took on the role doing what we would now call KM, but back then I just called it "the best job in the world where I got to use my legal skills contributing to my department but no longer having to work through the night."

I focused on creating a precedent system, identifying, collecting, and cataloguing reusable work product, drafting model precedents, creating a closing book library, and monitoring and writing about corporate and securities law developments. I also got involved in designing and developing some professional development programs for the department. After about five years of this role, I decided I wasn't quite ready to give up the practice of law entirely, so I went back to practice. Notwithstanding having been out of practice for almost five years, I felt that my KM work had enabled me to stay totally current on legal developments and drafting documents, and I certainly knew how to access all of the resources I needed to practice. I will admit my negotiating skills were rusty, but after my first deal I was fully back to speed.

A couple of years later, in early 2008, the firm went through a strategic planning process, and out of that they determined that the firm needed to invest in a number of talent areas. They created a new full-time, firm-wide role focused on professional development and precedents (since only the Corporate department had any precedents, and even those had been neglected since I had gone back to practice). Early on they saw the inherent symmetry between professional development and KM. They offered me the role, and I decided it was a real opportunity to have a larger impact. It soon became clear that one person couldn't achieve all that we wanted to, and after visiting with a number of U.K. firms, researching the role of Practice Support Lawyers, I proposed to the firm the idea of having KM lawyers embedded in the practice groups—not dissimilar to the role I had played earlier on. We started with one, and as other departments saw the benefits, the program extended so that we now have seven KM lawyers.

My role has evolved over time. KM is naturally very closely aligned with the library, as they are actively involved in cataloguing and sharing internal and external knowledge, and they play a great role in supporting training and awareness on all of our knowledge resources. So, eventually it was folded under our knowledge and learning umbrella. Under KM I also spearheaded our Opinions Committee, Boilerplate Committee, and an ad hoc committee looking at document standards. KM and all of these related activities have a common thread of being aimed at quality and risk management. Eventually, these drivers got me more involved in other risk management policies and activities until, most recently, I took over responsibility for our Conflicts and Records Department.

The challenge and opportunity now is to find new ways for all of these groups to find their common ground and integrate activities and knowledge assets as much as possible. KM and professional development have worked together the longest, with KM providing content for professional development programs. Now we are developing topic pages on the intranet that include the typical KM content of precedents and checklists, but also short e-learning nuggets to provide lawyers with focused, just-in-time practice resources. The Library is taking on an increasing role in collecting knowledge resources, providing user support for accessing internal and external resources, and pushing content to practice group pages. This year we hope to start expanding the Records team's role to help lawyers manage their electronic content, and the Conflicts/New File Opening team is working with Client Development and Finance & Accounting to build a more integrated view of our clients and matters.

One of the most exciting developments in KM over the last few years, for me, is the expansion into legal project management and process improvement. One of the basic KM drivers has always been efficiency—providing lawyers with easy access to the resources they need when they need them, in the context in which they need them. This is process efficiency. We started down this road almost eight years ago when we developed our client and matter pages on our intranet, providing lawyers with real-time access to the financial information about clients and matters. Then about five years ago we added additional matter tagging so we could start searching for matters by type, or industry, or size, to support fee estimates, finding expertise, pushing precedent content, and responding to RFPs. With the development of the firm's Practice Management and Innovation initiative in 2010 (out of the firm's most recent strategic planning process), KM has been a core part of the team since the start.

I think the best element of being in KM is the ability to get involved in so many different aspects of the firm. Certainly, this is not the legal career I envisioned for myself when I started out. Although my Bachelor of Commerce degree and MBA provided me with a solid financial and business background that helps immensely with budgeting and strategy development, like most lawyers, I never expected to use those skills in a practical business environment, and I still am not sure I am qualified to manage the teams that report to me. When I first took on this role, one of the lawyers said to me "So, you have gone over to the dark side now!" There are challenges to being in a nonbilling role. You have to be flexible, tenacious, service-oriented, and comfortable with the value you believe you bring to the organization. But like most organizations, if you step up, offer to help, and provide a solution to a problem, you can have a positive impact. I still no longer have to pull all-nighters, but anyone on the senior administrative side of a law firm likely overall ends up putting in the same kind of hours as most practicing lawyers. But law firms are increasingly operating like other business organizations and putting in place the support systems and processes that go with that. And KM, with its focus on understanding and standardizing business processes, identifying and addressing areas of risk, and leveraging knowledge across the organization (legal and administrative), can play a key role.

Scott Rechtschaffen

Scott Rechtschaffen is Chief Knowledge Officer at Littler Mendelson, P.C. He has held this position since 2009.

What Do You Do?

I lead a national team of KM professionals dedicated to enhancing and innovating the way our firm delivers legal services to its clients. I help develop KM products and services that enable our attorneys to share their knowledge and experience, collaborate on client matters, and work more efficiently for the benefit of our clients. I also focus on developing innovative solutions that enable clients to directly access online Littler's collective knowledge and expertise.

How Did You Get Started in KM?

I took a somewhat convoluted path to become the Chief Knowledge Officer of an AmLaw 100 law firm—more of an accident than a planned career path. Although, in retrospect, there was a certain inevitability to where I have wound up. I joined Littler Mendelson in 1984, right out of law school. At the time, Littler was a regional labor and employment law firm with about 50 attorneys in five offices in California. I initially trod a traditional path—handling union organizing cases, labor arbitrations, employment litigation, and advice and counseling work—but I soon gravitated toward outside-the-mainstream projects.

Littler has always been a very entrepreneurial firm and encouraged innovative approaches to delivering client services and marketing the firm's services. Littler was one of the first firms to really understand "content marketing," and it began hosting major client conferences and investing significant resources into publishing substantive publications and client alerts. I became involved with many of these client conferences and publications. Then, in the early 1990s, I became involved in several fairly creative projects: I helped develop (1) a video series educating employers about litigation risks, (2) sophisticated software that helped employers build employee handbooks and employment agreements, and (3) a pre-Internet system to provide employers with automated answers to questions delivered through telephone decision trees and fax-back memos. Over time, our attorneys came to see me as the go-to resource for any wacky project they could dream up.

Then, in 1996, this reputation culminated in one of the more unique projects any attorney could claim as the origin of their second career: I designed and built a board game. We were preparing for The Employer Conference, our annual client conference, which, at the time, typically attracted about 1,000 human resources and in-house counsel attendees. That year, the theme of the conference was going to be the law of training—why employers needed to train their managers and employees about sexual harassment, workplace violence, diversity, workplace safety, and other subjects. One evening, Garry Mathiason, one of Littler's visionaries and the driving force behind our conferences and publications, asked to see me. He told me that he wanted to create something that we could give to conference attendees to take home to their workplaces to help them train their employees. I blankly nodded in agreement and asked what he had in mind. He said that he had been in Toys"R"Us the night before with his daughters and had been in the aisle with all of the board games. He wanted my help in creating a board game that we could give out at the conference that would help companies train their employees about employment law issues.

Law school had prepared me to deliver oral arguments, analyze court decisions, and prepare creative written advocacy; law school had not prepared me to design a board game. How exactly does one create a board game? Well, I soon learned. I contacted the owner of the company that produced the Trivial Pursuits board game. I told him I wanted to make a board game. Now, at the time, board games were very popular and big sellers. His first response to me was "Yeah, you and everybody else. How are you going to finance your game?" I was somewhat taken aback and, frankly, had not thought about financing. I asked him how much he needed. He said that he needed $10,000 just to get started. I told him I would FedEx him a check the next day. Needless to say, he and I developed an excellent business relationship.

I spent the next several months designing and building a board game. It was much like the board games that were popular at the time: Players would work their way around the board answering employment law questions in an effort to become "team leader of the year." We gathered a panel of HR experts to advise us, and we engaged some great graphic designers to help us make the game attractive. We rolled out the game—Winning through Prevention®—at our annual conference to a tremendous reception. Our clients and guests were blown away by it; what law firm actually creates a board game? We were, frankly, astonished by the reaction. What we had thought was merely a marketing tool quickly became an actual product. We were selling the games for $100 apiece, and the demand grew pretty heavily. Soon, we created a Training Edition, complete with a how-to video and a facilitator's guide.

At some point, we realized that there was a market for practical hands-on products created by a law firm. This led us to create an ancillary business, Employment Law Training (ELT), which would initially exploit the sales opportunities arising from our board game but then go on to create a comprehensive suite of online training programs on employment law topics. The visionaries at our firm correctly saw that online training would soon become a major business. I was asked to move over to ELT, on a part-time basis, to build out their live training division. I would spend the next two years as ELT's Sr. Vice President of In-Person Training, generating revenue for the company as it developed its online training products.

As ELT focused more heavily on its online training catalog, we decided to bring the live training business back into the law firm, and I transitioned back into a full-time role within Littler. Initially, I was asked to explore other possible ancillary businesses that the firm might consider. However, in about 2001, the firm engaged in a strategic planning process involving senior firm leadership, firm visionaries, and some outside consultants. We spent time examining all of the various nonbillable activities the firm was engaged in: our ancillary businesses, publications, conferences, and partnerships with third parties. As we worked through the process, it became evident that the best use of these resources was in providing our working attorneys with greater resources to enable them to serve their clients more efficiently and effectively. We had stumbled on the basic principles of knowledge management, without really knowing what knowledge management was.

At one point, during our strategic planning meetings, one of our firm leaders observed that if we were to grow to 60 offices and 1,000 attorneys (yes, the vision for the firm we are now was foreseen in 2001), we would need to have some structure to create a viable community of interest among our offices, a way for attorneys to share their collective knowledge and a way to ensure consistent quality across all of our offices. I recall very distinctly one of our leaders saying, "I think there is this discipline called knowledge management." He then pointed to me and said, "Why don't you find out about that and make it work here."

At the time, needless to say, I knew nothing about knowledge management, but I set out to learn and soon discovered that, in addition to the concept of knowledge management, there were a lot of people writing and talking about the future of law and how the traditional law firm model would be inalterably affected by technology and process improvement. I read Richard Susskind's *Transforming the Law* and went to conferences where I learned from early prognosticators like Jeff Rovner, Peter Krakauer, Ron Friedmann, and Michael Mills. Eventually, I became a convert; I became firmly convinced that the traditional law firm model was broken. And, I became convinced that the real role of knowledge management was to help shape the future of how law firms would effectively deliver services to their clients.

I have spent the last decade or so building out a fairly robust KM function at Littler. I have been blessed to work with some really visionary law firm leaders and have their trust and support. And I have benefited enormously from their understanding that KM is not just about technology. KM at Littler has always partnered with IT; we have never been part of the IT department. Our leadership has always believed that effective KM requires us to have dedicated human resources; this is what has enabled me to develop the unbelievably dedicated team of KM attorneys (now over 12 attorneys with an average of 13 years of labor/employment law experience) that has made our program so successful. I am convinced that the complete adoption of KM as a critical department within Littler is attributable to our having an incredible team of Knowledge Management Attorneys who have gained the trust of our working attorneys.

I used to be a practicing attorney—serving clients, billing hours, generating receipts. At some point, through a series of unplanned occurrences—and a board game—I got a new job. My wife likes to say that I'm the only person she knows who completely changed careers without ever leaving his office. I owe that to a remarkable, entrepreneurial law firm and far-sighted law firm leaders who were willing to trust me and my vision of how legal services could be delivered differently.

Jeffrey Rovner

Jeffrey Rovner has been the Managing Director for Information at O'Melveny & Myers, LLP since May 2006.

What Do You Do?

I oversee and coordinate four information-rich functions in my firm: IT, KM, Library, and Records. To paraphrase Google's mission statement, my job is to organize the firm's information, and—subject to appropriate confidentiality measures—make it accessible and useful to our personnel and clients.

How Did You Get Started in KM?

My story begins in the early 1990s, when I was a young partner at Morrison & Foerster, doing municipal bond financings. I'd been a lawyer for about 10 years at that point, and I was struggling with the tedium of the practice. So I bought a personal computer and taught myself how to create databases and form documents that minimized the repetitive aspects of my work. Tasks that had previously taken hours to accomplish, such as preparing the pitch materials to compete for a new deal, could now be done in a few minutes.

The chairman of the firm, Carl Leonard, saw what I was doing, and he said all of the firm's lawyers should be using my techniques. The only problem was that the rest of the firm was still using mini-computers, rather than PCs. So Carl put me in charge of the firm's technology committee and gave me a mandate to introduce personal computers and software to the firm—in my spare time.

While I was trying to introduce personal computing to the legal masses, I faced another problem. The firm assigned me a first-year associate to work on each bond project, but the work was so mind-numbingly tedious that nearly every associate quickly moved on to more interesting work at the earliest opportunity. As a result, I found myself spending a lot of time training young lawyers, only to lose them within a few months. Because I couldn't make municipal bond law more interesting, I decided I needed to find a way to deliver my training course in less time. So I deconstructed each type of bond transaction into its fundamental elements (e.g., the timeline of the transaction, the participants, the documents that must be drafted, the legal sources that must be consulted, the issues that must be negotiated) and gathered all of these elements into a packaged training course. Armed with this package, I could bring a first-year associate up to speed much faster than before, and I discovered that the same package of materials helped me to complete my own legal work more quickly and with less boredom.

I then came across a book by Yale computer scientist and Unabomber victim David Gelernter that seemed to explain why my packaged training course had been successful. In *Mirror Worlds*, Gelernter argued that all human beings crave what he called topsight, or the ability to see the big picture of a place or a subject, so they can understand how the parts fit together. It's the reason people love to climb the Eiffel Tower or any other tall structure. Aha! My training course succeeded because it gave a young lawyer topsight over the topic of municipal bond financing. The lawyer could see the big picture and then drill down into the details. I found this very interesting.

Around this time, in the fall of 1996, I got a call from an old friend who had left Morrison & Foerster to become a partner at the Brobeck firm. We spoke regularly, so he knew I'd become much more interested in my technology and process work than in doing bond deals. He invited me to leave my practice and come to Brobeck, where my full-time job would be to apply my new skills to the lawyers in Brobeck's emerging company practice. It was a chance to spend my days indulging the hobby that I'd come to enjoy, for about the same pay I was making as a Morrison & Foerster partner. I struggled with the decision for nearly two minutes before jumping ship. At Brobeck, I was given the title of Counsel and Director of Practice Development for the Business & Technology (B&T) Group. There was no job description for my role, so I was free to write my own. But what should I focus on? What sort of problems should I try to solve?

To answer those questions, I set out to immerse myself in the B&T Group, just as an anthropologist might immerse himself in a primitive tribe. I called this my walking-around phase. I traveled to each office and conducted one-on-one, 30- to 60-minute interviews with every lawyer in the group. At the beginning of each interview, I explained that I would hold our discussion in confidence. I then peppered my interviewee with questions:

- How would you describe your practice?
- In what areas are you an expert?
- Who are the other top experts in various aspects of the group's practice? (If my interviewee was reluctant to answer this question, I could get my answer by asking the question differently: "If you had a particularly thorny venture capital problem and needed advice, whom would you call first? How about an M&A problem? A 1934 Act problem?")
- What are the biggest frustrations you face in your practice?
- Is there another firm that is better than we are? If so, what do you think makes them so successful?
- If you were chair of the firm for a day, what's the first thing you would do?

After conducting several of these interviews, themes began to emerge. I tested these themes in my remaining interviews to determine whether they were widely shared. When I concluded my discussions, I had amassed a treasure trove of useful information, as follows:

- I learned the biggest problems that afflicted my group, and I knew the specific lawyers who would be my allies as I tackled a given problem.
- I learned several good ideas, and knew whom to publicly thank when I implemented each idea.
- I learned which lawyers were most widely admired in each of the group's specialties. In the parlance of Malcolm Gladwell's *The Tipping Point*, these were the group's mavens. I knew that if I could persuade one of these mavens to endorse my work, then the rest of the group would fall into line.

I now had my marching orders, but I lacked an efficient way to communicate with the group and to publish my solutions. Brobeck's CIO, Marty Metz, came to my rescue. Marty and I had joined Brobeck on the same day. In his prior job, Marty had built one of the first intranets in the legal industry. He persuaded me that he should build an intranet for Brobeck, and I should publish my work on that platform. (Marty has since become a dear friend. I'm indebted to him for a lot of wise advice over the years.)

Shortly thereafter, BrobeckNet was born. In its initial incarnation, it focused exclusively on the B&T Group. For each of the group's practice topics, it provided the rough equivalent of the packaged training courses I had developed in my former life. Each training course was based on input from the group as a whole but bore the endorsement of the group's acknowledged experts in that topic. For each topic, I provided forms of the documents that were most common, and each form document was annotated to explain what each provision meant and how to negotiate it against a skilled adversary. BrobeckNet was a great success, because it offered something for everyone. The associates loved it, because it made them knowledgeable and efficient. And the partners loved it, because they no longer had to worry about the quality of the work their associates were producing.

Around this time, I accepted an invitation from the Professional Development Consortium to speak about BrobeckNet at their annual conference. As I was waiting for my turn to speak, I perused the printed conference materials. I came across an article describing something called knowledge management and was startled to discover that it described exactly what I had been doing at Brobeck. Eureka! Now that I knew the name for my job, I could learn better ways to do it. I felt like an adopted child who had found his birth mother.

I quickly devoured all of the books I could find on knowledge management. Although the legal industry had yet to adopt KM, other industries were implementing KM with great success. I discovered the companies whose programs were most admired, and I met with many of their KM leaders to learn what they had done and what they were planning. I recall that I learned a huge amount from my meeting with the CKO of McKinsey & Co. It is said that imitation is the sincerest form of flattery. If that's so, then I flattered several companies profusely as I adopted their KM ideas in my work at Brobeck.

The following year, the chair of Brobeck, Tower Snow, asked me to present BrobeckNet at a meeting of all of the firm's practice group leaders. By the end of the presentation, the group agreed that I should relinquish my role with the B&T Group and lead an effort to extend BrobeckNet to all of the firm's practice groups. At that point, I was given a new firm-wide title, one that was the first of its kind in the legal industry: Director of Knowledge Management.

The rest of my tale can be summed up briefly. I recruited four terrific lawyers to introduce KM to the firm's other practice groups. Together we designed a new BrobeckNet to deliver our KM tools to the firm. The new system was very sophisticated, even by today's standards. In 2002, the *National Law Journal* reported that BrobeckNet "may well be the most advanced legal knowledge management system in use."[1]

Later that year, I accepted an offer to lead Clifford Chance's KM program in the United States. The opportunity to take on the challenges of knowledge transfer in a firm of 3,000 lawyers across dozens of offices was irresistible. I knew I would learn a lot, because my new boss, Paul Greenwood, had come to the firm from McKinsey, where he led a highly regarded KM program in their London branch. I stayed at Clifford Chance for four years, honing the ideas I had developed at Brobeck and learning how to deliver KM solutions on a global scale. I was a kid in a candy store.

In 2006, I was invited to join O'Melveny & Myers. I was offered leadership not only of KM but also Information Technology (Library and Records were added later). My task would be to integrate the two functions, with two overarching goals: (1) to ensure that the firm's IT investments were spent primarily to enhance the firm's legal practice, rather than on back-office systems, and (2) to identify all of the information that passed through the firm (much of which was visible only to administrative staff) and to present that information, in context, to the lawyers in useful ways. This was a golden opportunity, particularly because I had been an associate at O'Melveny from 1983 to 1988 and still had many friends at the firm. So I rejoined O'Melveny eight years ago and have worked there very happily ever since. My current KM delivery system is ommni, an intranet that strives to live up to its tagline: "Your one source for Firm information."

1. Ashby Jones, "Brobeck Rolls Out Legal Knowledge Management System," *American Lawyer Media*, April 8, 2002.

In addition to my duties at O'Melveny, I accepted an offer from my former Morrison & Foerster mentor, Carl Leonard, to teach KM and IT each year at George Washington University's Master's Program in Law Firm Management.

During my 18 years leading KM programs in law firms, I've distilled a few principles:

- Never forget the myriad pressures of practicing law in a large law firm—of finding the right answers to difficult questions, of operating under severe time constraints, of competing with determined adversaries, of navigating the path to partnership, of satisfying the firm's administrative and bureaucratic expectations, and of winning (and keeping!) clients. Remember that a chief aim of KM must be to relieve these pressures as much as possible. To the extent we can do that, our KM programs will always be relevant and popular.
- Strive to develop KM solutions that (a) do not depend upon lawyers taking any actions beyond their day-to-day client work, (b) can be delivered at scale (i.e., to all offices and practice groups simultaneously), and (c) automate that which can be automated (but not more).
- When delivering multiple technologies to a firm, design them so they appear, collectively, as a single system that can be easily understood. (Most people think of Google's search tool as a single system, and therefore find it simple to understand and use. Yet that tool incorporates hundreds of underlying technologies.) If that system happens to act just like another system with which the users are already familiar, so much the better. (That's why O'Melveny's ommni intranet borrows heavily from successful online shopping principles and designs, such as the long-tail and faceted search.)
- When designing a technology solution, focus exclusively on how to make it delightful to its users, no matter how much behind-the-scenes effort that will require. In other words, it's all about the effect, not the method. (That's a lesson I learned from my lifelong interest in sleight-of-hand magic.)

Evan Shenkman

Evan Shenkman is Senior Knowledge Management Counsel at Ogletree, Deakins, Nash, Smoak, & Stewart, P.C., which happens to be where I serve as the Director of Knowledge Management. Here, he shares his story about how he got started in knowledge management. Evan started his role in June 2011.

What Do You Do?

I help design, promote, and maintain our firm's internal and client-facing KM tools; manage the firm's KM legal resource center of model documents, templates, exemplar documents, and practice guides; assist attorneys in issue-spotting complex labor and employment issues; provide our attorneys and clients with substantive legal news updates; provide training to attorneys on KM tools and services; and supervise the firm's KM Counsel.

How Did You Get Started in KM?

In 2010, I was elected shareholder at Ogletree Deakins, a labor and employment litigation firm. I was also a husband and a father of two active boys under eight, who—as boys that age should—expected me to spend my nights and weekends with them, both physically and mentally. It was difficult to oblige. The life of a litigator has many virtues (satisfaction of intellectual curiosity, wonderful client relationships, and camaraderie among my peers topped my personal list), but downtime is not among them, particularly as a shareholder. And when I finally found myself at home with the boys, I was anything but carefree; the adversarial nature of the practice caused my mind to continually churn about that nasty letter awaiting a response, a looming argument, or ongoing gamesmanship. By early 2011, after nine years of practice, I decided I wanted a change.

Although most career changes in law involve leaving one's firm, my goal was to find a possibility that existed within. I explained to our senior management that, "my first choice [rather than the usual progression of, for instance, going in-house] would be to stay with Ogletree in some different professional capacity. I love the people, it's a great firm, and the firm has been great to me. And I know I can bring a lot to the table—energy, creativity, my experience and success working up the ranks here, etc.—especially in a position in which I feel I am making positive changes for the firm, its attorneys, and clients."

Although I didn't know it at the time, my firm was in the early stages of establishing a KM department, and firm leadership concluded it would be a great fit for me. Legal KM closely aligned with my skills, interests, and personality. As a known commodity in the firm, it was expected my role (as Senior KM Counsel) would help give the new department instant credibility. Furthermore, I like to teach and train, and I already had intimate familiarity with the way our firm operates, what it takes to be a successful attorney, what makes our clients happy, what caliber and style of work product is expected, and who our firm's subject matter experts are—all topics at the heart of many KM initiatives. I became the firm's first full-time KM employee on June 1, 2011.

I didn't know any other KM professionals before starting my KM role at Ogletree, but fortunately, the legal KM community was promptly welcoming. Days after I started in my new role, a client suggested I contact his colleague, Patrick DiDomenico, to learn more about legal KM. Patrick, who several months later would join our firm as Director of KM, flooded me with guidance and materials on all things legal KM. He also connected me with a large group of fellow legal KM professionals in New York City with whom I now meet for monthly strategy and knowledge-sharing meetings. Finally, I've also met many KM professionals at industry events, such as ILTA, ARK, and LegalTech, as well as at vendor social events.

What I liked best about the practice of law remains in my KM role: I still get to issue-spot and problem-solve complex puzzles (i.e., I think like a lawyer); develop relationships with my firm's clients; work with great attorneys; and put my knowledge of labor and employment law, and tech-savvy skills, to good use. I also spend a good deal of time training and mentoring our junior attorneys, which is especially rewarding. Best of all, those aspects of the practice of law that kept me up at night and away from my family (namely, the constant animosity and argument for the sake of argument) are completely gone in the KM world. I now spend my days helping our attorneys and clients—rather than fighting with adversaries—and my nights and weekends coaching soccer and enjoying my family.

Euan Sinclair

Euan Sinclair has been the Director of Knowledge Management at Lawson Lundell, LLP since January 2011.

How Did You Get Started in KM?

My first interest in KM stems from when I was working as a lawyer for the British government in the early 1990s. At that time, Tony Blair and New Labour were campaigning to be elected to government in the 1997 election. I remember being fascinated by a program that they had deployed to great effect called Excalibur, which was a database that used fuzzy logic to retrieve information on any point. It was used by the party's rebuttal unit to find any facts, figures, or quotes to quickly rebut any stories by the opposing parties before their version made the 6 o'clock news or the next day's headlines.

I wondered what would happen if we had a database of all our legal department's knowledge and experience and could search that database with Excalibur. Although it sounded fantastical to my bosses at the time, it's pretty standard now. Time moved on, as did my legal career, but I consistently collected interesting articles, materials, agreements, or language that I came across and kept it in a binder. This is actually a traditional Scottish practice (they are called "styles" in Scotland).

My practicing career has mainly been as an in-house lawyer. I've seen the "more for less" pressure from the other side of the fence, since I regularly instructed external counsel, who just did not understand the budgetary pressure the organization faced. I have always had an interest in management, and graduated with an MBA from Edinburgh University. Then I graduated LLM (Master of Laws) in IT law from Strathclyde University, where Richard Susskind is a professor and was a tutor on the retreats. Richard is an extraordinary advocate for technology in legal practice, and it amazed me that lawyers were not more receptive to his theories at that time.

Over the years, I stayed in touch with a good friend from the government. When I was in Edinburgh one day attending an in-house lawyers' conference at his firm, I arranged to meet him for a coffee during the break. He was a professional support lawyer (PSL), and I was interested to know more about what he did. He explained all about knowledge management to me. I told him that if there was ever a vacancy, he should call me. About six months later, my friend did in fact call to let me know that he was leaving that firm to move to another firm as PSL. Therefore, there was a vacancy for his job, was I interested? Although moving to a law firm would be turning from poacher to gamekeeper, I jumped at the chance and was grateful to be selected.

The role centered around the real estate department (around 80 lawyers) and consisted of maintaining the KM database, which by that time was fairly mature at around ten years old, developing new precedents, updating the lawyers on any new developments, and organizing training. PSLs in Scotland are deep subject matter experts (sometimes referred to as "gurus") and are embedded within the practice groups. During this time, an associate returned as a part-time PSL, as the department grew. I branched out to include support for the growing construction and infrastructure projects department (around 20 lawyers). I have gained quite a bit of experience in projects and procurement.

And then we had the credit crunch and the great recession. Liquidity disappeared, the real estate market corrected sharply, and development projects were cancelled. All through the recession, the firm did not cut back on knowledge management, although almost every other area was scaled back. The firm had the experience from the previous recession in the early 1990s that when the recession is over, the economy can rebound sharply. Some colleagues lost their jobs, alas. Most of the others opted to work a four-day week to save their jobs. In fact, KM activity increased during this time. The firm saw it as an opportunity to review the precedents. If associates had any capacity, then they were expected to be working on precedents.

The firm realized that if it was going to grow, it had to be better at proposals and pitches. I was seconded to the business development team, where I developed precedent systems for proposal writing and project managing the collation, collaboration, and delivery of the proposal to our prospects.

The process was mapped and optimized from the go/no-go decision, to forming the team, having a kick-start meeting to agree on the team's commitment, and then setting regular milestones for deliverables. This initiative turned out to be a highly successful adaptation of knowledge management and project management to directly impact the bottom line. As a published author, I was also encouraged to write compelling proposals and assist in pitch preparation. Our success rate was measurable and significant: The ratio of pitches won went from 1:8 to 1:3. The firm actually managed to grow its business during the recession and continues to grow. It is now one of the top firms in Scotland.

I was always interested in living and working overseas. Fed up with the economic rollercoaster and equipped with my new KM toolkit, I actively sought opportunities abroad. There were no suitable legal vacancies, but it turned out that Lawson Lundell, based in Vancouver, were looking for a KM professional to lead their new KM program. I applied for the job and was successful. I started at Lawson Lundell in January 2011, and my young family moved over in April. When setting the strategy, I focused on people and process more than technology. We partitioned our space in our document management system (iManage) to create the new repository. This has been a highly successful system, which was achieved at no cost. The culture is slowly turning into a collaborative and sharing environment, although challenges remain. My work in developing precedents is ongoing, and I'm also now looking at implementation of legal project management, process improvement, and document automation.

Acknowledgements

Peer Reviewers:
Thomas Clay
Ron Friedmann
Don MacLeod
Evan Shenkman
Dr. Silvia Hodges Silverstein

LPM Section Peer Reviewers:
Tom Mighell
Carol Greenwald
Jack Bostelman

Editorial:
Jonathan Malysiak
Meredith Hall
Jason Stauter

Content Contributors:
Alexis Adair
Carolyn Austin
Felicity Badcock
Tom Baldwin
Oz Benamram
Chris Boyd
April Brousseau
Flyn Flesher
Lisa Gianakos
John Gillies
Sally Gonzalez
Richard Gordon
Mark Gould
David Gurteen
Angela Hickey
Milena Higgins
David Hobbie
Eric Hunter
Ari Kaplan
Paula Kluth
Rick Krzyminski
Steve Lastres
Tanisha Little
Charlotte Logullo
Sean Luman
Randi Mayes
Jennifer Mendez
Nick Milton
Chris Mixon
Catherine Monte
Julia Montgomery
Mara Nickerson
Jean O'Grady
James Pennington
Nina Platt
Scott Rechtschaffen
Scott Reid
Dr. Larry Richard

Jeffrey Rovner
Kate Simpson
Euan Sinclair
Anne Stemlar
Shawn Swearingen
Debbie Ting
Pamela Woldow

Index